THE ETHICS OF GRACE

T&T Clark Enquiries in Theological Ethics

Series editors
Brian Brock
Susan F. Parsons

THE ETHICS OF GRACE

Engaging Gerald McKenny

Edited by Michael Mawson and Paul Martens

LONDON • NEW YORK • OXFORD • NEW DELHI • SYDNEY

T&T CLARK
Bloomsbury Publishing Plc
50 Bedford Square, London, WC1B 3DP, UK
1385 Broadway, New York, NY 10018, USA
29 Earlsfort Terrace, Dublin 2, Ireland

BLOOMSBURY, T&T CLARK, and the T&T Clark logo are trademarks of Bloomsbury Publishing Plc

First published in Great Britain 2023
Paperback edition published 2024

Copyright © Michael Mawson and Paul Martens, 2023

Michael Mawson and Paul Martens have asserted their right under the Copyright, Designs and Patents Act, 1988, to be identified as Editors of this work.

For legal purposes the Acknowledgments on pp. 5–6 constitute an extension of this copyright page.

All rights reserved. No part of this publication may be reproduced or transmitted in any form or by any means, electronic or mechanical, including photocopying, recording, or any information storage or retrieval system, without prior permission in writing from the publishers.

Bloomsbury Publishing Plc does not have any control over, or responsibility for, any third-party websites referred to or in this book. All internet addresses given in this book were correct at the time of going to press. The authors and publisher regret any inconvenience caused if addresses have changed or sites have ceased to exist, but can accept no responsibility for any such changes.

A catalogue record for this book is available from the British Library.

Library of Congress Cataloging-in-Publication Data
Names: Mawson, Michael G., editor. | Martens, Paul Henry, editor.
Title: The ethics of grace : engaging Gerald McKenny / Michael Mawson, Paul Martens.
Description: London ; New York : T&T Clark, 2022. | Series: T&T Clark enquiries in theological ethics | Includes bibliographical references and index. |
Identifiers: LCCN 2022012363 (print) | LCCN 2022012364 (ebook) | ISBN 9780567694676 (hb) | ISBN 9780567708335 (paperback) | ISBN 9780567694706 (epub) | ISBN 9780567694683 (epdf)
Subjects: LCSH: McKenny, Gerald P. | Christian ethics.
Classification: LCC BJ1278.5.M35 E84 2022 (print) | LCC BJ1278.5.M35 (ebook) | DDC 241–dc23/eng/20220615
LC record available at https://lccn.loc.gov/2022012363
LC ebook record available at https://lccn.loc.gov/2022012364

ISBN: HB: 978-0-5676-9467-6
PB: 978-0-5677-0833-5
ePDF: 978-0-5676-9468-3
ePUB: 978-0-5676-9470-6

Typeset by Deanta Global Publishing Services, Chennai, India

To find out more about our authors and books visit www.bloomsbury.com and sign up for our newsletters.

For Gerald McKenny—
teacher, mentor, and friend

CONTENTS

INTRODUCTION
    Michael Mawson and Paul Martens   1

Chapter 1
THE DIALECTIC OF GRACE
    Gilbert Meilaender   7

Chapter 2
TO LIVE BY GRACE: THE ROLE OF A DISTINCTIVE REFORMATION PSYCHOLOGY IN BARTH'S ETHICS
    Angela Carpenter   19

Chapter 3
BETWEEN ETHICAL SINGULARITY AND SOCIAL SOLIDARITY: THE ROLE OF CONSCIENCE IN KARL BARTH'S *ETHICS*
    Jeffrey Morgan   35

Chapter 4
SUPEREROGATION FOR PROTESTANTS?
    Eric Gregory   53

Chapter 5
VOCATION IN A MORAL VACUUM: PROTESTANTISM IN A DIVIDED SOCIETY
    Robin W. Lovin   69

Chapter 6
BODY MATTERS: SOME BRIEF REMARKS IN PRAISE OF JERRY MCKENNY
    Stanley Hauerwas   81

Chapter 7
"THE WORD BECAME FLESH": WHAT ARE THE IMPLICATIONS OF AN AUGUSTINIAN INCARNATIONAL ECONOMY FOR BIOTECHNOLOGY?
    Travis Kroeker   87

Chapter 8
THE NORMATIVE STATUS OF HUMAN NATURE: BARTHIAN AND
THOMISTIC CONVERGENCES
    Stephen J. Pope   105

Chapter 9
NATURE AND GRACE: A CONTRIBUTION TO A LONG CONVERSATION
    Jean Porter   125

Chapter 10
ENCOUNTERING GRACE AFTER THE FALL: THE NORMATIVITY
OF NATURE IN PROTESTANT ETHICS
    Michael Mawson   143

Chapter 11
THE FULFILLMENT OF CREATURELY NATURE
    Jennifer A. Herdt   161

Chapter 12
ENHANCEMENT, QUANTIFICATION, AND THE IMAGE OF GOD:
A THEOLOGICAL ANALYSIS OF THE BIOSTATISTICAL VISION OF
HUMAN NATURE
    Paul Scherz   175

Chapter 13
THE NORMATIVE STATUS OF HUMAN BIOLOGICAL NATURE
AND ECOLOGY
    Paul Martens   189

List of Gerald McKenny's Publications   199
Bibliography   203
List of Contributors   215
Index   217

INTRODUCTION

Michael Mawson and Paul Martens

We conceived of this book several years ago in a pub in Aberdeen, Scotland. At the time we decided that the best way to honor Gerald McKenny for his contribution to Christian ethics would be to invite colleagues, former students, and friends to provide "high-level critical engagements" with his work.[1] Rather than just asking our contributors to celebrate McKenny and his legacy, we suggested that they either develop and present robust criticisms or display his influence by writing rigorous academic essays around themes central to his intellectual journey.

The title for this volume, *The Ethics of Grace*, is intended to capture and convey something of McKenny's own character and scholarship. Most directly, this title invokes one of McKenny's books: *The Analogy of Grace: Karl Barth's Moral Theology* (2010). In this book he draws on Barth to provide a rich reflection on the moral life as attesting to God's gracious work in and as Christ. As with all McKenny's work, it is meticulously crafted and carefully argued. One reviewer has observed, "McKenny writes with the patience of a pedagogue, rendering each chapter lucid in its trajectory and each paragraph crafted in its argument. He adopts a measured tone throughout that is at once both appreciative and critical of Barth."[2]

These comments can be extended to McKenny's broader contributions to Christian ethics. Across his many books, articles, and chapters, he has undertaken appreciative and critical engagements with a range of scholars and topics. When he does finally disagree with a given interlocutor, or break from a particular view, it is only after a patient and gracious reading. In a theological landscape that has become increasingly polarized and driven by confessional or ideological commitments, McKenny has the rare ability to inhabit different positions and consider them on their own merits, albeit without compromising the coherence of his own position.

Those of us who have studied or worked with McKenny will be familiar with the breadth of his reading and academic interests (a breadth illustrated by the list of his books, chapters, and articles included at the end of this volume). Over the decades he has drawn from a range of seminal theologians and philosophers, including Martin Luther, John Calvin, H. Richard Niebuhr, Emmanuel Levinas,

---

1. This quotation is from the invitation letter sent out to contributors.
2. See Paul Nimmo, "Reflections on *The Analogy of Grace* by Gerald McKenny," *Scottish Journal of Theology* 68, no. 1 (2015): 88.

Michel Foucault, Karl Barth, Dietrich Bonhoeffer, and Alasdair MacIntyre. He has carefully and critically engaged some of the most important contemporary figures in Christian ethics: James Gustafson,[3] Stanley Hauerwas, Oliver O'Donovan, Jean Porter, Jennifer Herdt, and many others. And McKenny's work touches on such topics and areas as responsibility, ethical genre, phenomenology, technology, disability, bioethics, and medical ethics.

Despite these wide-ranging interests, McKenny's most significant contributions have focused on two tasks: (1) developing an account of ethics that gives priority to God's grace, often in conversation with Barth's theology, and (2) attending to the normative significance of nature and the body, with a view to issues and challenges in medicine and bioethics. Given the centrality of these two tasks for his work (and for this volume), it is worth considering each in turn.

Retrieving an Ethics of Grace

In an important essay from 2016, McKenny observes that Protestants have "lost confidence in the viability of their most distinctive theological commitments."[4] He suggests that there has been a loss of confidence in the idea that God acts apart from human beings, as was evident in older Protestant understandings of justification. The notion that God acts in this way, according to McKenny, is increasingly seen as compromising human agency and hence as "deeply unattractive."[5]

In McKenny's reading, this loss of confidence is at least partly due to deep tensions in Protestant theology itself. While Luther and Calvin gave clear priority to God's freedom and action, they were less clear about how this related to human agency and creaturely capacities. As he observes, "Luther and Calvin believed that creaturely capacities are renewed by the working of grace" but neglected to provide an "explicit account of the renewal of these capacities of our creaturely nature."[6] This stands in contrast to the more sophisticated and substantive account provided in the Thomistic tradition.

In this context McKenny proposes that Karl Barth's theology indicates a way forward. Or he at least proposes that Barth retains (even radicalizes) Luther's and Calvin's commitment to God's free and gracious action, while directly reflecting on how this action establishes human beings as agents and covenant partners: "God is

---

3. James Gustafson was McKenny's own doctoral supervisor at the University of Chicago.

4. Gerald McKenny, "The Plight of Protestant Ethics," in *The Freedom of a Christian Ethicist: The Future of a Reformation Legacy*, ed. Michael Mawson and Brian Brock (London: T&T Clark Bloomsbury, 2016), 17.

5. Ibid., 18.

6. As McKenny observes, "they ignored matters that were worked out with great sophistication and precision in the Thomistic tradition." McKenny, "The Plight of Protestant Ethics," 19.

God with and for humanity, and humanity is the one whom God is with and for."[7] In this essay—and in more detail in *The Analogy of Grace*—McKenny develops an account of ethics that keeps God's gracious action at its center: "Barth's God is indeed everything, but only in order that as such we, too, may be everything in our own place, on our own level and within our own limits."[8]

Responding to this thread in McKenny's thought, several chapters in this volume engage and reflect upon this ethics of grace. For example, in Chapter 1 Gilbert Meilaender contends that McKenny, by following Barth, gives insufficient attention to how God's Word is pardon *but also power* in Reformation theology: "there is a needed place for grace as power in our lives—and, hence, for moral instruction that does more than simply show us our sin and our continuing need for pardon."[9] In addition, Meilaender insists that the tension or dialectic between God's action and human action in Reformation theology is necessary: "that simply *is* the structure of the Christian life." He therefore questions the prudence of McKenny's (and Barth's) attempt to resolve or move beyond this tension.

The chapters by Angela Carpenter and Jeffrey Morgan aim to supplement and expand on McKenny's ethics of grace. Carpenter focuses on the issue of growth in the moral life. She attends closely to Barth's account of a "psychological transformation that is foundational to human agency in order to articulate redeemed human action."[10] By contrast, Morgan expands on McKenny's ethics by retrieving Barth's theory of conscience, formulated most clearly in his 1928–9 *Ethics*. Morgan claims that this theory provides a useful counterpoint to communitarian approaches to ethics: "Conscience, for Barth, sets the individual singularly before God, but in a way that accompanies and undergirds the more socially mediated forms of God's command."[11]

Eric Gregory's chapter focuses on the place of supererogation in recent philosophical and Christian ethics. Surprisingly, Gregory suggests that McKenny may have something to offer to this ongoing work.[12] In advancing this claim,

---

7. McKenny, "The Plight of Protestant Ethics," 22.

8. Ibid., 33.

9. Furthermore, Meilaender suggests that Luther's and Calvin's theology may be more viable on its own terms than McKenny's reading suggests: "We can hardly hold it against the Reformers that, until the day when God pulls down the curtain on human history, we will always experience both continuity and discontinuity between who we are now and who we will one day be," Meilander, "The Dialectic of Grace," in *The Ethics of Grace: Engaging Gerald McKenny*, ed. Michael Mawson and Paul Martens (London: T&T Clark Bloomsbury, 2022), 18.

10. Angela Carpenter, "To Live by Grace: The Role of a Distinctive Reformation Psychology in Barth's Ethics," 20.

11. Jeffrey Morgan, "Between Ethical Singularity and Social Solidarity: The Role of Conscience in Karl Barth's *Ethics*," 52.

12. That is, Gerald McKenny, "The Rich Young Ruler and Christian Ethics: A Proposal," *Journal of the Society of Christian Ethics* 40, no. 1 (2020): 59–76.

Gregory engages a recent essay by McKenny that focuses on Jesus' response to the rich young ruler. "Though McKenny does not set out to use this biblical passage to analyze the problem of supererogation," Gregory observes, "his approach suggests a promising strategy for those who might wish to do so."[13]

Robin Lovin's chapter, "Vocation in a Moral Vacuum," builds on McKenny's ethics of grace by promoting the need for better Protestant vocational formation, particularly in light of recent political failures in the United States and a resulting temptation for Christians to withdrawal: "vocational formation . . . responds to what is missing in our contemporary context, rather than resisting what seems to be wrong with it."[14] In other words, gracious ethics involves participation in and commitment to the world and its problems.

The Normativity of Nature

While one of McKenny's main tasks in his work has been developing an ethics of grace, the other has been attending to the ethical significance of human nature and the body. This was the focus of his very first book, *To Relieve the Human Condition: Biotechnology and the Body* (1997). In this book McKenny argues that standard approaches to bioethics proceed as part of the "Baconian project," that is, with the underlying imperative of modern medicine to relieve suffering and expand individual choice. Moreover, McKenny reviews several important critics of standard bioethics and this Baconian project: Stanley Hauerwas, Hans Jonas, James Gustafson, Leon Kass, Drew Leder, Richard Zaner, and Michel Foucault.

In his chapter in this current volume, Stanley Hauerwas recounts the significance of McKenny's first book in relation to his own *Suffering Presence* (1986). Furthermore, Hauerwas insists that the central claims of McKenny's first book remain relevant for today: "We cannot forget the lesson that McKenny so urgently teaches us: we are bodily creatures whose vulnerable bodies make illness and death a given."[15]

In line with this concern with bodily vulnerability, McKenny's more recent book, *Biotechnology, Human Nature, and Christian Ethics* (2018), explores different ways of understanding the ethical status or normativity of human nature. Specifically, he outlines four ways in which nature has been understood and appealed to by ethicists in response to challenges posed by biotechnology. The first view is that nature is normative or has ethical status simply in its givenness (a position McKenny labels "NS1"). The second is that it is normative as a basis for rights and human flourishing (NS2). The third is that nature is normative in its

---

13. Eric Gregory, "Supererogation for Protestants?," 65.
14. Robin Lovin, "Vocation in a Moral Vacuum: Protestantism in a Divided Society," 70.
15. Stanley Hauerwas, "Body Matters: Some Brief Remarks in Praise of Jerry McKenny," 85.

indeterminacy, open-endedness and susceptibility to alternation (NS3). Finally, drawing on Kathryn Tanner and Karl Barth, McKenny presents his own view (NS4), that nature has normative status in how it equips and prepares us for life with God.

A number of the chapters in this present volume respond to McKenny's *Biotechnology* by challenging his readings of particular figures and where he locates them in his typology. For instance, Travis Kroeker argues that Augustine is better read as a version of NS4 than NS2; he proposes that Augustine's messianic, apocalyptic account of the *imago dei* can be used to expand McKenny's version of NS4, thereby providing additional resources for negotiating and resisting biotechnology. Stephen Pope contends that Thomas Aquinas, when read carefully, displays an understanding of grace that is much closer to Barth and NS4 (rather than fitting with NS2, where McKenny locates him). Along similar lines Jean Porter provides a robust reading of Aquinas' conception of the relationship between nature and grace in response to McKenny's criticisms of Aquinas in *Biotechnology*. She too suggests that he comes closer to NS4 than McKenny himself recognizes.

In his chapter, Michael Mawson aims to expand McKenny's account of NS4 by drawing in Dietrich Bonhoeffer as a new interlocutor. He argues that Bonhoeffer's understanding of human nature in the *Ethics* manuscript, "Natural Life," provides a version of McKenny's NS4 that avoids the shortcoming in Tanner's and Barth's versions. Jennifer Herdt expands on McKenny's version of NS4 by attending to insights from evolutionary and comparative anthropology and psychology. Focusing on theories that suggest that human beings have actively embraced and shaped their own pro-social tendencies, she suggests that there are forms of human agency that can support and attend to God's eschatological transformation of our nature into the divine likeness.

Also engaging *Biotechnology*, Paul Scherz takes up and expands on McKenny's critiques of biostatistical and quantitative understandings of human traits, which as he notes have become pervasive in biotechnology and medicine. Scherz is alert to the dangers of this development: "such a quantitative understanding subtly shifts how we think of these traits, especially insofar as it requires us to eliminate many of the qualitative aspects of mental life."[16] Finally, Paul Martens' chapter critically engages McKenny's work by considering the ecological entailments of his appeal to the normative status of human biological nature.

Acknowledgments

We are grateful to all those who contributed to this volume and wrote their chapters during an extremely difficult two years. Thank you for accepting our initial

---

16. Paul Scherz, "Enhancement, Qualification, and the Image of God: A Theological Analysis of the Biostatistical Vision of Human Nature," 176.

invitation and then for the care and thought that went into your contributions. As editors it has been a pleasure to read and engage with your work.

We acknowledge financial support from the Centre for Public and Contextual Theology at Charles Sturt University in the form of a grant to assist with editing and indexing costs. On this note Brandin Francabandera deserves mention for his meticulous and careful assistance. Additionally, Brandin provided comments and suggestions that improved and tightened many of the chapters.

We are grateful to Brian Brock and Susan Parsons for their willingness to include this collection in the *T&T Clark Enquiries in Theological Ethics* series, for their patience with repeated delays and missed deadlines, and for their enthusiasm and encouragement. We are also thankful to Anna Turton at T&T Clark Bloomsbury for her ceaseless work in support of academic theology and Christian ethics.

Many of us have benefited from Phimpmas (Toy) Bunnag's generosity and hospitality over many years. Toy, thank you for your willingness to open your home to successive waves of doctoral students. And for the small yet significant ways that you've supported students, partners, and families.

Finally, we—along with all those who have contributed to this volume—wish to acknowledge the generosity and grace of our friend, mentor, and colleague: Gerald McKenny. Jerry, while words are never enough, we hope that the words that we have collected here convey just a little of how much you have given.

Chapter 1

THE DIALECTIC OF GRACE

Gilbert Meilaender

Among Christian theologians who think and write about the moral life, it would be hard to find any who read texts more carefully or write more precisely than Gerald McKenny. Although his interests are wide-ranging, I think it is fair to say that over several decades the focus of his work has been on two issues: the place of grace in the Christian life (especially, of course, in the thought of Karl Barth) and the question whether human nature is normative (in the sense that it provides guidance for, and limits upon, our actions).

These concerns have been apparent in his work for a long time. His first book, published in 1997, while examining with sympathy the efforts of Hans Jonas and James Gustafson to limit the "technological utopianism" of the "Baconian project," concluded that neither quite developed "a normative conception of the human" sufficient to accomplish that aim.[1] Some years later, but still more than a decade before publication of his important, recent work on biotechnology,[2] McKenny wrote that, insofar as technology may become able to replace some human traits, "the ethical task [is] remarkably clear. . . . It is . . . to come up with a normative conception of the human."[3]

Likewise, the belief (in Barthian fashion) that human life should be lived "in correspondence to divine grace," as an analogy of grace, has been germinating in McKenny's work from the start.[4] A long endnote in *To Relieve the Human Condition* takes issue with Leon Kass's strong emphasis on lineage and biological kinship by noting that "Barth rejects the absolute claim of the natural," because "the true human is humanity as elected, justified, and sanctified by God in Jesus

---

1. Gerald McKenny, *To Relieve the Human Condition: Bioethics, Technology, and the Body* (Albany: SUNY Press, 1997), 213.

2. Gerald McKenny, *Biotechnology, Human Nature, and Christian Ethics* (Cambridge: Cambridge University Press, 2018).

3. Gerald McKenny, "Technology," in *The Blackwell Companion to Religious Ethics*, ed. William Schweiker (Oxford: Blackwell Publishing, 2005), 465.

4. Gerald McKenny, *The Analogy of Grace: Karl Barth's Moral Theology* (Oxford: Oxford University Press, 2010), 5.

Christ."[5] And, of course, in *The Analogy of Grace*, noting the common worry that Reformers such as Luther and Calvin had difficulty relating moral requirements to their understanding of justifying grace, McKenny examines Barth's theology in detail, discerning in it "a way that brings ethics unambiguously into the domain of the theology of divine grace."[6]

These two focal points—the place of grace in the moral life and the search for a normative concept of human nature—might seem to be quite different topics for scholarly attention. In McKenny's thinking, however, they come together. His understanding of divine grace undergirds his preferred concept of human nature, and that concept of human nature suggests that the grace-given life is not formless. There is much to be learned from his scholarly project, not least in those moments when it may not fully persuade us.

I will examine McKenny's project, focusing especially on the nature of ethics within a strong theology of grace and considering the structure and limits of moral theology as he envisions it. In particular, he seeks, with the aid of Barth, to do better than did the magisterial Reformers when they sought to unpack the relation between justification and sanctification. In a recent essay that extends still further his treatment in *The Analogy of Grace*, he considers the implications of the fact that grace is something God does apart from our activity.[7] How then are we engaged as agents in the grace-given life, and does it matter whether we are? And from where do we get guidance for the living of this life?

I will approach these questions by noting something that seems puzzling to me in McKenny's work. Central to his examination of biotechnological intervention is the question whether its effects on human nature should matter when we consider the moral appropriateness of such intervention. "Most bioethicists today," he writes, "flatly deny that normative status attaches to human nature."[8] By contrast to such standard bioethical approaches, he examines and seeks to defend the claim that human nature does have "normative status" and therefore must count in some way and to some degree in our evaluations. But he also emphasizes that to say this is not to say that human nature alone counts. We have to consider it in relation to "other morally significant factors, including autonomy, safety, and fairness" (the primary concerns of standard bioethics).[9]

Very near the end of the biotechnology book McKenny returns to the fact that most bioethicists today would evaluate biotechnological interventions on the basis of those three factors—autonomy, safety, and fairness—and he acknowledges that

---

5. McKenny, *To Relieve the Human Condition*, 249.
6. McKenny, *The Analogy of Grace*, 21.
7. Gerald McKenny, "Karl Barth and the Plight of Protestant Ethics," in *The Freedom of a Christian Ethicist: The Future of a Reformation Legacy*, ed. Brian Brock and Michael Mawson (London: Bloomsbury T&T Clark, 2018), 18.
8. McKenny, *Biotechnology, Human Nature, and Christian Ethics*, 6.
9. Ibid., 13.

these considerations are important.¹⁰ Concluding that we can neither rule out all interventions aimed at altering our nature nor simply view them as acceptable expressions of our nature's openness to such intervention, he suggests that, with respect to any possible intervention, we simply have to examine whether it will "actualize or subvert the meaning and purpose of our creaturely nature." How shall we do this? "In a morally well-ordered society, principles of autonomy, safety, and fairness will establish appropriate ethical conditions for Christians to make these determinations. But to make these determinations well will require a great deal of discernment, deliberation, and prayer."[11]

And just there is my puzzle. When, having made my way as best I could through the very careful arguments in *Biotechnology, Human Nature, and Christian Ethics*, I came to those last sentences on the last page, I found myself a little baffled, uncertain whether I could really be understanding what seems to be a curiously muted conclusion. How shall we evaluate possible biotechnological interventions? The answer seems to be: via standard bioethics (autonomy, safety, fairness), laced with a good dose of prayer. One might have hoped for something more.

Perhaps, of course, that is just the truth of the matter, but it led me to another puzzle. If we seem to be back where we began, balancing (albeit prayerfully) the several standard bioethical norms, might that have anything to do with the other central focus of McKenny's scholarly work—the understanding of divine grace that he has painstakingly developed from the thought of Barth? Could it even be that the Reformers did better than he thinks?

Beyond the Reformers?

McKenny writes,

> It is difficult to deny that the Protestant Reformation in its Lutheran and Reformed versions found it difficult to establish a stable relationship between divine grace and human moral action capable of providing a genuine alternative to the broadly Augustinian tradition that prevailed in Catholic theology with its understanding of justification and sanctification as two aspects of a single process.[12]

That "broadly Augustinian tradition" pictured the Christian life in terms of a pedagogical understanding of grace. That is, empowered and directed by God's grace we are more and more able to grow in holiness and to act in ways that please God (though, of course, we may sometimes backslide). This picture of the Christian life displays a certain continuity—growth from what we are here and now to what,

10. Ibid., 190–1.
11. Ibid., 192.
12. McKenny, *The Analogy of Grace*, 291.

thanks to the pedagogy of grace, we will be when our created but sinful nature has been transformed and perfected. By contrast, the Reformers—Luther most of all, no doubt—saw not gradual transformation but a great rupture, a death and resurrection. Before we talk of grace as power for progress in holiness, we must, they believed, think of it as pardon. Buried with Christ, sinners are raised with him to a new and righteous life, a life in which his righteousness becomes theirs.

Of course, in thus magnifying the grace of God we may seem to marginalize the moral life. If we do wrong, grace will cover our failings; if we do right, it is still only the new life in Christ that makes us pleasing to God. And if such assertions make us uneasy, and we try then to emphasize the necessity of living in ways that please God, we risk undermining or compromising the sovereignty of grace. That is why McKenny believes the Reformers "found it difficult to establish a stable relationship between divine grace and human moral action." And it is this instability that McKenny hopes, drawing on Barth, to overcome.

It might initially seem strange to turn to Barth in order to do this. To be sure, Barth does, on McKenny's reading, dispense with a pedagogical understanding of Christian ethics. Instead, "[b]y establishing and fulfilling the good in our place, grace interrupts all our striving for the good and calls it into question."[13] Not only our justification but also our sanctification is already accomplished in Christ. Divine grace enacted in Christ is forgiveness for our failures to keep the moral law, and it is also "the source and content of the ethical requirement itself."[14] This makes clear, first, that all our moral striving is in vain if we think that we could actually achieve a moral worth that would make us pleasing to God, but grace also demonstrates that the good has already been accomplished in Christ. Now the moral law presents us not with obligation ("you must") but with permission ("you may").

At first sight this strong depiction of grace—with both our justification and our sanctification already accomplished in Christ from eternity—appears to exacerbate the instability said to characterize Reformation understandings of grace. Hence, it might seem "futile or even perverse to call on Karl Barth for a solution."[15] The pedagogical Augustinian tradition at least left a place for our own activity (empowered by the Holy Spirit) in the quest for holiness, honoring thereby the very capacities given us by the Creator, whereas the Reformers had struggled to leave any such place. The question to be answered with Barth's help is therefore the following: Given that in Jesus Christ God has already accomplished the good for us and in our place, what can be the point of our own moral reflection and striving?

McKenny examines in far more depth than need be traced here the gradual development of Barth's answer to this question and the form his developed answer takes, but it is clear that central in McKenny's explication is Barth's thoroughgoing

---

13. Ibid., 21.
14. Ibid., 167.
15. McKenny, "Karl Barth and the Plight of Protestant Ethics," 21.

(and, I am inclined to say, strikingly imaginative) understanding of election. Because from eternity humankind has been elected in Christ to be God's covenant partner, the whole of human history—not only our justification but also our creation and our sanctification—is understood as the work of divine grace. From beginning to end of our history, "Christ acts in the place of all other humans and apart from their action."[16] Hence, the gracious Word of God to us is the language of permission—"you may live." What is required of us has been accomplished in Christ, and we need only live in faith as people for whom this has, in fact, been accomplished.

We should note in passing how nicely this dovetails with the manner in which, according to McKenny, human nature can play a normative role when we are considering the possibility of biotechnological interventions. When we are elected in Jesus Christ as God's covenant partner, our nature needs to be neither destroyed (as the Reformers were sometimes inclined to say) nor perfected (as the Augustinian tradition suggested). It is to us precisely in our created nature that God's "you may live" is addressed. Our nature "does not need to become anything other than what it is, as created by God, in order for humans to enjoy covenant fellowship with God."[17] It functions as a norm in our moral deliberations simply because, as it is, it suits us for a life in which we image God. It is worth noting that this normative function of human nature gives relatively little guidance when we consider the morality of biotechnological enhancements. It does not rule out "the possibility that biotechnological alteration might contribute to life with God," as Barth envisions it.[18]

After all, that God has from eternity claimed us in Jesus Christ does not in itself tell us whether any particular action does or does not respond properly to the divine permission to live. Moreover, if we ourselves try to judge any particular action as right or wrong, we seem to be making a determination that only God can make. This sets stringent limits on what we can ask from ethics. "The task of moral theology is not to try to determine the particular actions God commands but to explicate this encounter of our free human decision with the free decision of God."[19] When we reflect morally on possible courses of action, we should focus less on what should be done than on how God has claimed us. "Barth thus transforms ethical deliberation into a spiritual practice."[20] We are, in fact, back to prayer, and perhaps we can understand why it is that, despite the rigorous detail of McKenny's examination of different ethical evaluations of biotechnological interventions, he leaves us in the end with autonomy, safety, and fairness as the ethical conditions that will have to be balanced in our thinking.

16. Ibid., 22.
17. Ibid., 28.
18. McKenny, *Biotechnology, Human Nature, and Christian Ethics*, 178.
19. McKenny, *The Analogy of Grace*, 229.
20. Ibid., 237.

This means that moral theologians do not seem to have much to offer those seeking guidance about bioethical issues—or, at least, not much that is not also available elsewhere. Perhaps we should not be surprised that this is as far as McKenny can or will take us. As is well known, Barth thought that—without usurping God's freedom to command—ethics could provide us with "instructional preparation," a general sense of what God might command. No more than that, however. God remains free, and we cannot in advance say of any possible course of action that God will surely require it of us or will surely not require it of us. Ethical inquiry simply helps us wait to hear what God commands, and "[t]he name for this practice of testing and waiting . . . is prayer."[21]

Returning to the Reformers

Without in any way denying the architectonic beauty of Barth's approach (or McKenny's explication of it), we may wonder whether a considerable price has not been paid in order to safeguard the freedom of God and reject any use of a pedagogical understanding of grace. Of no possible action are we to say without exception that God would never command it. Still more important, because not only our justification but also our sanctification has already been accomplished in Christ, how are we to say with St. Paul that, though Christ Jesus has made us his own, we are not yet perfect, but must press on to make our own what Christ has accomplished?[22] Or with St. Peter that we are newborn babes, still needing to "grow up" to salvation?[23] Indeed, the countless exhortations to holiness in the New Testament epistles are addressed chiefly to those who are baptized and belong to the Body of Christ but who still need to grow in holiness through the power of divine grace.

Near the outset of his examination of Barth's moral theology McKenny had characterized it very clearly as the opposite of a pedagogical vision of grace: "The moral life is not a human journey from here to there; rather, it is the concrete signification in our conduct of God's movement from there to here."[24] Yet, to do justice to the New Testament witness, Barth himself had to complicate—or break with?—the architectonic structure built upon his understanding of election.[25] For,

---

21. Ibid., 265.
22. Phil. 3:12-14.
23. I Pet. 2:2.
24. McKenny, *The Analogy of Grace*, 14.
25. Here we encounter complex issues in the interpretation of Barth's project in the *Church Dogmatics*, issues about which I can claim no expertise. McKenny points to them in passing in his Preface to *The Analogy of Grace* when he writes that his account of the development of Barth's ethics "assumes, controversially, that the development of his position in the fourth volume of the *Church Dogmatics* is an extension of the position worked out in the second and third volumes rather than a distinct stage in his thinking," McKenny, *The Analogy of Grace*, x.

as McKenny notes, a complete picture of Barth's vision must be somewhat more "complex," since "the pedagogical emphasis on growth in grace will be given a place" within the *Church Dogmatics*.[26] Especially in volume IV/2 Barth is careful to make place for this growth. There he emphasizes that "the coexistence of the 'old man' of sin and the 'new man' of righteousness is not a static dualism but a dynamic history." Therefore—and very much to the point—"[j]ustification is not merely forensic but sets us in motion from one state to another [dare we say, from here to there?]."[27]

Suppose, then, we grant the need to speak of grace in pedagogical terms—as the power of the Holy Spirit helping believers in their thoughts and their deeds to grow in grace. Must we then abandon that "one very distinctively Protestant commitment, namely, the notion that God acts apart from our action" to save us?[28] Or, can we find a way to talk of justification that does not mire us in any of the three problems that, in McKenny's eyes, continued to plague the views of the classical Reformers—namely, that a strong view of grace seems to undermine human agency, that the emphasis on justification may seem to leave no need for sanctification, and that a strong view of grace seems to bypass rather than renew our created nature?

In my view the difficulty is not that the Reformers thought of the work of grace in forensic rather than pedagogical terms. In fact, they characterized it in both ways. For example, confusing though it may seem, Luther can write of our alien righteousness, which "swallows up all sins in a moment," and "our own actual righteousness," which "goes on to complete the first" alien righteousness.[29] And for Calvin, because "regeneration is a renewal of the divine image in us . . . , the lives of believers, framed to holiness and righteousness, are pleasing" to God. Therefore, "God 'accepts' believers by reason of works only because he is their source."[30]

The problem arises when forensic justification is understood primarily through the language of imputation, which, to be sure, Reformation theology did use, and which tends to leave no place for the pedagogical image. This language invites us to think of the righteousness of Christ imputed to sinners in what we might call substantive terms. God looks at sinners through the cross and sees them covered

---

26. McKenny, *The Analogy of Grace*, 15.
27. Ibid., 221–2. And McKenny adds his own comment at this point (223): "We may legitimately question whether the denial [that any evidence of moral good can be discerned in our action] does justice to the work of the Holy Spirit in our lives."
28. McKenny, "Karl Barth and the Plight of Protestant Ethics," 17.
29. Martin Luther, "Two Kinds of Righteousness," in *Luther's Works*, vol. 31, ed. Harold J. Grimm (Philadelphia: Fortress Press, 1957), 298–301. For more detail, see chapter 5 of Gilbert Meilaender, *The Theory and Practice of Virtue* (Notre Dame: University of Notre Dame Press, 1984).
30. John Calvin, *Institute of the Christian Religion*. The Library of Christian Classics, Vol. XX (Philadelphia: The Westminster Press, 1960), III, XVII, 5.

(substantively) by the righteousness of Christ. And, of course, one cannot get any more righteous than that.

Once we set foot on this path, all the standard difficulties with forensic justification (and McKenny's worries) will quickly arise. Surely there can then be no point in talking of progress in the Christian life. Those who now have as theirs the righteousness of Christ must, indeed, be righteous. It cannot be that God simply plays a game of pretense, treating us "as if" we were something other than the sinners we actually are. To think that way would be to undermine the reality of the justifying verdict. Yet, when we look honestly at our lives, judging our thoughts and actions, we may easily doubt that we are really righteous in God's eyes. How shall we deal with those doubts, if we are thinking primarily in terms of the language of imputation?

We might, of course, pivot to thinking of grace in pedagogical terms, supposing that we still need in our behavior to complete ethically (and make real?) what God has begun in our justification. But that would seem to betray the reality of justifying grace. To avoid that, and to avoid thinking that our own moral progress is needed to make us wholly righteous before God—to deal with our doubts—the only thing we can do is return time and again to the word of the Gospel, which reassures us that in Christ we truly are substantively righteous.

Consider, though, what the structure of the Christian life then looks like: Convicted of our failure to be the holy people God calls us to be, we turn to hear the promise that our sin is covered with the righteousness of Christ. Renewed by that promise we seek to please God in our thinking and our doing, only to be struck by our failures. So once *again* we turn from what we see to what we hear—that in faith the righteousness of Christ is imputed to us. Energized by that word we seek to please God—and fail. Yet *again*, therefore, we take refuge in the promise that Jesus' blood and righteousness is the wedding garment we wear. Again and again and again, without end in this life. That simply *is* the structure of the Christian life. It goes nowhere (for this is no pedagogical image of grace). It simply returns time and again to where it began.[31] With respect to such a depiction of the Christian life we may want to borrow McKenny's judgment of Barth's insistence on the hiddenness of sanctifying grace and express some doubt whether it "does justice to the work of the Holy Spirit in our lives . . . , thus failing to do full justice to the power of grace to transform us."[32]

The Dialectic of Grace: The Truths of Reality and Experience

It seems, then, that Barth has not entirely avoided a problem that regularly besets Reformation ethics. Is there a way to give proper place to movement and growth

---

31. See chapter 2 of Gilbert Meilaender, *The Freedom of a Christian* (Grand Rapids: Brazos Press, 2006).

32. McKenny, *The Analogy of Grace*, 223.

in the Christian life without undercutting the truth that in Christ a gracious God is well pleased with us?

In describing the righteousness of God that becomes ours in Christ, we need to turn from substantive to relational language. As Bultmann put it, the perplexities that regularly come to mind when we think of justification "rest upon the misunderstanding that 'righteousness' denotes the ethical quality of a man, whereas in truth it means his relation to God."[33] In what is surely relational language, St. Paul writes in 2 Corinthians (5:19), that "in Christ God was reconciling the world to himself, not counting their trespasses against them." To be justified—or "rightwised," as Bultmann has it—is to be forgiven, accepted, and reconciled to God. It is to be at peace with God.[34] If I forgive someone who has wronged me, that says nothing about how substantively righteous he is. But it does restore the broken relationship and commits me to doing everything I can to bring this reconciliation to fruition in our lives. Similarly, the righteousness of Christ by which God justifies sinners "does not mean the ethical quality of a person. It does not mean any quality at all, but a relationship."[35] Moreover, this gracious justification of sinners not only restores peace, but it also announces God's commitment to restore the relationship in its fullness. "I am sure," St. Paul writes, "that he who began a good work in you will bring it to completion at the day of Jesus Christ."[36]

God's reconciling grace meets us, then, as both pardon and power. "Which is easier," Jesus asks, "to say to the paralytic, 'your sins are forgiven,' or to say, 'Rise, take up your pallet and walk'?"[37] The truth is that in the fullest sense both can only be said by God and must be said by God if his gracious intent to be reconciled with us is to come to completion. When we understand the word of grace as both pardon and power, we may be able to address McKenny's three concerns about Reformation theology without drawing the whole of the Christian life into the divine decree of election in eternity.

"Your sins are forgiven"—that is, you are pardoned and at peace with God. "Take up your pallet and walk"—that is, by the power of the Spirit of Christ, be reconciled to God in all your thinking and your doing. There is no lack of human agency here, for it is precisely as agents called to be reconciled to God that we are forgiven and accepted.[38] Nor are our creaturely capacities ignored or bypassed—or,

---

33. Rudolf Bultmann, *Theology of the New Testament*, Volume I (New York: Charles Scribner's Sons, 1951), 277.

34. Rom. 5:1: "Therefore, since we are justified by faith we have peace with God through our Lord Jesus Christ."

35. Bultmann, *Theology of the New Testament*, 272.

36. Phil. 1:6.

37. Mark 2:9.

38. In general, the concern that Reformation theology risks a loss of human agency may be overstated. With respect to Luther, for example, Simeon Zahl argues that Luther's well-known claim that human beings are passive before God in the matter of salvation is not primarily a philosophical argument but, instead, "a pastoral and empirical one." Zahl, "Non-

at least, no more so than the Gospel of the death and resurrection of Christ requires. After all, in the same context where St. Paul clearly depicts God's "rightwising" of sinners in relational terms, he also declares that "if anyone is in Christ, he is a new creation; the old has passed away, behold, the new has come."[39] We can hardly hold it against the Reformers that, until the day when God pulls down the curtain on human history, we will always experience both continuity and discontinuity between who we are now and who we will one day be. That is simply what it means to be "in Christ," who lives the resurrected life of the new age, but lives it still with the nail marks of our history in his hands. What will one day be seen to be the transformation and perfection of our creaturely capacities must sometimes be experienced by us here and now as more like their destruction. As Josef Pieper (a Thomist, after all!) reminded us, the "transformation" that our nature must undergo "perhaps resembles passing through something akin to dying," and it is therefore "much more than an innocuous piety when Christendom prays, 'Kindle in us the fire of Thy love.'"[40]

This leaves us yet with that third aspect of "the plight of Protestant ethics," the relation between justification and sanctification. About this we would probably be foolish to try to say anything radically new. Insofar as Barth attempted that, I noted earlier that even as sympathetic an interpreter as McKenny concluded that he had probably not "done justice to the work of the Holy Spirit in our lives."[41] The simple truth is that we have two ways in which to talk about God's grace in Christ, and we genuinely need each of them. There is the language of pardon—the forgiveness, acceptance, and reconciliation accomplished and offered in Christ. And there is the language of power—the power of Christ's Spirit to bring us ever more fully into that holiness of life without which no one will see the Lord. Although this holiness is not a condition for fellowship with God, it is a description of what we will be in the new creation. How are these two (equally necessary) ways of speaking about divine grace to be held together?

Perhaps the most honest answer to that question is: This is simply the continuing project of Christian moral theology and pastoral care. Insofar as that is the case we can only be grateful for McKenny's attempt, drawing on Barth, to see both pardon and power, justification and sanctification, as fully accomplished in Christ, apart from any human action—and ours by participation in Christ through faith

---

Competitive Agency and Luther's Experiential Argument Against Virtue," *Modern Theology* 35 (April 2019): 206. Or again (on 217): "For Luther . . . the doctrine of predestination is not about the coherence of human moral responsibility before God. Rather, it is about pastoral consolation."

39. 2 Cor. 5:17. Hence Bultmann rightly says that the saving work of Christ "is the *eschatological event* by which God ended the old course of the world and introduced the new aeon." *Theology of the New Testament*, Volume I, 278.

40. Josef Pieper, "On Love," in *Faith, Hope, Love* (San Francisco: Ignatius Press, 1997), 281.

41. McKenny, *The Analogy of Grace*, 223.

and love.⁴² I myself, however, am more inclined to take seriously the Barth of volume IV of the *Church Dogmatics*, where, or so it seems to me, the contrasting languages of pardon and power, and the tensions that contrast produces in the Christian life, come more to the fore.

We have two languages, of pardon and power, by which to describe the one work of God in Christ, reconciling the world to himself. My own way of holding them together (albeit in some tension) is to think of the language of pardon as speaking to our experience. In this life—unless we attain John Wesley's Christian Perfection!—we will continue to experience the lure and grip of sin in our lives. When we do, and especially when we are genuinely troubled by our seeming captivity to sin, there is little point in assuring us that God's grace is powerfully (pedagogically) at work in us, when, even though that is true, the opposite so clearly seems to be what we experience. At such times—and this seems to be especially important for pastoral practice—what we need to hear is the language of grace as pardon. Not "take up your pallet and walk," but "your sins are forgiven." That language of pardon addresses the truth of our experience in such moments.

But such moments are by no means the whole of the Christian life. Hence, we also, and often, need to hear that God's grace is at work in us as the pedagogical power for holiness of Christ's Spirit. We need to hear that God is truly committed to enabling us to walk in newness of life.⁴³ For whatever our experience at any moment may say to us, that, in fact, is the truth of reality, which Christians do need to hear. But not always, of course. Not at those times when they are unable to see grace powerfully at work in their lives, when, weighed down by the sin that clings to them, they need to hear only one gracious word: that they are pardoned and accepted. The ability to distinguish the truth of reality from the truth of experience, to know when we should speak of grace as power and when as pardon, is at the heart of moral theology—and, even more so, at the heart of pastoral care. How these two languages of grace can themselves be reconciled as the one Word of God to us is God's own eschatological mystery, not ours to solve.

To be sure, when almost a decade ago, in the course of an email exchange about a dissertation we had both read, I suggested this approach to Jerry McKenny, he was not quite prepared to agree, though he was quick to give a charitable reading to my suggestion. "I hesitate," he wrote in our email exchange, "to say anything pastorally that conflicts with what we say theologically, if theological statements are truth claims." There perhaps—I am not quite certain—the Calvinist drew back a bit from the Lutheran. But charitably, he added, "In any case, I don't see any problem here. What the person you describe needs to know is that by faith in Christ he is in a right relationship with God despite his lack of progress, that God is committed for Christ's sake to maintaining and strengthening that relationship, and that the Holy Spirit does not always work in visible ways."⁴⁴ All true, of course.

---

42. McKenny, "Karl Barth and the Plight of Protestant Ethics," 24.
43. Rom. 6:4.
44. Gerald McKenny, email to Gilbert Meilaender, April 27, 2011.

The question is whether the tensions of the Christian life—and of Christian pastoral care—can be smoothed out quite that readily.

I was therefore heartened to note in *The Analogy of Grace* how McKenny responds to Barth's view that, because the law that obligates us presents us with what Christ has already done, it takes the form of permission. Since it does, obligation ("you must") and permission ("you may") are therefore identical. Having said this, McKenny then has to note that while this may be the truth of the matter, it is not necessarily what we experience. "This coincidence of permission and obligation is paradoxical, and for good reason. Barth points out that it is only in Jesus Christ and therefore eschatologically that the coincidence occurs; for us, this coincidence is a matter of faith rather than a fact of experience."[45] If we are caught within this tension between what we experience and what we believe is the truth that will one day be revealed, what are we to do? "The best moral theology can do . . . is to tack dialectically back and forth . . . in the confidence that they do indeed coincide in the Word of God."[46] Not so much, then, an analogy of grace as a dialectic of grace.

I take this to mean that at different moments and in differing circumstances the language of permission will sometimes be needed and appropriate, while at other times we will need the language of obligation. This seems on target to me, and it suggests that, in addition to the reconciling word of pardon, there is a needed place for grace as power in our lives—and, hence, for moral instruction that does more than simply show us our sin and our continuing need for pardon. To be sure, such moral guidance will not be the whole of the ethical task, but it will have its important place. This may even mean that moral theology can sometimes do more than prayerfully provide instructional preparation for the ethical event. Perhaps sometimes it can direct us to the path of growth in righteousness—not least, even, when we ponder the morality of biotechnological interventions.

---

45. McKenny, *The Analogy of Grace*, 188.
46. Ibid.

Chapter 2

TO LIVE BY GRACE

THE ROLE OF A DISTINCTIVE REFORMATION PSYCHOLOGY IN BARTH'S ETHICS[1]

Angela Carpenter

Gerald McKenny's scholarship on Karl Barth is undertaken with the conviction that Barth's theology offers something important to Christian ethics, something beyond a cohesive and intellectually satisfying theological system.[2] Barth has diagnosed some of the most profound spiritual sicknesses of modernity (which have by no means disappeared even as modernity itself has waned), and he articulates a powerful response. With a keen eye to the field of contemporary Christian ethics, and without ignoring Barth's weaknesses, McKenny seeks to make Barth's unique contributions visible. His argument is thus not simply that of a Barth scholar, but that of a moral theologian. Barth's ethics is not merely workable and coherent for McKenny but also attractive and worthy of further exploration by other scholars in the field.

This chapter is an initial foray along these exploratory lines. Specifically, I will pursue an area that McKenny identifies as a weakness for Barth—the absence of an account of moral formation. While Barth ultimately affirms human agency and the integrity of human action, his primary theological priorities lead him to resist the notion that human beings engage in a process of incremental improvement. Can one, however, largely share Barth's theological priorities and his framing of human agency, yet also make a case for a gradual growth in the moral life? I contend that one can provide such an account by making use of an aspect of Barth's theological anthropology that is implicit in, but not a primary focus of, McKenny's work. This element is what I will refer to as the distinctive Reformation psychology of

---

1. This chapter was made possible through the support of a grant from the John Templeton Foundation. The opinions expressed in this publication are those of the author(s) and do not necessarily reflect the views of the John Templeton Foundation.

2. See Gerald McKenny, *The Analogy of Grace* (Oxford: Oxford University Press, 2010); and Gerald McKenny, "Karl Barth and the Plight of Protestant Ethics," in *The Freedom of a Christian Ethicist: The Future of a Reformation Legacy*, ed. Brian Brock and Michael Mawson (London: T&T Clark, 2018), 17–37.

grace.[3] Barth, like Luther and Calvin, relies on a psychological transformation that is foundational to human agency in order to articulate redeemed human action. Specifically, Barth's account of human moral action requires a person to have an understanding of grace and, even more importantly, a sense of the self in relation to God as constituted by grace. When this psychological aspect is brought to the forefront, it affords new options for thinking about growth and formation. The approach I suggest goes beyond what Barth himself articulates, but I will argue it is consistent with his understanding of grace and human agency. The structure of the chapter proceeds as follows: first, for the reader who is less familiar with McKenny's work on Barth, and perhaps wondering if a Barthian ethic is worth the trouble, I review his various arguments for its distinctive contribution and ongoing relevance. Next, I provide an account of the Reformation psychology of grace by examining its appearance in the earliest writings of Martin Luther and then tracing the shape this psychology takes in Barth's ethics. Lastly, I think through how an explicit formulation of this psychology can provide resources for talking about moral growth or formation.

The Appeal of a Barthian Ethic

As the title of McKenny's book *The Analogy of Grace* indicates, the defining feature of Barth's ethics is the centrality of grace. God in Christ graciously accomplishes the good on behalf of humanity, so that it is not left to us to bring about, and God then summons human beings to confirm this grace. McKenny notes that Barth's ethics at this point resembles the teleological structure of Aristotelian-Thomist accounts that many find appealing.[4] God has created human beings for a specific purpose—to be covenant partners. When humans are then summoned to confirm grace, the content of this response is simply "being with God" or "being with Jesus."[5] Grace gives the person permission to be who she is—to be the one determined for fellowship with God. As with traditional Aristotelian accounts, this linkage of action to human purpose means there is the possibility for joy in human action. Here grace leads to an alignment between permission and obligation. What a person is summoned to be (God's covenant partner) is also what a person is created and permitted to be. Obligation does not divide the person so that obedience is a struggle or burden. Rather, obligation coincides with the person's true being and is thus a permission to joyfully be with God. While human desire is not, for Barth, a clue to determining right action, the emphasis

---

3. Krister Stendahl refers to this psychological aspect of the reformers as "the introspective conscience of the west." See Stendahl, "The Apostle Paul and the Introspective Conscience of the West," *The Harvard Theological Review* 56, no. 3 (1963): 199–215. I refrain from using this term in order to highlight the role of grace.

4. McKenny, *The Analogy of Grace*, 187.

5. Ibid., 194, 198.

on permission and joy suggests that the actions that correspond to God's grace are ideally actions the agent desires to take.[6]

This correspondence of human action to God's grace is itself a distinctive way of being in the world, as Barth's reading of the Sermon on the Mount indicates. Because God has accomplished the good, and because God cares for human beings, there can be an absence of fear or anxiety in human action. Humans are actually capable of seeking first the kingdom, rather than obsessing about their own needs. Because God has forgiven, those who affirm grace likewise forgive one another. Because the earth has been promised as a gift, those who recognize this gift can live a life that is meek and humble and generous.[7] They need not attempt to dominate others for personal gain. Grace does not simply liberate human action and enable the person to "be with God," but in so doing it also shapes the life that is lived in response.

Another appealing feature of Barth's ethics is that the way in which grace establishes human agency serves to liberate human action from the dangers of moral certainty and the burden that moral perfection imposes on human finitude. In ethical frameworks that assume humans possess an unambiguous knowledge of the good and an obligation to realize it in society, the moral subject is beset by multiple dangers. If she thinks she must realize the good and attempts to do so, she will soon discover the world is more complex than anticipated. Her efforts to control and perfect society, however well intentioned, might cause pain and destruction. Even when not met with such dramatic failure, human moral effort can be burdened by the disjunction between finitude and perfection. For the one who takes goodness seriously, the demands of the good on moral agency are unending and exhausting. On the flip side, the agent is then tempted to diminish the good— to look at human capabilities and to search for a more attainable goal. An ethics that is a response to grace avoids these difficulties.[8] God has accomplished the good absolutely and human action cannot add to or take away from it. Rather, human action responds to, signifies, or affirms the good that God has brought about.

According to McKenny, Barth's ethics is also appealing in its ability to address ongoing tensions in Christian ethics, such as the tension between an ethic of ordinary life and one that focuses on the supernatural end of salvation, or the many tensions between nature and grace.

Regarding the former, Barth's insistence that authentic human action is simply "being with God" prevents his ethics from falling prey to the "narrative of

---

6. Ibid., 186–9. As McKenny notes, for Barth the coincidence of permission and obligation is only in Jesus and therefore in its fullness only an eschatological reality for the ordinary person.

7. McKenny, *The Analogy of Grace*, 19, 211 and Karl Barth, *Church Dogmatics*, II/2 (Edinburgh: T&T Clark, 1957), 694–6.

8. McKenny, *The Analogy of Grace*, 98–102, 293.

secularization."⁹ For Barth, the moral life is always about life with God because it is fully realized in God's covenant with humanity, but at the same time fellowship with God does not entail escape from the world or ordinary human life. Barth affirms the significance of the ordinary because for him the everyday unfolding of life is a sign of God's grace in the world. It reflects or attests, in a fully human way, the good that God has brought about in Jesus. Thus, participation in ordinary activities like a vocation or raising children is itself a correspondence to God's gracious action. For McKenny, Barth thereby overcomes tensions in both Catholic and Protestant theology between a desire to affirm a general humanistic ethic while also recognizing specifically Christian claims about salvation and supernatural ends.[10]

Regarding the relationship of grace to nature, McKenny argues that a major contribution of Barth's ethics is that it provides an account of human action as both genuinely human and simultaneously a work of God's grace. As we have seen, for Barth God has acted decisively to accomplish the good in Christ and now calls human beings to confirm it in action that does not complete or contribute to what God has already done. For Barth, human nature does not need to be altered in order for a person to express this confirmation or agreement. Because God created humanity for fellowship with God, human nature is already suitable for this end. The human response to God's action in Jesus is thus genuinely human action. God's grace does not need to change or add to human nature in any way for this purpose to be realized. But at the same time, human action is never independent of grace. Human nature cannot attain fellowship with God on its own, but it is always this nature (and not some other nature or some altered nature) that graciously enjoys this fellowship.[11]

In sum, Barth's ethics is attentive to ordinary human life and human nature, while strongly affirming its transcendent purpose of fellowship with God. It is an ethic that recognizes human finitude and the psychological burden of perfection without reducing divine goodness and holiness. And it is an ethic with its own distinctive shape—including a grace-centered affirmation of Jesus' Sermon on the Mount—that is at once joyful and uncompromising. For McKenny and others, this depiction of Christian ethics is immensely appealing, but it is not without its weaknesses. McKenny devotes an entire chapter of *Analogy of Grace* to Barth's approach to moral discernment, an area Barth's critics frequently reference. He concludes that Barth does offer a kind of moral discernment—one which occurs in the context of prayer and with a robust understanding of the ways in which human finitude and sin should prevent claims of moral certainty. But even with this important defense, Barth's ethics is not without its limitations. Specifically, McKenny sees the absence of moral formation and virtue to be a weakness, especially given the current appreciation for virtue theory within Christian ethics,

---

9. Ibid., 288.
10. Ibid., 289–90.
11. McKenny, "Karl Barth and the Plight of Protestant Ethics," 25–32.

and he laments Barth's lack of sacramental mystery.[12] In what follows, I take up the first of these issues and reflect on the possibility for a distinctive Reformation psychology to ground an account of moral formation.

Reformation Psychology of Grace

Implicit throughout Barth's ethics, and crucial to its appeal outlined earlier, is the extent to which the human action that he commends is characterized by a specific psychology. First articulated by Luther, but employed by Calvin and other Reformed figures, this distinctive account of moral agency has elevated and made foundational the idea that God's gracious action has a corresponding psychological effect on the recipient of grace. In this section, I look at how this dynamic was originally described in Luther's early writings and then show how aspects of it are also critical for Barth's understanding of agency. While there are certainly differences, many of the crucial features are the same. Both Luther and Barth are concerned with the crushing weight on the moral agent who is constantly aware that she could do more. Both seek the authenticity of human agency and a vision in which God alone accomplishes the good for human beings and is glorified in this action. And for both, these concerns are addressed by emphasizing the primacy of grace in human action. Crucially, it is not simply the case that the moral agent must *receive* grace. In addition to this, she must be *aware* of grace. She must have an ongoing grasp of grace as constitutive of her being and act out of this self-awareness. While Luther is more well known for the psychological role played by one's awareness of grace, highlighting the continuity between the two on this point will make Barth's commitment to this notion more explicit.

The psychology of grace appears clearly and forcefully in Luther's early writings, particularly *On the Freedom of a Christian* and the *Treatise on Good Works*, both written in 1520. In these and other writings, Luther distinguishes between the person who does good works in order to secure God's approval and the person who "lives by faith," trusting that God already loves and forgives her. The former, who has not learned of God's grace in Christ, really only worships a God of her own imagination, a God who, she assumes, hates sin and is pleased by good works. In her fierce desire to gain God's approval, she even invents good works beyond those required in scripture. This moral agent is idolatrous because she uses her good works to control and manipulate a God of her own invention. For Luther, such individuals actually act "as if God were in our service or debt and we were his liege lords."[13] But Luther is also sympathetic to this moral agent, seeing many of these individuals as "weighed down by all this to the point of despair" and "miserable

---

12. McKenny, *The Analogy of Grace*, 293.
13. Martin Luther, *The Large Catechism*, trans. Robert H. Fischer (Philadelphia: Fortress Press, 1959), 11.

with anxiety."[14] Even if a person is somewhat successful in keeping her own high standards, her posture toward such a God cannot be one of love, but only one of fear. Nor can she glorify God, for her good works are her own accomplishment over and against the God who demands them.[15]

By contrast, the person who lives by faith is transformed through the knowledge of grace and by the Word of God which tells her that she is forgiven. This knowledge produces several effects. First, the conscience is no longer crushed by the burden of unending works, especially, for Luther, those "many and useless" ones that have not been commanded by God.[16] Next, the recognition of grace means that the glory of human salvation is exclusively God's.[17] God commands, but God through faith also fulfills what is commanded.[18] Lastly, and most significantly for our purposes, when people in faith choose to do good works, those works are genuine and "free." Previously, good works (especially, for Luther, ceremonial works) were of ambiguous value, because the agent's objective was not love of God but rather establishing her own good reputation and being able to make a legitimate claim with God. For Luther, however, faith implies absolute trust in God and therefore makes people "genuine and lively children of God."[19] Any works like fasting or religious observance undertaken in the context of such faith will thus also be sincere worship. This sincerity means that the works are "free," though not in the sense that a person can do good works or omit them according to her choosing. Antinomianism might be a perennial risk in Protestant thought but it is explicitly not Luther's intention. In *The Freedom of a Christian*, he repeatedly states that Christians should do good works.[20] When Luther says that a person is free, he means that the person is not compelled to act in order to secure something for herself or to look good among God and others.[21] God's grace has ruled out these motivations by preemptively granting all that person ultimately needs, including God's love, forgiveness, and acceptance. Thus, the works are free because they can be undertaken for the sake of the work itself, which is to say out of love for God and neighbor.[22]

The psychology I'm describing here is no doubt familiar to most readers of Reformation theology. What is particularly important to underscore is that this is

---

14. Martin Luther, *Treatise on Good Works*, trans. Scott H. Hendrix (Minneapolis: Fortress Press, 2012), 23.

15. For a thorough exposition of this psychology, see Randall Zachman, *The Assurance of Faith* (Louisville: Westminster John Knox Press, 2005).

16. Martin Luther, *Luther's Basic Theological Writings*, ed. Timothy Lull (Minneapolis: Fortress Press, 1989), 601.

17. Ibid., 603, 615.

18. Ibid., 601.

19. Luther, *Treatise on Good Works*, 30.

20. Luther, *Luther's Basic Theological Writings*, 610–12, 621, 624–5, 628.

21. Ibid., 615.

22. Ibid., 619.

not simply a rational knowledge, but, in the terms of contemporary psychology, it more closely approaches the idea of self-concept. For psychologists, a self-concept refers to the set of core understandings one has about oneself, which, among other things, shapes one's interpretation of reality and guides behavior.[23] Luther is describing a foundational sense of self that he believes will enable and shape behavior in particular ways and that can and should be cultivated and strengthened. This distinction between rational knowledge and self-understanding comes out most clearly when Luther speaks of the "inner man" or the "heart." He criticizes those who would preach of Christ's life and teaching as "historical facts, as if the knowledge of these would suffice for the conduct of life."[24] Rather, Luther is after a much more intimate connection that is transformational, "that he may not only be Christ, but be Christ for you and me, and that what is said of him . . . may be effectual in us."[25] When this takes place, Christians learn that they are "kings and priests and therefore lords of all."[26] On the basis of this realization about the self who is united to Christ, one will, in turn, react differently in the world:

> Who would have the power to harm or frighten such a heart? If the knowledge of sin or the fear of death should break in upon it, it is ready to hope in the Lord. It does not grow afraid when it hears tidings of evil. It is not disturbed when it sees its enemies. This is so because it believes that the righteousness of Christ is its own and that its sin is not its own, but Christ's, and that all sin is swallowed up by the righteousness of Christ.[27]

Here it is not only knowledge of Christ but also an understanding of who the person is in relation to Christ that is crucial for human agency. It is when such faith is "strong and substantial" that believers are able to bear knowing other truths about themselves, such as the sinfulness and inadequacy of their actions.[28]

Before turning to see how this psychology is deployed by Barth, it is worth pausing to note that Luther's account of agency has not been unproblematic for Christian ethics. Luther, for instance, rejects the very notion of virtue or habituation, and yet one of his central analogies—that of the good versus bad builder of houses—could, in fact, be better utilized to promote virtue theory.[29]

---

23. See Carolin J. Showers and Virgil Zeigler-Hill, "Organization of Self-knowledge: Features, Functions, and Flexibility," in *Handbook of Self and Identity*, ed. Mark R. Leary and June Price Tangney (New York: The Guilford Press, 2003), 47–9.
24. Luther, *Luther's Basic Theological Writings*, 609.
25. Ibid.
26. Ibid.
27. Ibid.
28. Luther, *Treatise on Good Works*, 36.
29. Luther, *Luther's Basic Theological Writings*, 613. Here Luther argues for an internal transformation as the basis of moral action by observing that good builders build good houses and that one must first be a good builder to build a good house. But, surely, good

Nor should one deny that his account of agency has the potential to mire the agent in passivity and introspection, never arriving at the point of action.[30] And these critiques are merely the start of a longer list. Whether these concerns can be addressed satisfactorily goes beyond the scope of this chapter. What I wish to affirm here is that Luther's core insight is valuable enough to warrant the effort this would require. What Luther is really proposing here is a solution to a problem that plagued the author of Job. How can one truly know God and love God when we all simultaneously need or want things from God, and when we think we can secure them through our action?[31] Luther's response to this question, which is fundamentally one about human nature and psychology, is also one that respects the integrity of that nature and psychology and does not attempt to bypass it. For Luther, one can experience this kind of freedom for genuine friendship with God because God acts decisively to save humanity apart from human action.

As McKenny observes, Barth both located himself within this Reformation framework of grace and made it his mission to correct perceived errors and realize that tradition's full potential. A brief look at Barth's theological anthropology in his doctrine of creation, and particularly his discussion of gratitude, will serve to illustrate how for Barth, like Luther, a person's response to grace involves a subjective understanding, a sense of self, that goes beyond mere cognitive assent. For Barth, one must know who one is in order to be who one is.

Barth's commitment to grace in theology shares some of the fundamental concerns that motivated Luther, but these have been translated from a late medieval to a modern vernacular. Like Luther, Barth identifies self-assertion as the primary barrier to human fellowship with God.[32] This concern is framed not with the Reformation terminology of "works righteousness" but, instead, with attention to the modern bourgeois determination to accomplish the good in human life and society.[33] Human beings are "for themselves" in this effort and therefore unable, in their self-enclosure and self-sufficiency, to be who they are meant to be—creatures in covenant fellowship with the God who is for them. Humans in this state cannot truly be in relationship with God because in their self-assertion, they can have no true knowledge of a God of grace. Or, to put it differently, the posture of self-assertion, of establishing oneself over and against God, is inherently antithetical to fellowship with the God who has determined from eternity to be with and for

---

builders have learned over time, through much practice and perhaps even some "bad houses" to become good builders?

30. See Jennifer Herdt, *Putting on Virtue: The Legacy of the Splendid Vices* (Chicago: The University of Chicago Press, 2008), 192–6.

31. See Gustavo Gutierrez, *On Job: God-Talk and the Suffering of the Innocent*, trans. Matthew J. O'Connell (Maryknoll: Orbis Books, 1987).

32. Karl Barth, *Community, State, and Church: Three Essays* (Garden City: Anchor Books, 1960), 85.

33. McKenny, *The Analogy of Grace*, 21.

humanity.[34] In their self-assertion, humans misuse God's law to establish their own worth, but as with Luther they experience a law that is unending in its demands, and they are plagued by anxiety.

Also like Luther, Barth is concerned with the freedom of human agency and sees this as directly related to God's grace. In McKenny's explication of this complex theme, the subject who encounters the law of God's grace is free from the burden of establishing her own moral worth and from condemnation for failing to do so.[35] But even more importantly, this subject is given a permission that is not a neutral freedom of choice, but, rather, a freedom *for* fellowship with God. Because Jesus has fulfilled the law, and thereby ruled out any possible space for the subject to use the law in the dynamics of self-assertion, a new space is opened up. The subject is now able—free—to be who God intended, to exist as the covenant partner of the God who is for human beings. And, in fact, in this very confrontation with the law of God's grace, with the fulfillment of the law by Jesus, the subject is already this covenant partner. He is the person God is for and is free to live in this reality.[36] As McKenny puts it, this is a freedom "to fulfill the divine determination of human beings to be covenant partners of God, a freedom which grace has already won for us, in which it has established us, and which it summons us, as law, to confirm in our conduct."[37]

While there are here many echoes of the pattern we observed in Luther, Barth does not deploy the same explicitly psychological language. Luther imaginatively narrates the transformation of thought, intention, and action of the person who learns of God's grace. Barth's discussion of freedom focuses more on the ontology of the person: in union with Christ, the moral agent is objectively God's covenant partner and freed to live as such. One must therefore ask whether Barth's account, for all its similarities with Luther, is actually an example of the Reformation psychology of grace. Is an *awareness* of grace, and a self-concept of the person as a recipient of God's grace, important for her understanding of agency? In Barth's discussion of gratitude as the paradigmatic response to grace, we find an assumption of just such a psychology throughout his analysis.

Barth's discussion of gratitude is found in his theological anthropology, where he locates the distinctiveness of human nature not in some intrinsic characteristic, but in hearing the Word of God, the substance of which is "the grace of God in which He espouses the cause of His creature."[38] Gratitude is the paradigmatic human action in response to hearing the Word of God. In the ensuing discussion, it is important for Barth not merely that this word is spoken in the existence of Jesus, but also that it is heard and realized by the creature. "Man is, as he hears this

---

34. Ibid.
35. Ibid., 192.
36. Ibid., 193.
37. Ibid., 196.
38. Karl Barth, *Church Dogmatics*, III/2, ed. Geoffrey William Bromiley and Thomas F. Torrance (Edinburgh: T&T Clark, 1956), 166.

Word. He is, as he is awakened by this Word. He is, as he raises himself to this Word. He is as he concentrates on this Word."[39] Everything that Barth then says about gratitude as a response to God's grace in the following pages relies on this very specific realization and understanding of grace by the creature. The psychological language of understanding, recognizing, acknowledging, becoming aware, realizing, affirming, and accepting permeates this discussion. With this language, Barth is not simply talking about the acquisition of information or a cognitive assent. It is a knowledge that is "insight rather than factual or philosophical" and involves "active participation."[40] The specific content of this insight, in which one actively participates, is, again, a kind of self-concept. It is an understanding of who one fundamentally is in relation to God. One knows oneself to be someone who has received not merely existence from God but also election—one has been chosen as God's covenant partner. And one must grasp this precisely as a gift, as "a good which one could not take for oneself but has in fact received, as an action which one could not perform for oneself but which has nevertheless happened to one."[41] In fact, for Barth the whole mystery of self-knowledge, the problem of how we become an object to ourselves, is a function of the human encounter with God's grace. "Coming from where I can have nothing behind me but the Word of God, I find myself on the way to God, my Saviour and Keeper, apart from whom I can have nothing before me. There alone do I have the future of my being. There alone do I find myself before myself."[42]

The self-knowledge that results from this encounter with God is such that it is substantial enough, and deep enough, to establish action. A person must "accept permanently and unreservedly" that he cannot do without God's grace.[43] It is an acceptance that "has a depth and abandon and constancy."[44] For Barth, gratitude is not just an action of humans, but the reciprocity of grace and gratitude is where we find the "being of man."[45] Gratitude, and the insight into God's grace that grounds and inspires it, is thus always present, infiltrating and shaping all other action. As Barth says:

> With anything more or less or other than this, man could only be grasping in relation to God, and could and would only draw down upon himself wrath and perdition. Obedience without gratitude would be nothing. Love without gratitude would be nothing. The best and most pious works in the service of

---

39. Ibid., 167–8.
40. Ibid., 179.
41. Ibid., 167.
42. Ibid., 178.
43. Ibid., 169.
44. Ibid.
45. Ibid.

God, whatever they might be, would be nothing if in their whole root and significance they were not works of gratitude.[46]

Here we find echoes of Luther's insistence that a particular posture toward God (faith for Luther and gratitude for Barth) is necessary for a work to be an adequate response to God. Otherwise, the work distorts the divine–human relationship. Like Luther, Barth finds that other foundations for human action lead to a manipulative relationship to God, or one in which the human agent tries to posit himself independently as an equal.[47] In any situation where God has not established human agency, human beings will attempt to do so over and against God, precluding any possibility of a free, genuine, loving relationship. Of course, Barth also differs from Luther in his understanding of the grace to which the human agent responds, and, as McKenny highlights, this difference is critical for Barth's ethics. Whereas Luther emphasizes grace as God's response to sin and to the violation of the law, Barth has a much more totalizing concept, embracing creation, redemption, reconciliation, and even the law itself. Specifically, when it comes to sanctification Barth differs from both Luther and Calvin in making it, along with justification, alien to the person. Sanctification occurs in Jesus as the human fulfillment of God's command and in other humans only by virtue of their participation in Christ. This difference is especially crucial for Barth's ethics. Because sanctification is accomplished in Christ, the moral agent can recognize it is not up to her to determine or accomplish the good. But because God calls the person to confirm grace in her own life, grace also establishes human action and secures its significance.

In sum, for both Luther and Barth, God's action in Christ is meant to fundamentally shift human psychology and, consequently, the foundation of human action. The human person is meant to not only receive grace but also to live by it, to grasp that God has acted on her behalf and that she should not attempt to earn or deserve what God has freely given. This knowledge is not, for either theologian, a matter of mere cognitive assent or philosophical proposition. Rather, it is a stable and deeply rooted self-understanding that grounds one's being and action in the world.

It is noteworthy how many of the appealing aspects of Barth's ethics rely on this psychology. Genuine fellowship with God as a God of grace presupposes a personal awareness of grace and a recognition that God in Christ is "for me." A person must also have a deep sense of grace if she is to avoid experiencing God's command as a burden that exceeds her capacity. The specific content of Barth's ethics, with its compelling affirmation of Jesus' Sermon on the Mount, also finds its rationale in the recognition of grace—we forgive others because we ourselves have experienced God's forgiveness. And lastly, the responsive and relational dynamic

---

46. Ibid., 170.
47. Ibid., 190.

that allows Barth to so robustly affirm the integrity of human nature also rests on a person's experience and recognition of God's grace.

Barth's Ethics and Practical Theology

If the psychology of grace is so foundational for Barth's ethics, and particularly for the strengths McKenny has identified, can it also help us reflect further on the weak points of his ethics? It is no coincidence that the primary weaknesses McKenny detects in Barth's theological ethics are in the arena of practical theology. Because Barth prioritizes grace and divine action, he must constantly wrestle with the implications for human agency. If one wishes to reimagine Barth's practical theology, to ask if moral formation or a different kind of sacramental theology is possible on Barth's terms, one could hardly do better than to begin with the psychology of grace. It is here that Barth's most prominent theological priority most clearly aligns with subjective human experience. In this final section, I will reflect on how Barth's psychology of grace is suggestive of an account of moral formation.

It should come as no surprise to the attentive reader of Barth that he would be resistant to more familiar accounts of moral formation, especially virtue theory. Such programs tend to rhetorically privilege human action and suggest that goodness can be an attribute of the person. Instead of a process that gradually approaches (even if never quite reaching) moral perfection, Barth prefers to speak of good human action as episodic.[48] God's grace is truly made manifest in human action, but not with regularity or with increasing stability. Should Barth's approach here, in fact, be considered a weakness? Some readers might wish to defend Barth on this score, but on the whole, the numbers of Christian ethicists who would wish to deny all accounts of growth in the moral life are likely few.[49] As McKenny notes, Barth's account of moral decision making presupposes certain dispositions or character traits that enable moral agents to make decisions and act on them. And yet, without some account of how one might come to embody such traits, his ethics is incomplete.[50]

I suggest here a vision of moral formation that places the psychology of grace front and center. Let us presume for the moment that Barth is correct—that an awareness and understanding of grace along the lines that he describes does,

---

48. See George Hunsinger, "A Tale of Two Simultaneities: Justification and Sanctification in Calvin and Barth," *Zeitschrift Für Dialektische Theologie* 18, no. 3 (2002): 316–18, for a discussion of the "again and again" aspect of sanctification for Barth.

49. See Angela Carpenter, *Responsive Becoming: Moral Formation in Theological, Evolutionary, and Developmental Perspective* (London: T&T Clark, 2019) for a Reformed account of moral formation.

50. McKenny, *The Analogy of Grace*, 275–7.

indeed, have the effects on human agency that Barth claims.[51] If this is the case, what would it mean to grow in the moral life? In the first instance, it would simply be to grow in grace. It would entail a richer understanding of what it means to say that God is "for me," and of how God's commitment to human beings is manifest in election, creation, redemption, and reconciliation. More importantly, and in addition to an intellectual understanding, "growing in grace" would have a personal dimension. The person would have a deeper, more robust sense that she most fundamentally *is* the person God is for, and this sense of herself would, more and more, shape her encounter with the world and her action.

But how would one experience such a growth in grace? For Barth, it is absolutely crucial that any such change in a person is always the work of the Holy Spirit, and he tends to speak of it as an event rather than a process. Barth, of course, is extremely reluctant to portray a divine agency which could possibly be construed as sharing power with creation, and thus his discussion of receiving grace or encountering the divine Word focuses on the direct activity of the Spirit.[52] Even so, he also insists that "in the encounter with the community of Jesus Christ [one] encounters Jesus Christ Himself."[53] It thus seems plausible that a process of spiritual formation of the self as the recipient of grace could be understood to occur in the course of the preaching, praying, and even the sacramental life of the church.[54] In other words, a person grows in grace through the ongoing encounter with Christ in the Spirit, and this encounter, while not reduced to or in any way manipulated by human action, is generally understood to take place in the ordinary life of the community of Jesus. From this perspective, moral formation would be very closely aligned to (and, indeed, an outgrowth of) spiritual formation, but this close connection would make sense given the existing relationship between dogmatics and ethics in Barth's thought.

What would be the advantages of theorizing formation along these lines? At the most basic level, instead of restricting the human correspondence to grace to individual acts, it would allow an account of character growth over time in which certain dispositions (humility, generosity, gratitude, etc.) might become relatively stable. The process whereby this occurs, however, resists implications of self-assertion or individual accomplishment. This resistance comes in part because the awareness that is cultivated is always one of the self as the recipient of God's grace. More importantly, however, claims of individual accomplishment are difficult

---

51. Whether or not this is the case would then need to be a key point of debate between a Barthian account of formation and other options in contemporary Christian ethics.

52. Barth, *Church Dogmatics*, IV.4, 33. See also IV.4, 32 and IV.1, 760.

53. Barth, *Church Dogmatics*, IV.1, 759.

54. The latter would depend on the extent to which one shares Barth's anxieties about the sacraments and divine agency. See John Webster, *Barth's Ethics of Reconciliation* (Cambridge: Cambridge University Press, 1995), 116–47. In the account I sketch here, I believe there is space for a sacramental theology that focuses on encounter with divine mystery.

because the process suggests an interaction in which human agency participates while remaining dependent. One cannot manufacture a sense of the self as a recipient of God's grace but must again and again receive this from the Spirit as one experiences "life with Jesus." In McKenny's terms, this formation is not a gradual journey from "here to there," from human effort to holiness, but, rather, always from the "there" of divine holiness to the "here" of human need. In this way of thinking, "growth" or "formation" occurs in a way that is stable but not as an irrevocable attribute of the person. Just as one can have a deepening awareness of grace and who one is as God's covenant partner, a person could also experience a lessening of trust. Relationships, after all, can get closer or become distant and cold. Thus, a version of formation that takes a psychology of grace as foundational still has some resistance to a straightforward and exclusively linear account.

Another advantage to seeing moral growth as growth in grace is that such a developmental understanding of the Reformation psychology resists the impression of moral passivity that so many readers find in Luther. If the recognition of grace (perhaps like the faith of a mustard seed) is expected to grow and deepen, then it seems like one can dispense with any anxiety about whether one is sufficiently aware of God's grace or truly acting on the basis of faith rather than trusting in one's own effort. After all, a growth in grace is by definition not perfect or complete at any point along the way. To even inquire of oneself something along the lines of, "Is my action a confirmation of grace?" itself implies some degree of awareness of God's grace. Because the growth model expects such complexities of the human psyche, it is not troubled to discover them. Nor does it require that these be resolved before action, for one can act in the confidence that God's grace is sufficient.

But what of the struggle of the moral life, and the concern for oneself as a moral agent that characterizes so much work on moral formation and virtue? Could a person, on Barthian terms, be concerned with her own moral self? Is something like habituation an option in this paradigm? While moral formation is in the first instance growth in grace, it could secondarily, and within the psychology of grace, also include actions and intentions of this sort. Barth does not discuss how a person acquires virtues, but he does take great pains to depict authentic moral discernment as an encounter with God in prayer. In other words, moral discernment takes place within the psychology of grace, within the awareness of who one is in relation to God. The key to including concern for one's own moral agency is that it would need to occupy the same conceptual space in Barth's moral theory. In other words, it would need to be understood as a response to God's definitive actualization of the good, a response that confirms and attests what God has done. So, for example, one might recognize that one has a tendency to discriminate against certain groups of people and ask as part of a prayerful encounter with God, how one might begin to cultivate different attitudes and dispositions. Concern for moral agency would then simply be one aspect of hearing the divine command.[55]

---

55. McKenny makes a similar suggestion. See *The Analogy of Grace*, 279.

The preceding description is not, of course, a complete account of Barthian moral formation but is, rather, intended to sketch one possible direction such an account might take. Because the psychology of grace is the point at which Barth's theology most clearly connects with human experience, it is the most logical starting point for a further exploration of practical theology. For Barth, moral formation would have to be a way in which human beings live by God's grace. One way to accomplish this is to portray moral growth as growing in grace.

Chapter 3

BETWEEN ETHICAL SINGULARITY AND SOCIAL SOLIDARITY

THE ROLE OF CONSCIENCE IN KARL BARTH'S *ETHICS*

Jeffrey Morgan

The reception of conscience in Christian ethics for many years now has been mixed. Its status in predominantly Thomistic Catholic moral theology as the practical application of prudence seems secure, but many Christian ethicists since at least the early twentieth century have worried about the way conscience can act to buoy the autonomous individual of modern life.[1] This is the individual who thinks of his personal identity and moral accountability as ultimately up to himself. "Hercules at the crossroads" is how Karl Barth describes the "mad autonomism" of this individual who flaunts the authority of his conscience.[2] Barth fears that appeals to conscience might encourage us to think that we each innately, as autonomous individuals, hold "the norm of God in our hands."[3] John Webster explains that Barth finds conscience complicit in "most of the moral traditions of modernity" wherein "conscience has been an authoritarian and autonomous faculty of self-governance, increasingly detached from rational considerations of moral order."[4] If Barth's fears are at all representative, then despite a long and dignified lineage in the history of Christian thought, conscience has become a significant problem for Christian ethicists, as it aids and abets the subjective caprice of the modern self.

The overwhelming response by Christian ethicists to the specter of this modern self has been the communitarian assertion that we are contingent, historically determined, primordially social beings whose moral agency depends upon the communities that shape us. If there is a role for conscience in this paradigm, it must be as a way to describe the personal internalization of the mores and self-understanding of the community that has given to a person her moral identity

---

1. To take a prominent example, see Oliver O'Donovan, *Resurrection and Moral Order: An Outline in Evangelical Ethics*, 2nd ed. (Grand Rapids: Eerdmans Press, 1994), 119.

2. Karl Barth, *Ethics*, trans. Geoffrey Bromily (New York: Seabury Press, 1981), 479, 485. Cf. 74.

3. Ibid.

4. John Webster, *Karl Barth's Moral Theology: Human Action in Barth's Thought* (Grand Rapids: Eerdmans, 1998), 58.

and that holds her accountable to it. H. Richard Niebuhr offered such a social theory of conscience in an account of moral agency that has proven to be influential in its affirmation of the communally contingent and socially mediated quality of our lives.[5] But attention to conscience waned after Niebuhr, and my suspicion is that the stain of its association with a certain notion of autonomy makes conscience seem to be more trouble than it's worth. A focus on conscience might promote an unhealthy interiority that encourages a person to take an antisocial, inward turn toward a supposedly a-historical, noncontingent location in the self.[6] It would be better, we might infer from Stanley Hauerwas's work, to keep the focus on the tradition-bearing community that examines itself in order to discern if its "practices are consistent or . . . inconsistent in light of its basic habits and convictions or whether these convictions require new practices and behavior."[7] Hauerwas does not explicitly reject the value of something like Niebuhr's social theory of conscience, but it makes sense why conscience, with its individualistic baggage, finds no place in a communitarian ethics like Hauerwas's and why, generally, it has fallen out of favor.

Barth has not been seen to be inimical to the kind of narrative, communitarian theology so prevalent in Christian ethics over the past few decades that has tacitly dismissed conscience. Hauerwas himself has appealed to Barth for much of his career.[8] His idea, for example, that theological ethics must proceed from the sociolinguistic conventions entrusted to the church by God's Word is one he develops with significant debts to Barth.[9] Furthermore, in concert with Hauerwas, Barth vigorously denies the detached interiority of the modern moral subject.[10] But, as Webster writes, Barth also "does not undermine the primacy of interiority by exploring the embeddedness of moral self-hood in a public world—in the ethical self-descriptions which the Christian agent absorbs from participation in the linguistic and social conventions of the church considered as a form of moral culture."[11] Barth is certainly worried about modern moral autonomy, about a "subjectivity that regards itself as truth."[12] But Barth considers

---

5. H. Richard Niebuhr, *The Responsible Self: An Essay in Christian Moral Philosophy* (New York: Harper and Row, 1963). See also Francis Schussler Fiorenza, "Theology as Responsible Valuation or Reflexive Equilibrium," in *The Legacy of H. Richard Niebuhr*, ed. Ronald Thiemann (Minneapolis: Fortress Press, 1991).

6. See Stanley Hauerwas, *The Peaceable Kingdom: A Primer in Christian Ethics* (Notre Dame: University of Notre Dame Press, 1981), 39–44.

7. Ibid., 120.

8. See, for example, *Hannah's Child: A Theologian's Memoir* (Grand Rapids: Eerdmans, 2010), 37, 59, 108; see also "How 'Christian Ethics' Came to Be," in *The Hauerwas Reader*, ed. John Berkman and Michael Cartwright (Durham: Duke University Press, 2001), 45–9.

9. Hauerwas, "How 'Christian Ethics' Came to Be," 49.

10. Webster, *Karl Barth's Moral Theology*, 42.

11. Ibid.

12. Karl Barth, *Fragments Grave and Gay* (San Francisco: HarperCollins, 1971), 99.

human moral agency to be constituted by the "self-bestowing, communicative personal presence" of a God who claims each of us individually.[13] Barth resists the dichotomy of the atomistic, autonomous individual, on the one hand, and the historically determined, narrative, and socially formed self, on the other hand. As Gerald McKenny argues, Barth's moral theology does not accommodate this dichotomy between "individualistic and communal forms of ethics"; rather, Barth strives to affirm the ethical singularity—the irreplaceable singular accountability—of each individual before God and the social solidarity intrinsic to the universality of God's command.[14] What I argue in this chapter is that, despite Barth's worries about conscience, he does develop a theory of conscience in his 1928-9 ethics lectures (posthumously published as *Ethics*) that nicely captures his commitment to ethical singularity and social solidarity that McKenny identifies.[15] This chapter will therefore hopefully be a resource for Barth scholars interested in Barth's only sustained treatment of conscience, as well as for those looking for a theory of conscience that resists some of the prevailing trajectories which have pushed conscience to the margins of contemporary Christian ethics.

Defining Conscience

Conscience is predicated for Barth on the basic premise that God speaks to us, that the Word of God claims us every moment of our lives, and makes us responsible for the quality of our lives before this claim.[16] As McKenny explains, by the time Barth delivers the lectures that would become *Ethics*, the Word of God "is the *command* of God insofar as it not only directs a pronouncement to its human addressee, but in doing so also claims the later entirely in her life conduct."[17] Barth frames ethics in terms of the command of God, because he "wants to emphasize ... that to grasp human life from the standpoint of the Word of God is to grasp it in terms of its determination by God's grace."[18] Living and active, the Word of God's grace comes to the human addressee with an indicative pronouncement, a decisive claim, that makes her responsible. And so it is a claim that comes as a command. Specifically, Barth writes, it is Jesus Christ who is "the goodness of God which

---

13. Webster, *Karl Barth's Moral Theology*, 42.
14. Gerald McKenny, *The Analogy of Grace: Karl Barth's Moral Theology* (New York: Oxford University Press, 2010), 274–5.
15. As Nigel Biggar argues, since Barth was never able to write the planned fifth volume of *Church Dogmatics* on God the Redeemer, the 1928 ethics lectures are an especially important resource to help us conjecture what he would have said in that volume, which is where we most likely would have found Barth's final account of conscience (Nigel Biggar, *The Hastening that Waits: Karl Barth's Ethics* [Oxford: Oxford University Press, 1993], 3).
16. Barth, *Ethics*, 35.
17. McKenny, *The Analogy of Grace*, 55.
18. Ibid.

confronts us" and who comes to us as a command.[19] To say command, then, is to say that God's Word, God's self-revelation in Christ, comes to a person, claims her, and questions her again and again in every day of her life.[20]

Barth is clear that God's self-revelation indicates the characteristic contours of what God will command of a person.[21] In Christ God is revealed as creator, reconciler, and redeemer and, correspondingly, the human being is revealed to be God's creature, reconciled sinner, and redeemed child. What Barth insists upon in *Ethics* is that the one Word of God—Jesus Christ—comes to the human addressee in three ways: "the one total thing is said three times," Barth writes, because Jesus Christ, "stands at the controlling center of the thought of reconciliation, and in this [is] also the presupposition and quintessence of the thought of creation and the thought of redemption."[22] The Word of God reveals God to be this God, human beings as claimed by God in this way, and so whatever God says will be coherent in these terms. The specific thing God says to a person each moment, that is, bears witness to this three-part movement of the one Word, or command, of God.[23] In *Ethics,* Barth identifies a distinct organ, or voice, through which God speaks to a person from each of these three standpoints.[24] Conscience is one of these organs. The section on conscience in *Ethics* opens by identifying conscience with God's command: "God's command strikes me as my own strictly moment by moment co-knowledge of the necessity of what I should do or not do in its relation to his coming eternal kingdom. In this concrete fellowship of mine with God the Redeemer it claims me and I have to listen to it."[25]

The Word of God claims us from the standpoint of our redemption through our conscience. The reality of our redemption is the indicative, the "decisive truth" about ourselves, that comes to us through our conscience and through our conscience makes us responsible.[26] What we know with God in our conscience is that God has redeemed us, and in light of our redemption we know with God how we ought to act and how well or poorly we have acted. It is, in fact, only as we live with God in eternity as God's redeemed children that we have a conscience, that we know what God knows.[27] Eternity—our eschatological future—seems like a strange place to locate conscience but, with good Pauline warrant,[28] Barth asks where else can we know with God what God knows about us except on the

---

19. Barth, *Ethics*, 332.
20. Ibid., 38.
21. See McKenny, *The Analogy of Grace*, 59–60.
22. Barth, *Ethics*, 53.
23. Ibid., 55.
24. Ibid., 53–6.
25. Ibid., 475. Cf. Karl Barth, *The Holy Spirit and the Christian Life*, trans. R. Birch Hoyle (Louisville: Westminster John Knox, 1993), 65.
26. Barth, *Ethics*, 480.
27. Ibid., 477.
28. 1 Cor. 13:12 (NIV). Emphasis added.

other side of history, where with Christ we participate in the divine nature and have our being in God.[29] To have a conscience, "to know what is in God, to know his judgment on our conduct," Barth writes, is to "reach beyond the limits of our creatureliness and our reconciliation,"[30] to the reality of our promised future as God's redeemed children.[31] Conscience, then, is the knowledge we have with God of our beatitude, of our eternal fellowship with God as God's beloved children who live as citizens of the heavenly kingdom. It is the redeemed child of God who has a conscience, who has genuine co-knowledge with God, who knows herself as she is fully known.

We know ourselves with God in our conscience as God's beloved children; this is the claim God makes upon us in conscience, the indicative according to which we know ourselves accountable in our conscience—accountable for what we are to do and for what we have done. What this means in particular is that in our conscience we know that in whatever we do we are to be glad, happy, grateful.[32] As God's children we find ourselves at the end of all God's ways with us, sharing with Christ in the beatitude of the divine life. And so what we know with God in our conscience is just what God knows and tells us: "It is given to you to belong to God. You live in and by the fact that you are the child of God, that you already stand by his side. . . . Act as one who lives in and by this gift. Know that your whole conduct is measured by this fact."[33] This is the claim conscience presents to a person moment by moment, the claim before which he is responsible.

But why does the redeemed child of God, who in eternity "does not sin,"[34] need to be held responsible for her actions? What real purpose does conscience serve in this case except to grant the child of God an eternal, joyful self-awareness of her perfect fellowship with God? This would be the case if conscience were confined to the eschatological future with no bearing on our present existence. It does belong to the eschatological future, but Barth insists that the eschatological self exists not merely "in the future" but "as the future in the present."[35] We already are this promised future self. Barth's thought here expresses his commitment to the idea that we are *simul justus et peccator*, simultaneously saints and sinners.[36] We already are what we shall be. We already live and move and have our being in Christ with God as God's child. We await an inheritance that has already been given to us. Our citizenship is both here on earth and in heaven and conscience

---

29. Barth, *The Holy Spirit and the Christian Life*, 65.
30. Barth, *Ethics*, 477.
31. Ibid., 478.
32. Ibid., 499.
33. Ibid., 501.
34. Ibid., 465.
35. Ibid.
36. Barth, *The Holy Spirit and the Christian Life*, 64. See also 62–3, where Barth offers a persuasive concatenation of biblical warrants for this claim. Cf. McKenny, *The Analogy of Grace*, 220–2.

bridges the two, acting as the place where the heavenly citizenship becomes directive for the earthly. When Barth says that conscience brings before me the reality of "my concrete fellowship with God the Redeemer," that this reality "claims me, and I have to listen to it," the "I" here clearly refers to the present self as that self is confronted by the "coming eternal kingdom."[37] In short, we already are the children of God who know ourselves with God as God knows us, and so the real point about accountability is that our eschatological self breaks into the present and holds us accountable to act as the glad, happy, grateful children of God that we are.

The Condition for the Possibility of Conscience: The Holy Spirit

But how is it possible that our eternal self from our promised future speaks to us in our present? This reaching into the present of our eternal future becomes a reality, Barth argues, by the power of the Holy Spirit. We have a conscience as we have our being with Christ in God in our promised future, and the Holy Spirit, the "vicar of the coming Christ," brings Christ to us and so brings to us our own future being in Christ.[38] "To have a conscience," Barth explains, "is no more and no less than to have the Holy Spirit. 'For no one knows what is in God except the spirit of God' (1 Cor. 2:11)." And, Barth adds, "to have a conscience is to know what is in God."[39] We do, indeed, have a conscience in the present, but only because by the power of the Holy Spirit "our divine future is present with us";[40] God bridges the gap,[41] as the Holy Spirit brings the distant eschatological self near.[42] Barth's language here about conscience can be a little slippery. By "conscience," Barth sometimes refers to our future co-knowledge with God, and at other times to the Holy Spirit-empowered event in which our present self encounters this future co-knowing self.[43] So, taken together, we will say that for Barth, conscience refers to the reality of our future co-knowledge with God and to the event of the encounter between our present and future self.

Both references clearly indicate the relational nature of conscience for Barth. Conscience exists in our "concrete fellowship with God" in the future and as the Holy Spirit brings this fellowship to the present.[44] It is crucial for Barth's theory

---

37. Barth, *Ethics*, 475.
38. Ibid., 478.
39. Ibid., 477.
40. Barth, *The Holy Spirit and the Christian Life*, 62.
41. McKenny, *The Analogy of Grace*, 284.
42. Barth, *The Holy Spirit and the Christian Life*, 60–1. See also John Webster, "God and Conscience," in *Word and Church: Essays in Christian Dogmatics* (Edinburgh, Scotland: T&T Clark, 2001), 258–9.
43. Barth, *Ethics*, 480.
44. Ibid., 475.

of conscience, then, that our co-knowledge with God becomes real in the present through a Spirit-empowered encounter with ourselves:

> When my conscience speaks to me, I am *addressed*. Someone *encounters* me, coming from outside into my present reality. But this someone is not another person, a fellow human.... In relation to an approaching or past moment of action *I* set myself under a final truth by which my action is measured. When conscience speaks, I find that I am on both sides, both listening and speaking.... The two partners are very dissimilar—on the one side I am in my present state... while on the other I am in a state of pure futurity which is a fact even though I can neither perceive nor grasp it—yet I am both partners.[45]

The idea that conscience represents a self-dialogue, an encounter within the self with an Other of some kind, has plenty of precedent in the history of Christian thought. But more often than not the language of an encounter with oneself as an Other in conscience is more analogical than literal; it is a way to describe how God has constituted human beings from creation to hold themselves accountable before God.[46] But for Barth, by the power of the Holy Spirit, I quite literally encounter myself as another person. The person my present self encounters is my glorified self who has his being with Christ in God, and who therefore speaks authoritatively with God's voice to my present self.[47]

Because Barth locates conscience in the event of a Spirit-enabled personal encounter, he insists that this makes the work of conscience "strictly occasional."[48] Barth compares conscience to a bolt of "lightning in a dark sky,"[49] and to the manna from heaven God daily gave to the Israelites in the wilderness.[50] It is not something over which we have control any more than we have control over the Holy Spirit. And so, like the manna from heaven, the declarations of conscience are new each day.[51] Or as he says in an earlier address, conscience "interrupts" us each day with its disclosure.[52] Conscientiousness is therefore not about casuistically following the wisdom of accrued verdicts of conscience; it is, rather,

---

45. Ibid., 480; emphasis original.

46. See, for example, the Apostle Paul's claim about conscience in Rom. 2:15; John Chrysostom, *On Wealth and Poverty* (Yonkers: St Vladimir Seminary Press, 1999), 88, 90; John Calvin, *Institutes of the Christian Tradition*, ed. John T. McNeill, trans. Ford Lewis Battles (Louisville: Westminster John Knox, 1960), III. 19. 15, 848; Immanuel Kant, *Metaphysics of Morals* (New York: Cambridge University Press, 1996), 6: 439, 189.

47. Barth, *Ethics*, 480–1.

48. Ibid., 495.

49. Ibid., 503.

50. Ibid., 495.

51. Ibid.

52. Karl Barth, "The Righteousness of God," in *The Word of God and the Word of Man*, trans. Douglas Horton (Gloucester: Peter Smith, 1978), 10.

Barth says enigmatically, "a fundamental openness and willingness to be guided by conscience."[53] What he means is that conscientiousness is about our openness to the word God lets us bring to ourselves again and again each day: you are God's child, now act accordingly and live with gratitude.[54]

Insofar as the individual's relationship to God is the fundamental basis for Barth's theory of conscience, it is appropriate to call it a social theory of conscience. But it is not a social theory of conscience like H. Richard Niebuhr's in the sense that social forces shape the conscience. For Barth, conscience is not at all shaped by the nexus of a person's relationships, as though it were an internalization of a social group's external mores. The relationship the individual has with God in conscience is a singular relationship, singular in the sense that the individual exists in a distinct and irreplaceable moral relation to God,[55] that God knows and claims that individual distinctly. Barth writes that the reality of conscience "depends upon our being the children of God, a being into which we cannot be educated but which we must have *directly from God*, and which we can have *not in relation to other people* but truly only in our own relation to God."[56] What Barth sees for the redeemed child of God, in the eschatological future where that child lives with Christ in God, is a direct relation to God, an "encounter of immediacy."[57] The child of God, that is, exists in a direct, singular relation to God. This relation is not mediated through other people or communities, but one that is constituted by God's claiming of that individual alone, making that individual singularly accountable.[58] From the standpoint of our redemption—from the standpoint where conscience addresses us—we have to acknowledge "that we are not so much bound to one another as to the Lord" who addresses the individual person in a singular fashion through that person's future self.[59]

As the image of the individual singularly accountable before God in conscience might suggest, Barth assigns to conscience a striking—perhaps unnerving—degree of freedom and authority. In our conscience we confront ourselves with freedom and authority, he argues, because in our promised future we are "like God" and our voice "undoubtedly" also is "God's voice."[60] And since freedom and authority are "one and the same" in God, to speak to ourselves in our conscience with God's voice, as one who shares in God's being, is to speak with a final freedom and authority, the freedom and authority of God.[61] Co-knowledge with God is

---

53. Barth, *Ethics*, 496.
54. Ibid.
55. McKenny, *The Analogy of Grace*, 274.
56. Barth, *Ethics*, 484; emphasis added.
57. Ibid., 498. See also Barth, "The Righteousness of God," 10.
58. Barth, *Ethics*, 84.
59. Ibid.
60. Ibid., 480–1. It is, Barth writes, our "*divine* future, that is present in our present through the Word" (*The Holy Spirit and the Christian Life*, 64; emphasis original).
61. Barth *Ethics*, 482. Cf. Webster, "God and Conscience," 259.

possible only in this glorified state which is not something we achieve but which is given to us by God. Because conscience entails an encounter with the future self who lives with Christ in God, Barth concludes that conscience cannot be in error and that it needs no formation. It is nonsense, he writes, to "speak about educating the conscience or about a public conscience (that of the nation or humanity)," because it is simply not something we have by formation or education, but by the gift of God.[62] It breaks into the present, according to Barth, unconditioned and infallible.[63]

In Barth's account, then, conscience comes with divine authority. And this means that conscience, as an authority we share with God over ourselves, ensures that "we can subject ourselves to *all* other authority only in and of ourselves, in freedom."[64] Since the freedom and authority of conscience comes to us with the freedom and authority of our eschatological relation to God, it reveals as lesser, penultimate, and provisional *any* other claim to authority: "Over against all the authority of church and state, i.e. over against the whole claim of others, the question and criterion is freedom of conscience, i.e. the authority of God from which that relative authority has its commission."[65] Indeed, he argues, "we have to say that conscience is, in fact, *the final court and ultimate criterion of obedience*."[66] According to Barth, the final court or last word about our accountability before God comes not from the state, our various communities of interaction, or the church, but from conscience, from our singular, direct, unmediated personal relationship to God.

Striking as this claim is, Barth does not make it without significant caveats.[67] While conscience needs no formation and comes with the infallible authority of God, "we err in our hearing of it."[68] Conscience itself may be "infallible," but the hearer of conscience—or the present self in the self-encounter of conscience—is highly fallible.[69] "What I say to myself as a child of God I hear as a sinner saved by grace . . . I say it out of my future into my present. What else can one expect but that I should hear it very differently from the way in which I say it to myself."[70] The "self-dialogue" in which the present self encounters the future self is "a constant self-misunderstanding. We hear the voice of our future I with the ears of the present

62. Ibid., 483–4.
63. Ibid., 485.
64. Ibid., 483.
65. Ibid.
66. Ibid.; emphasis added.
67. Caveats I did not sufficiently air when I first wrote about Barth's theory of conscience as a graduate student for Gerald McKenny. I take full responsibility for the interpretation of Barth I offer in this chapter, but I hope it reflects the many helpful conversations I have had with Jerry over the years about this subject matter.
68. Barth, *Ethics*, 485.
69. Ibid., 487.
70. Ibid., 481.

I."[71] And this "present I," Barth writes, is "impotent before the pronouncement of conscience."[72] Through the conscience we share in the final, ultimate authority of God over ourselves and all other authorities, but this "does not go well with the present power we would like it to have."[73] In the act of hearing, the hearer of conscience is, as Barth repeatedly insists, weak, defenseless, and frail.[74] Our fallibility before the pronouncements of conscience is not absolute, Barth is clear, but it is nonetheless "relatively very" high.[75] Consequently, we cannot "make a great parade of our co-knowledge of God's truth as we have it in conscience, in the present in which it is given to us."[76] This is not to say conscience has no power in the present. We can really be disclosed in it and directed by it. But this "prophetic possibility" is "the miracle of God himself."[77]

Conscience Among Other Voices

The profound fallibility of the present self who hears the infallible voice of conscience is not the only caveat Barth places on the authority of conscience. As the future self—the reality of conscience—comes into the present, it joins other, clearer voices through which God directs us and holds us accountable. Here and now in the present we are what we shall be—God's redeemed children—but we are not only that. We are also creatures and sinners saved by grace and God speaks to us as such. Specifically, as creatures God speaks to us through our calling and as sinners saved by grace God speaks to us through our neighbors. And so while conscience makes us accountable to a final truth about ourselves, while it speaks a decisive word to us, it is not the only truth or word that comes to us and that we must strive to hear. Rather, we must strive to hear it as one voice among these other two voices that address us in a harmonious chorus. Our calling, our neighbors, and our conscience are, Barth claims, three distinct organs that speak in unison.[78] To say, as Barth does, that these three voices speak in accord with each other, that they relate to each other like "concentric circles,"[79] means that what each says has a bearing on what the others say. And so we will come to a more precise understanding of conscience's call to gratitude and to the nature of its authority as we briefly consider the form and content of these two other voices.

---

71. Ibid., 485.
72. Ibid., 492–3.
73. Ibid., 495.
74. Ibid., 492–3, 497, 503.
75. Ibid., 493.
76. Ibid. See also *The Holy Spirit and the Christian Life*, 66.
77. Barth, *Ethics*, 493.
78. Ibid., 53–5.
79. Ibid., 467.

Barth's concept of calling refers to the providentially given specificity of a person's life as the indication of how God will address that person.[80] Calling is about one's own life as the organ of God's speaking to us. The life we live, Barth claims, is the life given to us by God and to say that we have a calling is to say that God has determined our existence in very particular ways. The foil of calling, in this regard, is fate or chance.[81] To say that we have a calling is to say that it is God, not fate or chance, that orders our days. The life we live is the life God fashions for us anew each day.[82] And so calling refers to the fact that "God will find us where he has put us."[83] A person discerns her calling not so much by introspection as by looking to the external circumstances and relations that constitute her life. The "general ethical meaning of the concept of calling," Barth writes, is a person's own "reality understood in its specificity as a pointer . . . to God's command."[84] In this regard, the providentially sustained givenness of our own reality each day, bears authority over us as the indication of what God will say to us. This does not mean that faithfulness to God's command is simply, willy-nilly, living our lives as we see fit; it means that God finds us and claims us in the very particular givenness of the lives God has granted us to live.[85]

To say that our own reality points to what God asks of us each day indicates, for Barth, that what God asks of us through our calling is to submit to certain constancies and regularities in life, certain "orders" as he calls them in *Ethics*.[86] This

---

80. Ibid., 177; see also Webster, *Karl Barth's Moral Theology*, 54.
81. Barth, *Ethics*, 201.
82. Ibid., 196–7.
83. Ibid., 190.
84. Ibid., 177.
85. Ibid., 374.
86. Dietrich Braun explains that Barth decided not to publish his 1928 ethics lectures because his use of "orders" made him at least appear still to be an advocate for the doctrine of "the orders of creation" that he rejected (Braun, "Editor's Preface," in Barth, *Ethics*, vii). Among the many reasons the lectures were eventually published as *Ethics*, Braun writes, is that the "general sketch of theological ethics" Barth offers clearly anticipates what he would develop in the *Church Dogmatics* (Braun, "Editor's Preface," vii). And as McKenny explains, what Barth worried most about with the "orders of creation" doctrine, such as that offered by Bonhoeffer and Brunner, was that the orders, "because of their institutional form and historical nature," would be readily identified with "current forms of social and political life." Consequently, with this conflation, the orders are then taken "as the command of God itself" and "obedience to them is equated with obedience to God—a monstrous equation to make" (McKenny, *The Analogy of Grace*, 252). But, McKenny explains, Barth is clearly already occupied with this concern in *Ethics* and he formulates his conception of orders, "somewhat ambiguously," against formulations like Bonhoeffer's and Brunner's by emphasizing that the "orders are not themselves commands, and any natural knowledge we might claim to have of these orders in their givenness is not itself knowledge of them in their relation to the command of God" (McKenny, *The Analogy of Grace*, 253). However,

submission to orders is the content of what God asks of us through our calling. By "orders" Barth explains that our lives are "claimed for a certain regularity,"[87] that there are certain kinds of relations, such as marriage, family, friendship, and work, through which God will claim us.[88] "God will find us where he has put us" simply means that God sets us in certain relationships in specific places at specific times and gives us certain orders or standards through which God claims our obedience.

As God's children God speaks to us through our conscience, summoning us to live in gratitude, and as God's creatures God speaks to us through our calling, summoning us to certain orders or regularities in life through which we affirm the life God has given us. But we are not just redeemed children and creatures. We are also sinners saved by grace, and as such, alongside these other forms of God's speech to us, God speaks to us through our neighbors. The neighbor is God's appointed vessel to speak to us from the vantage of our reconciliation because our reconciliation has to do with the reestablishment of fellowship with God and with one another in God. Christ's reconciling work for us discloses the fundamental truth that God is for us: "God in Christ," Barth writes, "is not good for himself. This is the divinity and reality of his goodness."[89] But God's being for us is just what we reject. We want to be for ourselves, to be our own masters, and this self-enclosure is our sin.[90] But "God maintains his goodness" for us and contradicts our sin. God's goodness "is not the goodness that triumphs by being self-enclosed, self-separated, and self-differentiated. God is really good *for us*. He is good wholly and utterly in turning to us who are not good."[91] Despite my sinful will to be for myself, then, despite "everything that speaks to the contrary . . . God counts me his."[92]

And if God counts me as God's own, as a member of Christ, how can I possibly deny this of my neighbor? It should be no question for me "whether my neighbor who has come to me is himself a member of Christ."[93] However "ungodly" my neighbor appears to me, Barth insists that "Christ . . . has perhaps been pleased to call this . . . neighbor his brother." Consequently, "I necessarily deny the Christ

---

McKenny concludes, "what distinguishes Barth's position in *Ethics* from his later position is the view that the orders are aspects of creation apart from and prior to grace," something that Barth will later reject, since to extract creation from the covenant of grace "can only mislead" with the idea that the theological significance of creation is intelligible beyond the Word of God (McKenny, *The Analogy of Grace*, 253). So this is something we would need to keep in mind in any attempt to formulate what Barth's final word on conscience might have been.

87. Barth, *Ethics*, 214.
88. Ibid.
89. Ibid., 339.
90. Ibid., 340.
91. Ibid., 339.
92. Ibid., 435.
93. Ibid., 434.

living in me" if I regard my neighbor as "unworthy of Christ." This means, on the one hand, that I am given the responsibility to bear witness with my life and words to the neighbor that she belongs to God, that we are united together in Christ.[94] But this also means, on the other hand, that the neighbor has this *authority* in relation to me, that the neighbor I encounter, the neighbor given to me, "can and should remind me of my commitment as a member of the people of God."[95] I must regard my neighbors as those whom Christ counts as his own and so I must regard them as "Christ's messengers to me."[96] In their humanity I must see Christ's humanity—the humanity in which we see the truth of God's being for us and our determination to be those whom God is for.[97] And so as my neighbor confronts me, Barth claims, "Jesus Christ confronts me."[98] "I cannot evade these wonderful saints," Barth writes about our neighbors, "if I am not to evade Christ."[99] My relationship to Christ will, consequently, "constantly have to take place concretely in the relationship to my neighbor." We cannot be without our neighbor if we are to live as those who are reconciled. We "stand or fall" with this person whom we must regard as one God has taken seriously enough "to set him up over against me as a proclaimer of God's word."[100]

But I must confess, Barth insists, that my life moves by a very "unsavor like orientation to itself."[101] There is always the *peccator* of the *simul* formula Barth endorses. In this light, as I am here and now, it is true of me (though this not the only or final truth) that I do not want to grant the neighbor this claim. And so as God speaks to me through the neighbor, the neighbor is invested with an alien authority, an authority that contradicts our sinful will and stands over against us as a heteronomous law. In this heteronomy, again and again, Christ comes to me through my neighbor, asking me if I will be "fundamentally open to others"—to this particular other before me—"in and with their sin."[102] Christ has brought us into fellowship with each other through our fellowship with him. Through our reconciliation we are "completely linked."[103] And this means, if we are to hear God speaking to us as our Reconciler, we have to accept that we are bound in solidarity to this particular neighbor who comes to me with the authority of our common Lord.

Consequently, as God speaks to us through our neighbors God asks us to be humble, to surrender to the claim they make on us, to serve them, and not to

---

94. Ibid., 343.
95. Ibid., 382.
96. Ibid., 335.
97. Ibid.
98. Ibid.
99. Ibid., 348.
100. Ibid., 348–9.
101. Ibid., 344.
102. Ibid.
103. Ibid., 425.

consider ourselves better than them. The humility required of us by our neighbors is what corresponds to conscience's call to gratitude and calling's call to submit to certain orders. Through the neighbor, God asks us "to want to live together with the sinner, not ignoring his deepest plight, as though with a little good will it might not exist, but taking it into account that this is how he is . . . and accepting him as such," as Christ has accepted us.[104] Barth's point, in this light, is that as a messenger of Christ, my neighbor reminds me of Christ's humility, points me to it, and charges me to imitate Christ in my life in my relation to the neighbors God has set before me. Of course, Barth's claim is that Christ's humility is for our sake, for the reconciliation of our sin. Our humble submission to the claim of our neighbor is therefore "the attitude of one who knows himself to be one who is upheld by grace."[105] To be humble is not merely to imitate Christ's humility but also to act in the penitent consciousness that Christ humbled himself to save us from our sin. Therefore, it is an act of humble repentance before God to acknowledge the neighbor's authority and to submit to her claim as the claim of Christ over me.[106]

An important point that is implicit for much of Barth's treatment of the neighbor is that the authority the neighbor bears in relation to us *is* the authority of the church. Whether purposively or not, Barth consistently muddles the neighbor and the church together in *Ethics* without a systematic account of their relation. But it is clear that since I am to humble myself before my neighbor as one who belongs to Christ, I must regard the neighbor as one who lives with me "in and with the reality of church."[107] Likewise, Barth writes that my neighbor "is given to me in the church as a member of the people of God."[108] To reject the neighbor's authority as one through whom God speaks would be, consequently, a rejection of Christ, the community of Christ's members, and so a rejection of Christ's church.[109] And this is true even if my neighbor "be the worst of pagans." Even so, she nonetheless has over me "the right . . . of the church, i.e. the domestic order of the community of Christ which is fulfilled by him in relation to me and which I have to acknowledge as a member of the community."[110] We are united with our neighbors in the "community of Christ." We stand with them under the authority of Christ, whose work on our behalf claims us for a life of humble openness to others. And under Christ, in his church, we are entrusted with this authority over one another, to bear witness to Christ's authoritative claim on us. The invisible church, the church that is hidden with Christ in God, is the apparent object of this muddling of church and neighbor. Short of a full-fledged ecclesiology, the point Barth wants to stress is that the authority of my neighbor as an organ of God's voice is the authority of

104. Ibid.
105. Ibid., 402; cf. 405.
106. Ibid., 405.
107. Ibid., 351.
108. Ibid., 420.
109. Ibid., 370.
110. Ibid., 283.

the community of those whom Christ counts as his own, the church. And this is to say that for Barth, in one sense, the claim that God makes upon us and before which God holds us accountable is a claim that comes to us mediated through our very concrete relationships with our neighbors. It is a claim, in a certain sense, that comes mediated to us through the church.

Conscience, with its absolute authority, is therefore far from the only voice through which God speaks to us here and now. God speaks to us through our calling, claiming us in certain orders of life, and God speaks to us through our neighbors, directing us humbly to respect the claim they make on us as members of the community of Christ. Conscience is a decisive voice with final authority, but it does not stand alone and we do full justice to the systematic structure of *Ethics* to situate conscience alongside calling and the neighbor, as these voices significantly qualify the authority of conscience as conscience breaks into our present life. This is an important qualification, that there are these other voices that do have degrees of authority. We must remember, Barth insists, that God does not speak to us only through our own direct relation to God as God's children.

But these other voices are not simply distinct voices through which God speaks to us alongside conscience; they are distinct voices but their significance for conscience is not simply as a qualification. We noted earlier that Barth claims that these voices relate to each other like "concentric circles" and that what each voice says has a bearing on the meaning of what the others say. This is a point Barth makes above all with respect to conscience which is, he claims, the "innermost of three concentric circles."[111] The voice of conscience comes to us from the site of our final relation to God, where we, as God's children, live in glad, grateful agreement with God's will. This is the end of all God's ways with us as creatures and reconciled sinners. "The point" of our creaturely calling and our membership in the body of reconciled sinners is "our heavenly and eternal calling."[112] What God commands of us through these other voices finds its fulfillment in what God commands of us through our conscience. Beyond "orderliness and humility," Barth writes,

> gratitude means specifically that I am gladly, i.e. voluntarily and cheerfully, ready for what God wills of me in acknowledgement of what is given to me by God and as my necessary response to God's gift. This responsive "gladly" is not necessarily contained in the concepts of orderliness and humility. Orderliness might be grudging and humility forced, although, naturally, in such cases, they could not be claimed as a fulfillment of the divine command. Gratitude, however, is this responsive "gladly" which by going beyond them makes all orderliness and humility right and complete.[113]

---

111. Ibid., 467.
112. Ibid., 470.
113. Ibid., 500.

As God claims us through our calling and through our neighbors, God lets us through our conscience claim ourselves. God lets us direct ourselves to do everything God asks of us through these other voices gladly, cheerfully, and voluntarily. "Do we really obey," Barth asks, "if we do not obey as children?"[114] The distinction Barth makes between calling and the neighbor, on the one hand, and conscience, on the other, is a distinction between "secondary" and "primary and personal agreement" with God's will.[115] The child of God, who lives in this innermost circle in primary obedience to the will of the Father, "shows what obedience is in the two outer circles."[116] Conscience's own distinctive call, the call to gratitude, underwrites what is said to us through the other voices, so that we are asked in everything we do if we will act gladly. When we are asked to submit in certain orders of life or to submit to the claim our neighbor (the church) makes upon us, we can do so "grudgingly," but what God finally wants with us is that we submit to God's will gladly, happily, of our own accord. And so while Barth devotes considerably more attention to calling and to the neighbor than to conscience, when he finally does come to conscience he concedes that all "honor must be *quietly* paid to it."[117]

Conclusion: Conscience between Singularity and Solidarity

But the honor Barth tells us to pay to conscience must be quiet because its presence to us here and now is, as we have seen, faint and elusive. As creatures and sinners saved by grace we never hear the voice of our conscience alone. Barth is clear that God makes claims upon us that are, indeed, mediated, that come to us through our neighbors (the church) and through the interpersonal circumstances of our lives. We cannot know what God commands of us apart from these social contingencies. Conscience—the singular, unmediated relationship with God that constitutes conscience—is always there in the background making its final and decisive claim, asking us if we will submit to the claims made upon us by these other voices. But it is there in the background as a kind of translucent presence, something we should never assume we can fully grasp. If we assume otherwise and make a great parade of our conscience, and if we think with our conscience we "hold the norm of God in our hands,"[118] we are fools chasing a "will-o'-the wisp," almost certain to go astray.[119] Perhaps this qualification is too strong and makes conscience so marginal a concept for Barth as to be meaningless, at least with respect to its ability to inform our everyday conduct. And yet, however faint and elusive conscience

---

114. Ibid.
115. Ibid., 467.
116. Barth, *Ethics*, 467.
117. Ibid., 479; emphasis added.
118. Ibid.
119. Ibid., 472.

might be, Barth insists that it does break through. If only like a flash of lightning or a fleeting epiphany, conscience reminds us that even as we are here and now inextricably bound to one another, even as our relationship to God in Christ takes place in the present through the community of Christ that is the church, we are ultimately "not so much bound to one another" as we are each singularly bound to the Lord.[120] What Barth means is not that we are not bound to one another, but that we are first singularly bound to the Lord and only then bound to one another. Indeed, Barth is quite clear that the singularity we have with God in the relationship of conscience is a singularity each of us has. And this means, in turn, that it is through the very singularity of our relationship to God in conscience that we find a source of eternal solidarity with one another.[121] That is, according to Barth, the fact that God's command claims each and every human being—the fact of the universality of God's command and the universality of conscience—entails that we are first singularly bound to God but therein also indissolubly bound to one another. As McKenny writes, "to be *irreplaceable* in one's accountability is not necessarily to be *alone* in one's accountability."[122]

This concession to the fundamental solidarity Barth's theory of conscience affirms will almost certainly not satisfy the most ardent communitarian. And to say, in conclusion, that conscience in Barth's *Ethics* occupies a place between singularity and solidarity might need some qualification. The reality of conscience, again, for Barth, comes from a place of absolute ethical singularity in which the individual exists in a distinct, unconditioned, direct, and unmediated relation to God. Singularity is the dominant note in Barth's theory of conscience. And yet, when conscience comes to the individual, when it reaches out from her eschatological future into her present, it meets her in a place where her relation to God and God's command is highly mediated; to the creature and sinner saved by grace God's command comes "from one person to another," McKenny explains, as a "public, not . . . private occurrence."[123] If one takes Barth's theory of conscience by itself then it would, indeed, anchor a very individualistic ethics. But taking conscience by itself is something Barth strictly forbids. And so we return to McKenny's assessment that Barth's moral theology in general and, as I have tried to show in this chapter, his theory of conscience in particular resist any simple dichotomy between individualistic and communitarian forms of ethics. Barth reminds us that while the community of Christ, the church, plays an important role here and now to mediate God's presence and God's command, our personal accountability before God must never be collapsed into accountability to any community, ecclesial or otherwise. Barth's theory of conscience does not encourage a fideistic recourse to communal authority as the way to resist the lure of the modern self-asserting subject. But it also does not hold up the individual as a solitary sovereign who

---

120. Ibid., 84.
121. Ibid.
122. McKenny, *The Analogy of Grace*, 274.
123. Ibid.

has the power, here and now, to go her own way with the "norm of God" in her hands. Conscience, for Barth, sets the individual singularly before God, but in a way that accompanies and undergirds the more socially mediated forms of God's command. It is grounded in a person's singular relationship to God, as it directs a person toward her dependence upon and solidarity with others.

Chapter 4

SUPEREROGATION FOR PROTESTANTS?

Eric Gregory

Once upon a time the category of the supererogatory was a major division between Catholic and Protestant thought. Indeed, the rejection of the related distinction between precepts and evangelical counsels and a hierarchy between clergy and laity were signature themes of Reformation polemics. The reasons for this rejection were largely soteriological, bound up with debates about justification, sin, merit, and indulgences. But, as with most theological controversies concerning nature and grace or law and Gospel, disputes around the *opera supererogationis* involved dramatic reinterpretations of Christian liberty and the apparently radical demands of its biblical sources as law-like binding prescriptions for sinful humanity: especially the command to love God and neighbor. The diverse legacies of Protestant anti-supererogation are found in both its other-regarding moral strenuousness and its drawing together notions of Christian perfection, joyful vocation, and creaturely fulfillment.

Debates about supererogation crystalized many of the central theological disputes of the Reformation. A great deal of modern Protestant-Catholic dialogue has historicized these disputes and the terms on which they were once debated. But, apart from the particulars of Christian doctrine and ecclesial practice that now seem a matter for historical theology, Protestant denials of the supererogatory are often linked to profound changes in religious and moral sensibilities that exceed their distinct origins. They play an important role, for example, in what Charles Taylor has identified as both "the affirmation of ordinary life" and "a drive to make over the whole society to higher standards."[1] These changes, at times contradictory and unintended, launched various projects of social reform and issued novel ways of conceiving the sacred and the profane given contested notions of Christian freedom that could swing between moralism and antinomianism. Recent historical scholarship has emphasized their often-neglected salience for dramatic developments in early modern ethics and politics, especially for Protestant

---

1. Charles Taylor, *Sources of the Self: The Making of Modern Identity* (Cambridge: Cambridge University Press, 1989), 215; and Charles Taylor, *A Secular Age* (Cambridge, MA: Harvard University Press, 2007), 63.

conceptions of rights and natural law.[2] These religious origins are frequently, if briefly, mentioned in the resurgent interest in supererogation in modern moral philosophy.[3] One irony of this resurgence is the fact that supererogation now attracts the critical energies of moral philosophy much more than it does in the field of Protestant ethics. Why this need not, and should not, be the case is the topic of this chapter.

Reviving supererogation, even by way of invitation and reconstruction, may seem an unusual way to honor the work of a Protestant ethicist who seems to have no use for the term. Of course, issues raised by supererogation might best be discussed without the use of a term so burdened by history. But I think it is fitting to do so in this context for several reasons. Protestant theology and modern moral discourse are central themes in the work of Gerald McKenny. His scholarship, especially on Karl Barth's ethics, offers a confident yet irenic appreciation of Reformation distinctives in dialogue with the best of Catholic moral theology and secular philosophy. McKenny's work in bioethics, moreover, engages directly with the broad cultural changes identified previously by Charles Taylor with the Reformation.[4] Finally, McKenny's readings of Scripture in light of the moral law as revealed natural law reintroduces classical approaches that once made supererogation a central topic (even by way of its denial). In short, turning to supererogation might offer another way to challenge stereotypes and to frame key issues raised by McKenny for thinking about the relevance of Protestant theological ethics today. Or so I will argue.

My goals are threefold. First, I simply wish to call attention to the relative neglect of supererogation in religious ethics, especially among Protestants. Second, I point out that when it is addressed, Protestant ethicists of various stripes endorse the concept of the supererogatory (or something like it, as I later explore with reference to the notion of "imperfect duties"). And, third, I turn to a recent proposal for Christian ethics by McKenny that bears upon this topic by offering a generative way to reorient Christian ethics in light of Reformation commitments.

---

2. See, for example, Sarah Mortimer, "Counsels of Perfection and Reformation Political Thought," *The Historical Journal* 62, no. 2 (2019): 311–30; Johan Olshoorn, "Grotius on Natural Law and Supererogation," *Journal of the History of Philosophy* 57, no. 3 (2019): 443–69; and Greg Conti, "Jean Barbeyrac, Supererogation, and the Search for a Safe Religion," *Modern Intellectual History* 13, no. 1 (2016): 1–31.

3. See, for example, David Heyd, *Supererogation: Its Status in Ethical Theory* (Cambridge: Cambridge University Press, 1982); and Gregory Mellema, *Beyond the Call of Duty: Supererogation, Obligation, and Offence* (Albany: SUNY Press, 1991).

4. See, for example, Gerald McKenny, *To Relieve the Human Condition: Bioethics, Technology, and the Body* (Albany: State University of New York, 1997); and Gerald McKenny, *Biotechnology, Human Nature, and Christian Ethics* (Cambridge: Cambridge University Press, 2018).

Supererogation in Modern Moral Philosophy

By contrast to early Protestants, and their afterlife in figures like Kant and Mill, it seems natural to many contemporary philosophers to distinguish ordinary morality from its higher, more demanding perfections. While the features of supererogation are defined in various ways, let's begin with a minimal notion. A common attraction of the supererogatory is that it makes sense of acts that are neither required nor forbidden but are morally good. Supererogation opens space to value these actions (for moral reasons) without subsuming them under the category of duty, and, so it is thought, committing to a pathological altruism. Different vocabularies of justice and beneficence, or goodness and rightness, seem to capture something about a familiar division in our moral experience. Some things are demanded. We consider them obligations that trigger accountability in a relationship. Others are worthy of admiration. They might display virtuous excellence of character that excites the moral imagination. But we do not necessarily blame someone for failing to do their duty by their omission, especially when the sacrifice is difficult and great.

To trade in terms of J. O. Urmson's seminal 1958 article on this topic, there are compelling and intelligible reasons we find some people saintly or heroic. They go beyond what Urmson called "rock-bottom duties which are duties for all and from every point of view."[5] He argued that the ethics of his day, especially Kantianism and utilitarianism, had "no obvious theoretical niche" to accommodate them.[6] In fact, a dominant focus on obligation, permission, and wrongdoing obscured and even denied the basic distinction between duty and supererogation that he thought they revealed.

Finding that theoretical niche has occupied many philosophical efforts, and not simply in terms of acts of extraordinary self-sacrifice but more ordinary actions of everyday kindness that it seems odd to characterize as duties or requirements. Supererogation, for Urmson, pertains to a gap between what we are required to do and what would be even better to do (beyond duty's strict requirements for the sake of some good that is also worth caring about). While previous generations focused mainly on Kantian and utilitarian theories, we now find a variety of treatments that include what has come to be called virtue ethics and appears to have its own difficulties with accommodating supererogation.[7] But accounting for the apparent

---

5. J. O. Urmson, "Saints and Heroes," in *Moral Concepts*, ed. Joel Feinberg (Oxford: Oxford University Press, 1969), 60–73 (64). Originally published in A. I. Melden, ed., *Essays in Moral Philosophy* (Seattle: University of Washington Press, 1958), 198–216. Urmson's examples include a doctor who volunteers to join depleted medical forces in a plague-ridden city or a soldier who throws himself on an exploding grenade to save others.

6. Urmson, "Saints and Heroes," 67.

7. See, for example, Rebecca Stangl, "Neo-Aristotelian Supererogation," *Ethics* 126 (January 2016): 339–65. For a proposal that also seeks to "forge a symbiosis between religious ethics and a certain kind of secular ethic," see Andrew Flescher, *Heroes, Saints & Ordinary*

strangeness of the morally good or praiseworthy that is not strictly required has proved a conceptually difficult and controversial task. Philosophers refer to the "paradox of supererogation" in discussing actions that appear good, even the best thing to do all things considered, but if omitted are not considered a moral failure.[8] Some philosophers who believe morality is overriding have defended the intuitively strange idea that there are "morally permissible moral mistakes."[9] The status of supererogation is now seen to expose "deep problems about the nature of duty and its limits, the relationship between duty and value, the role of ideals and excuses in ethical judgments, the nature of moral reasons, and the connections between actions and virtue."[10] Contemporary moral philosophy, in fact, has been particularly vexed by questions about how to accommodate supererogatory actions that seem to go "beyond the call of duty," or to use biblical language, "to go the second mile."[11] A massive literature now exists, with increasingly technical proposals, examples, and definitions that probe the normative and meta-ethical dimensions of moral demands.[12]

Morality (Washington: Georgetown University Press, 2003), 18. Flescher offers a virtue-based imperative "which bids one to improve one's character over time and thereby reconceive the nature and scope of one's first-order moral obligations" (10). His modified account still distinguishes duty and supererogation. He describes it as "weakly 'perfectionist'" (11).

8. See Terry Hogan and Mark Timmons, "Untying the Knot from the Inside Out: Reflections on the 'Paradox of Supererogation,'" *Social Philosophy and Policy* 27 (2010): 29–63. Hogan and Timmons try to dissolve the paradox by refusing the assumption that "the only way in which a moral reason can favor an action is by tending to require that action" (62).

9. Elizabeth Harman, "Morally Permissible Moral Mistakes," *Ethics* 126 (January 2016): 366–93. Harman defends the supererogatory, but here distinguishes a moral wrong from a moral mistake. On this view the supererogatory is not simply in the realm of the permissible. In certain circumstances, failing to do something supererogatory invites criticism as a failure to respond to moral reasons even if it "falls short of blameworthiness" (392). On distinguishing supererogation and moral obligation, see also Stephen Darwall, *Morality, Authority, and Law* (Oxford: Oxford University Press, 2013).

10. David Heyd, "Supererogation," in *The Stanford Encyclopedia of Philosophy*, ed. Edward N. Zalta, Winter 2019 ed., Available online: https://plato.stanford.edu/archives/win2019/entries/supererogation/

11. Mellema notes the etymological (and conceptual) origins of supererogation in the Vulgate version of the parable of the Good Samaritan in the *supererogare* ("to overexpend or spend in addition"). Interestingly, he observes, "the Latin verb is used here in connection with the efforts of the innkeeper, not the efforts of the Samaritan" (Mellema, *Beyond the Call of Duty*, 14). It is the innkeeper who is asked to care for the wounded man even if the "two pence" are not sufficient.

12. Christopher Cowley, ed., *Supererogation*, Royal Institute of Philosophy Supplement 77 (Cambridge: Cambridge University Press, 2015).

Urmson's saints were "moral saints," to borrow a term from another influential article of modern moral philosophy that relates to supererogation. Like Urmson, Susan Wolf appealed to certain ordinary judgments that she thought were generally ignored by contemporary moral philosophy. But she did so in order to raise questions about "the moral point of view" and its place in a human life relative to nonmoral values.[13] She argued that "there seems a limit to how much morality we can stand" and questioned a prevailing assumption of ethical theories that "it is always better to be morally better."[14] Her concerns about the limits of morality were distinct from Urmson's interest in justifying an enforceable basic morality that was universal, yet limited in scope. They tap into ongoing debates about the overriding nature of morality, especially in relation to what makes for a good life *for an individual*. But, like Urmson, Wolf also held that "any plausible moral theory must make use of some conception of supererogation."[15]

This chapter does not aim to engage these developments directly or to assess their relevance for contemporary Protestant moral theology. However, I do think it would be helpful to do so, regardless of one's attitude to systematic moral theory. To be sure, like Wolf, influential strands of Protestantism have called into question a post-Enlightenment "moral point of view." Christians are no strangers to thinking about law and morality as bondage, especially this side of Luther's reading of Paul, where the justified sinner is set free for a life of gratuitous service to God and neighbor. Devotion to morality or a morally goodwill, let alone a moral theory, can be idolatrous on religious terms. Unlike Wolf, however, Christians have put morality in its place in order to contrast its anthropocentric assumptions to the theocentric logic of Christian faith. Supererogation, in fact, is sometimes framed only as a dilemma for a secularized post-Christian morality that privileges autonomy and the language of rights and duties. It is a problem for morality without God, without eschatology, and without grace. As one recent Protestant ethicist writes, "supererogation does not belong in the repertoire of moral concepts we can derive from the New Testament . . . for believers in Christ to act like the Good Samaritan is not to go *beyond* the call of duty but to experience the amplification of it."[16] Christian ethics here *is* simply this amplification: "you have heard that it was said . . . but I say to you" (Mt. 5:43-44). Nothing is deontologically open-ended or optional: "be perfect, therefore, as your heavenly Father is perfect" (Mt. 5:48) and "when you have done all that is commanded you, say, 'We are unworthy servants; we have only done what was our duty'" (Luke 17:10). Christianity is itself supererogatory, rendering the term superfluous. There is no moral extra credit, no greater and lesser righteousness, no reward for being good.

---

13. Susan Wolf, "Moral Saints," *The Journal of Philosophy* 79, no. 8 (August 1982): 419–39.

14. Ibid., 423, 438.

15. Ibid., 438.

16. James Mumford, "The Experience of Obligation: The Enduring Promise of Levinas for Theological Ethics," *Studies in Christian Ethics* 33, no. 3 (2019): 352–69 (369).

Even this way of putting it, however, may not go far enough for Protestant critics of supererogation. The intensification of moral demands might still seem parasitic on an austere conception of morality that is deontological all the way down or presumes a stable autonomous self against whom claims of the other are to be adjudicated. This kind of duty language, upon which supererogation finds intelligibility, is simply out of place given what Christians confess about God revealed in Jesus Christ. In his discussion of Christian *agape*, for example, Colin Grant claims to undermine the very notion of supererogation by contrasting, on the one hand, "the vision that sees life as a gift, so that we live as recipients, linked in common indebtedness, and on the other hand, the vision of life that sees it as our possession, to be shared to some reasonable extent and to be subject to our withholding or bestowal beyond that."[17] Insofar as supererogation poses a problem for modern moral philosophy, so much the worse for the "moral point of view" without religion. In the words of another theologian, "the language of morality is in need of a supplemental discourse, a theological understanding of the importance of excessive acts of generosity."[18] Or, more pointedly, "Christian morality is a thing *so* strange, that it must be declared immoral or amoral according to all other human norms and codes of morality."[19] I am sympathetic to these concerns. They resonate with calls to keep theological ethics theological. Protestants want an ethics that takes its priority from the story of a personal God and the Gospel narrative of salvation rather than moral philosophy. For Protestants, this story can sometimes be told in terms of a religion that demands everything but requires nothing because God has done it for us.

I am not persuaded, however, that questions about supererogation are wedded to problems with modern secular ethics, though no doubt secular views might feel their particular force in certain ways given a tendency to draw a sharp distinction between the right and the good as independent sources of normativity. First, the appeal of supererogation is both more ancient and more persistent than these claims suggest.[20] Second, many Protestants who affirm "goodness overflowing from a boundless source" also affirm the need for the category.[21] Third, questions about merit, let alone meriting salvation, can be distinguished from asking whether or

---

17. Colin Grant, *Altruism and Christian Ethics* (Cambridge: Cambridge University Press, 2001), 183. Later, however, Grant writes, "there is no place for a category of supererogation because there are no limits to the expectations of caring" (247).

18. Stephen Webb, *The Gifting God: A Trinitarian Ethics of Excess* (Oxford: Oxford University Press, 1996), 29. For a different account of a divine gift economy that retains a strong notion of obligations to others (but not to God), see Kathryn Tanner, *Jesus, Humanity and The Trinity* (Minneapolis: Fortress, 2001).

19. John Milbank, "Can Morality Be Christian?" in *The Word Made Strange* (Oxford: Blackwell, 1997), 219–32.

20. For the long history, see Joachim Hruschka, "Supererogation and Meritorious Duties," *Annual Review of Law and Ethics* 6 (1998): 93–108.

21. Robert Adams, "Saints," *The Journal of Philosophy* 81, no. 7 (1984): 392–401.

not the language of obligations and moral requirements exhausts Christian ethics. These three points suggest, at the very least, that it is appropriate for Protestant ethics to identify a way of addressing the issues that the pull of supererogation identifies. In any case, the aims of this chapter are much more modest than a full theological defense of supererogation.

Supererogation in Modern Protestant Ethics

One of the more theologically sensitive discussions of supererogation in moral philosophy once noted, "it is common to find theologians and philosophers of religion endorsing the contention of Luther and Calvin that no human creature ever performs good works over and above the fulfillment of obligation."[22] This contention may be common for some of the reasons given previously, or in light of alternative ways of construing the relationship between Christian faith and moral obligation. But, as with Gregory Mellema's own work, there are many trends that point in the direction of a Protestant revival of the supererogatory and a shift from anti-supererogation to pro-supererogation. One hope of this chapter is to call attention to this trend and its significance for Protestant ethics.

Modern Protestant ethics, to be sure, has focused on many issues adjacent to supererogation; these include the most discussed topics in the field. It would be interesting to tell the story of modern Christian ethics in terms of supererogation.[23]

Consider, for example, the centrality of debates about love and justice, virtue and obligation, doing and allowing, *agape* and special relations, self-regard and self-sacrifice, law and ethics, or mercy and forgiveness. All of these debates might usefully be organized by the concept of the supererogatory, or at least in relation to it as each of these topics is often framed in terms that at least recall supererogation debates. Does Christian charity, for example, go beyond what is owed to others by the claims of justice? Is forgiveness unconditionally required of Christians? Should the law promote virtue or merely prohibit certain kinds of

---

22. Mellema, *Beyond the Call of Duty*, 55. Mellema's examples of theistic opponents of supererogation were Karl Rahner and Joseph Allen. Both, he argues, expand the moral domain to include a "duty to be perfect" (Rahner) and a "duty to go the second mile" (Allen). In a later article, Mellema qualifies whether or not Allen's account of covenant love admits something like supererogation. See Gregory Mellema, "Supererogation and Theism," *International Journal of Philosophy and Theology* 5, no. 1 (2017): 1–7.

23. Debates about supererogation, for example, would be one way to think about how a previous generation of Protestant ethics discussed "situation ethics." See, for example, Gene Outka and Paul Ramsey, eds., *Norm and Context in Christian Ethics* (New York: Charles Scribner's Sons, 1968). The term explicitly appears several times in another influential volume for the field of Protestant ethics: see James Gustafson, *Ethics from a Theocentric Perspective*, Volume 2 (Chicago: University of Chicago Press, 1984), 11, 22, 114–15, and 171.

wrongs? How do eschatological expectations radically transform the duties that seem to go along with our ordinary (or natural) roles and responsibilities? The same holds for any number of issues in applied ethics, including bioethics, animal ethics, economic justice, the ethics of war and peace, and the more recent concern for structural injustice and collective responsibility. Supererogation, in one sense, is a way to name how Christian ethics deals with "the tension between creation as we know it and the new creation that God will bring."[24] But explicit reference to supererogation is relatively rare. The term itself barely appears in most standard reference materials.[25]

The reasons for this shift between the days of Luther and Calvin and contemporary Protestant ethics invite historical investigation. Of course, we no longer live in a world animated by the scholastic vocabulary of sixteenth-century Reformation debates. The professionalization of theological subdisciplines also likely plays a role. On the one hand, as we will see, Christian ethics in dialogue with moral philosophy does retain interest in the question; however, on the other hand, the relative isolation of Christian ethics from important developments in biblical studies and systematic theology might account for its relative absence. For example, few scholars in Protestant ethics have incorporated the controversial debates about Paul and the law that seem ripe for such analysis.[26] That said, I suspect the recovery of virtue ethics in Protestant ethics best explains its relative absence in the field. As we have seen, to the extent that supererogation is seen as a problem constructed by approaches to morality that focus on duties (as in Kant) or maximizing value in states of affairs (as in some versions of utilitarianism), the turn to "agent-centered" virtue ethics might be thought to dissolve its conceptual sting. One is hard-pressed, for example, to find sustained attention to supererogation in the work of influential Protestant thinkers like Stanley Hauerwas.[27] When mentioned, it is dismissed as inconsistent with the Christian story.[28]

---

24. David Clough, *On Animals: Theological Ethics*, Volume II (London: T&T Clark Bloomsbury, 2018), 80.

25. The lone entry that deals with supererogation in the *Blackwell Companion to Religious Ethics* (Oxford: Blackwell, 2004) is an article on Jewish ethics. A rare reference in the *Oxford Handbook of Theological Ethics* (Oxford: Oxford University Press, 2005) is in the context of the use of confessions in Anglicanism.

26. See, for example, John Barclay, *Paul and the Gift* (Grand Rapids: Eerdmans, 2015).

27. Of course, Hauerwas's relation to "virtue ethics" and "Protestant ethics" is complicated. See, for example, Stanley Hauerwas, "How To Do or Not Do Protestant Ethics," in *The Work of Theology* (Grand Rapids: Eerdmans, 2015), 52–64. On Hauerwas and virtue ethics, see Jennifer Herdt, "Hauerwas Among the Virtues," *Journal of Religious Ethics* 40, no. 2 (2012): 202–27. Herdt helpfully locates Hauerwas's subordination of an ethics of obligation or principle in its particular historical context.

28. Stanley Hauerwas and David Burrell, "From System to Story," in *Why Narrative? Readings In Narrative Theology*, ed. Stanley Hauerwas and L. Gregory Jones (Grand Rapids: Eerdmans Publishing, 1989), 170n17.

Yet, when discussed, some of the most prominent accounts in Protestant ethics *endorse* rather than *deny* the possibility of supererogation. These exceptions prove the rule.[29] For example, Gene Outka's *Agape: An Ethical Analysis* concluded with a discussion of the topic. While sometimes read as a broadly Kantian interpretation of the love commands that denies supererogation, Outka admitted, "the concept of supererogation can allow for certain complexities in the moral life which the typical notion of duty fails to include."[30] Here, he makes brief references to the debates in moral philosophy launched by Urmson. Outka's analysis focuses primarily on the way in which supererogation makes intelligible what he calls "agent-stringency." Agent-stringency involves morally relevant differences between an agent's relation to himself/herself and his/her relation to others. On his view, a person may "*exhort* others to go the second mile," but he/she cannot reproach others for failing to do so. Outka's discussion is admittedly undeveloped, but it was picked up by others, particularly by David Little who challenged an easy conflation of Protestantism and anti-supererogationism among modern moral philosophers. He argued, for example, that Calvin's idea of "Christian freedom" makes room for "what might be called a reconstructed view of supererogation."[31]

Timothy P. Jackson is another Protestant ethicist who favorably entertains the supererogatory in his treatment of *agape* as paradoxically "both a commandment and a gift, both required and heroic."[32] In *Love Disconsoled*, trading in both philosophical and biblical idioms, Jackson offers a typological scale of moral actions, motives, and effects. Liberation ("megavirtue") and abomination ("megavice") lie at the extremes of his analysis of love as a theological virtue, or what he calls a "metavalue." Liberation transcends obligation, like supererogation. It highlights a "prophetic capacity to transcend standing obligations and to redefine moral rightness in new and unexpected ways."[33] Jackson explicitly denies medieval Catholic ideas that supererogatory acts generate a treasury of merit. But

---

29. A recent doctoral dissertation notes this asymmetry between philosophical and theological ethics. See B. J. Condrey, "The Possibility and Role of Supererogation in Protestant Ethics," (PhD diss., University of Edinburgh, 2020). Condrey endorses Mellema's appeal to a Protestant doctrine of vocation in support of supererogation, but extends analysis to the divorce passages in Matthew (5:31-32 and 19:1-9).

30. Gene Outka, *Agape: An Ethical Analysis* (New Haven: Yale University Press, 1977), 297.

31. David Little, "The Law of Supererogation," in *The Love Commandments: Essays in Christian Ethics and Moral Philosophy*, ed. Edmund N. Santurri and William Werpehowski (Washington: Georgetown University Press, 1992), 160.

32. Timothy P. Jackson, *Love Disconsoled: Meditations on Christian Charity* (Cambridge: Cambridge University Press, 1999), 28. Jackson claims that the biblical love commandments are "holy oxymorons that can only be taken to heart by persons who have been touched by grace" (117).

33. Jackson, *Love Disconsoled*, 115–16.

he also denies the standard Protestant and Kantian denials of supererogation. Supererogatory virtues, for Jackson, reveal a kind of charismatic goodness that can outstrip mere dutifulness.

Still another Protestant endorsement of supererogation can be found in Robert Adams' *Finite and Infinite Goods: A Framework for Ethics*. Adams' approach to ethics is quite different from Outka's or Jackson's. Though each highlights the place of love in Christian ethics, Adams draws more from Calvin than Luther, and also more from Plato than Kant. For Adams, there is a difference between God wanting us to do something and God commanding us to do it.[34] Again, for those sensitive to such distinctions, Adams' framework might be considered theistic moral philosophy rather than Protestant ethics. But this is neither the place to parse such distinctions, nor to get into the relevant details of Adams' account of the semantics of obligation, excellence in resembling God, or vocation. I simply note that his version of divine command ethics distinguishes the good and the obligatory. In his words, "I think it is no virtue in a theistic metaethics to rule out supererogation as impossible by the very nature of obligation."[35] Other examples can be found, especially given the influence of these authors in Christian moral philosophy. I suspect growing attention to divine command and natural law ethics among a younger generation of Protestant ethicists might further expand its appeal or at least commentary. After virtue ethics, or at least after learning from virtue ethics, supererogation is back.

McKenny's "The Rich Young Ruler and Christian Ethics"

In various works, Gerald McKenny has focused on the significance of the Protestant Reformation for ecumenical moral theology and the church universal. In particular, his reading of Karl Barth suggests a distinctively Protestant account of justification and sanctification that relates divine grace and human moral action.[36] For McKenny, this account offers an alternative to the Augustinian-Thomist tradition for an age when "Protestants appear to have lost confidence in the viability of their most distinctive theological commitments."[37] In a recent essay, McKenny extends his proposal in part by turning to the kinds of phenomena that have swirled around debates about supererogation. McKenny's essay is generative in part because it situates these questions explicitly back within a biblical

---

34. Robert Adams, *Finite and Infinite Goods: A Framework for Ethics* (Oxford: Oxford University Press, 1999), 260.

35. Ibid.

36. Gerald McKenny, *The Analogy of Grace: Karl Barth's Moral Theology* (Oxford: Oxford University Press, 2010), and Gerald McKenny, "Karl Barth and the Plight of Protestant Ethics," in *The Freedom of a Christian Ethicist: The Future of a Reformation Legacy*, ed. Brian Brock and Michael Mawson (London: Bloomsbury T&T Clark, 2016), 17–37.

37. McKenny, "Karl Barth and the Plight of Protestant Ethics," 17.

framework.³⁸ He turns to the story of the rich young ruler rather than the even more familiar parable of the Good Samaritan.³⁹

In the story (Mt. 19:16-30; Mark 10:17-31; Luke 18:18-30), a wealthy man or ruler (Luke) asks Jesus what he must do to inherit eternal life. Jesus recites the commandments from the second table of the Decalogue, which the man claims to have kept from his youth. Jesus then says, "If you wish to be perfect, go, sell your possessions, and give the money to the poor, and you will have treasure in heaven; then come, follow me" (Mt. 19:20). The man went away grieving because he had many possessions.

According to McKenny, Christian ethics has interpreted the story in two different ways, each holding the biblical moral law as revealed natural law. They turn on the relationship between the commandments and Jesus' directive, which reflect different ways of relating the Decalogue, natural law, and the new law of the Gospel. First, as in Aquinas, Jesus' directive is seen as a counsel of perfection that goes beyond the Ten Commandments that are universally binding and is derived from fundamental principles of right reason. Counsels, as developed in the papal encyclical, *Veritatis Splendor*, are optional rather than obligatory. This remains the dominant reading despite McKenny's apt questions about how such a reading understands both the sadness of the rich young ruler and Jesus' famous declaration about the difficulty the rich encounter in entering the kingdom of God.

Second, the directive is actually to be found in the commandments that the man claims to have kept. For Calvin, God was a lawgiver not "a mere giver of counsel."⁴⁰ Jesus' call to discipleship does not add to the commandments so much as specify them. On McKenny's reading of this approach, Jesus reveals a "deficiency in his keeping of the commandments rather than pointing beyond them to a higher perfection" (60). Calvin, like Ireneaus, notes that Jesus does not

---

38. Gerald McKenny, "The Rich Young Ruler and Christian Ethics: A Proposal," *Journal of the Society of Christian Ethics* 40, no. 1 (2020): 59–76. Future references appear in the text.

39. Social historians have drawn attention to the importance of this story for early Christianity, even more than the Good Samaritan that captures contemporary imagination. See, for example, Peter Brown, *Through the Eye of the Needle: Wealth, the Fall of Rome, and the Making of Christianity in the West, 350–550 AD* (Oxford: Oxford University Press, 2012). Against the "high-minded language of the ascetic movement," Brown's work highlights the ways in which "humdrum acts of pious giving was just as important to Christian believers as was the occasional act of renunciation among the few" (xxv). For a contemporary reading, see Willie Jennings, "A Rich Disciple? Barth on the Rich Young Ruler," in *Reading the Gospels with Karl Barth*, ed. Daniel L. Migliore (Grand Rapids: Eerdmans, 2017), 56–66. Drawing on Barth, Jennings highlights the Markan reference to Jesus' love for the man, a love that challenges the captivity of his "imprisoned subjectivity" (61) and invites him to "covenant partnership" (62).

40. John Calvin, *Institutes of the Christian Religion*, ed. John T. McNeill, Volume I (Philadelphia: Westminster University Press, 1960), 419 (ii, viii, 56).

mention the tenth commandment against coveting. This implies that the man had failed to obey the commandments. But it does so by introducing what McKenny terms a "problematic internalization of discipleship" (61). McKenny does not linger on the problematic character of the interiorization; rather, he argues that Calvin fails to explain both how an external act ("sell your possessions, and give the money to the poor") overcomes the concealed interior disposition, and how the prohibition against coveting the goods of others relates to the man's coveting his own goods (60n5). By contrast, McKenny proposes that the rich man failed to satisfy the positive enjoinment implied in the eighth commandment against theft.

My point here is not to assess McKenny's interpretation of either Aquinas or Calvin, except to suggest that it is a familiar rendering that identifies potentially distinctive contrasts.[41] Again, McKenny raises important questions about each approach that would require some care in addressing matters of both textual detail and fundamental moral theology. What I find particularly notable for the purposes of this chapter is his reconstruction of Calvin's rules of interpretation, particularly in the notion that biblical moral law "contains positive enjoinments as well as negative prohibitions" (64). Others have identified the salience of Calvin's "rule of inference to the opposite."[42] McKenny argues that Calvin's emphasis on the *rationes* of the commandments extends beyond the acts explicitly prohibited or enjoined. Calvin understands the commandments as "testimonies of particular divine purposes for human life" (65). These purposes function as moral principles, liable to specification, and centrally governed by "the conformity of human life to the image of God" (66). Moreover, these principles and purposes can be identified, by a further "rule of extended reference," by attending to the whole of Scripture as an elaboration of the commandments (67).

Calvin's own application of his rules of interpretation yield promising, yet unsatisfying, results for McKenny. For my limited purposes, two claims are particularly relevant. First, McKenny argues that Calvin's equation of positive enjoinments and negative prohibitions risks a type of perfectionism that fails to guide the lives of believers or provide for their growth in righteousness. To relieve

---

41. McKenny's Thomas, at least in this chapter, is very much a "familiar" Protestant Thomas whose account of natural law appears divorced from the biblical drama of salvation. Familiar is not without controversy. Protestant readings that highlight Thomas' biblical commentaries and his discussion of the virtues would no doubt complicate McKenny's contrast. For a more evangelical and Christological Thomas, see, for example, Eugene F. Rogers, *Aquinas and the Supreme Court: Race, Gender, and the Failure of Natural Law in Thomas's Biblical Commentaries* (Oxford: Wiley-Blackwell, 2013), and John Bowlin, *Contingency and Fortune in Aquinas' Ethics* (Cambridge: Cambridge University Press, 1999).

42. The term is McKenny's, but see Mortimer, "Counsels of Perfection and Reformation Political Thought," 326–7.

this "overly demanding character of a moral life" (69), McKenny appeals to the familiar distinction between perfect and imperfect duties. Positive enjoinments, he claims, are primarily imperfect duties. They are binding, but "not at all times and not necessarily by the same acts" (70). He suggests that Calvin's discussion of neighbor-love and special relationships supports this revision, as does the pedagogical function of law in teaching and exhorting spiritual growth. Second, with particular attention to the eighth commandment, McKenny appeals to the work in biblical scholarship that finds "a progressive unfolding of the meanings of the commandments as their vectors proceed from the Decalogue through the legal codes to the prophetic and wisdom writings and ultimately to the New Testament" (71). While different from Calvin, McKenny argues that this extension is in the spirit of his identification of the biblical moral law within a wide range of acts that image God without separating precepts and counsels, thereby creating a two-tiered ethics. As he puts it, "in placing extraordinary acts that fulfill imperfect duties on a kind of continuum with more ordinary acts, it also insinuates the call to discipleship into our quotidian lives where it is always capable of disturbing our moral complacency" (75).

There is much to admire in McKenny's call to articulate moral principles that track the fullness of scriptural trajectories. His emphasis on biblical interpretation and the "continuum with more ordinary acts" is fertile ground for thinking about the place of the supererogatory in Protestant ethics. McKenny's reflection on this one story, for example, avoids reducing theology to ethics or pitting an ethic of law against an ethic of love because it joins discussion of law to reflection on the kingdom of God. It does not shy away from the demandingness of the commandment, even as it makes room for the ordinary and the extraordinary. Therefore, though McKenny does not set out to use this biblical passage to analyze the problem of supererogation, his approach suggests a promising strategy for those who might wish to do so. A fuller account would require further attention to a whole cluster of biblical texts and questions about them. For example, how should we read Jesus' *command* to the rich young ruler alongside the story of Ananias and Sapphira (Acts 5)? In that story, the judgment against those who fail to share possessions turns on lying about the deed, not withholding what was at their disposal. Is this a more apt example of an imperfect duty? Or, consider the familiar story of Mary and Martha, set just after the telling of the parable of the Good Samaritan (Luke 10). How might Mary's choice be read, if at all, in light of supererogation? What about the woman who brings the jar of costly oil to the house of Simon the Leper (Matthew 26), or Paul's teaching on marriage (1 Corinthians 7), renunciation of payment (1 Corinthians 9), and admonishment to "pray without ceasing" (1 Thess. 5:17)? These biblical stories, of course, should not be pressed into a narrow frame of supererogation. But they might give Christian ethics a new way of framing them.

These stories, like McKenny, do not mention supererogation. I suspect he might bristle at the term, perhaps for reasons similar to why many Protestants reject the eudaimonism of the Augustinian-Thomist tradition. The terms of that rejection, and its bearing on supererogation, would take us well beyond the scope of this chapter.[43] Moreover, it is not clear if his account of imperfect duties makes room for the category. Early modern Protestant natural lawyers, for example, relied heavily on the language of perfect and imperfect duties because it "made room for the operations of love which their religion made so important to them."[44] McKenny's revised version of Calvin's account of biblical moral law that admits a diverse range of moral acts and ways of describing them follows in this tradition. In one sense, imperfect duties are still duties, albeit in a particular sense that allows latitude in their mode of application given the contingencies of time, place, role, and circumstance. On the other hand, they seem to allow room for distinguishing morally good acts from morally required ones. Kant scholars, for example, differ on the relation between the supererogatory and acts of imperfect duty.[45] This chapter does not rest on resolving a question in Kant studies, or even how it relates to McKenny's proposal to read positive enjoinments exclusively in terms of commandments rather than virtues. McKenny himself raises several further unanswered questions about his proposal that turn on the relation between the Ten Commandments and the call to discipleship. But, to my mind, his emphasis on the pedagogical function of the law potentially bridges the deontic and aretaic in ways similar to how some thinkers have thought about supererogation. Duties are demanding, especially for those expected to pass through the eye of a needle. For Protestants, this is why we are compelled by grace to seek divine help for the life of Christian virtue. It may also be why the tradition has often prioritized negative prohibitions without losing sight of imperfect duties.[46] But the moral life for sinners and saints is such that we also need vocabulary to recognize the praiseworthy and the difficult, perhaps especially to recognize exemplars who extend received understandings of a positive enjoinment for us pilgrims on the way.

A still larger issue, and possible danger, remains largely unaddressed in McKenny's proposal that resists supererogation by resorting to a distinction between perfect and imperfect duties. McKenny is certainly aware of the historical injustices perpetuated by normative appeals to biblical commandments that are

---

43. See David S. Sytsma, "John Calvin and Virtue Ethics: Augustinian and Aristotelian Themes," *Journal of Religious Ethics* 48, no. 3 (2020): 519–56, and Joseph Clair, "Wolterstorff on Love and Justice: An Augustinian Response," *Journal of Religious Ethics* 41, no. 1 (2013): 138–67.

44. Jerome Schneewind, "Misfortunes of Virtue," *Ethics* 101, no. 1 (October 1990): 42–63 (49).

45. See, for example, Marcia Baron, "A Kantian Take on the Supererogatory," *Journal of Applied Philosophy* 33, no. 4 (November 2016): 347–62; Thomas E. Hill, Jr., *Dignity and Practical Reason* (Ithaca: Cornell University Press, 1992), 147–75; and Mark Timmons and Robert N. Johnson, *Reason, Value, and Respect: Kantian Themes from the Philosophy of Thomas E. Hill, Jr.* (Oxford: Oxford University Press, 2015).

46. See Millard Schumaker, *Sharing Without Reckoning: Imperfect Right and the Norms of Reciprocity* (Toronto: Wilfrid Laurier University Press, 1992).

thought to be binding on everyone. He concludes his essay by highlighting the importance of distinguishing judicial and moral laws. Roughly speaking, this move invites turning from moral theology to political theology. In his telling of the history of supererogation, Joachim Hruschka shows that distinctions between precepts and counsels that became the distinctions between perfect and imperfect duties are fundamentally "one history, namely the history of the differentiation between law and ethics."[47] For Hruschka, this differentiation ultimately has led to a positivistic approach to law wherein "the state and the state alone decides upon the contents of the law."[48] If Hauschka is right, McKenny's proposal has a history that is one more example of the secularizing consequences of the Reformation. No doubt McKenny the biblical natural lawyer would want to resist this fate, just as he wants to resist certain legacies of Calvin's legal philosophy that held all precepts of the New Law are just implicit in the natural law. But how so? All I have sought to do in this chapter is to show that Protestant ethics would do well to more explicitly tend to the supererogatory. It might be a further irony of the Reformation heritage should returning to supererogation enliven the uncertain field of Protestant ethics. That is something Gerald McKenny has certainly done.

---

47. Hruschka, "Supererogation and Meritorious Duties," 93.
48. Ibid., 107.

Chapter 5

VOCATION IN A MORAL VACUUM

PROTESTANTISM IN A DIVIDED SOCIETY

Robin W. Lovin

The diversity of faith in the United States has been celebrated by preachers, politicians, and historians as a testimony to the power of confessional Protestantism to shape both religious identity and religious toleration. In their worship and their creeds, today's congregations and denominations reflect the waves of immigration that first brought their forms of religious life to America in the early seventeenth century and set the terms for their relationship to the wider society.[1] Gerald McKenny's work, however, also reminds us that even the strongest expressions of Christian dogmatics are also shaped by modern thought and modern society.[2] In this, he continues the dialogical ethics of James Gustafson and H. Richard Niebuhr, and his ecumenical career is itself a model of definitive thinking in relationship to a variety of conversation partners.

In Protestantism, the interaction between modern context and confessional faith is evident in a social identity that hesitates between the church and the sect, uncertain whether it is the City on a Hill or the Treasure Hidden in a Field. This has been especially true in the United States, where a variety of religious traditions and abundant opportunities for social experiments have encouraged a full spectrum of possibilities, from established churches in New England, to circuit-riding revivalists, to utopian colonies on the edges of the frontier. Their theologies also covered the spectrum from classical Reformed theology taught in universities to homespun biblical narratives with a heavy emphasis on the power of the Spirit. But as H. Richard Niebuhr observed nearly a century ago, the ways in which denominational identities develop often depend as much on social context as on theological commitments.[3] Indeed, these forces continue to

---

1. David Hackett Fischer, *Albion's Seed: Four British Folkways in America* (New York: Oxford University Press, 1989).

2. Gerald McKenny, *The Analogy of Grace: Karl Barth's Moral Theology* (New York: Oxford University Press, 2010).

3. H. Richard Niebuhr, *The Social Sources of Denominationalism* (New York: Henry Holt and Company, 1929).

shape choices between a Protestantism that casts itself in resistance to society and one that finds its vocation within it. The compelling need for more effective Christian formation makes the sectarian approach particularly attractive today, but this chapter makes the case for a vocational formation that responds to what is missing in our contemporary context, rather than resisting what seems to be wrong with it.

The Search for Integrity in a Divided Society

The need for congregations and denominations to maintain a distinctive identity in a pluralistic society becomes theologically compelling when that society itself is divided. In the middle of the twentieth century, theologians worried about whether Protestants who were also part of a white, European culture, were losing a sense that their faith set them apart, even though many of their forebears had sectarian Protestant backgrounds. By the second or third generation, they were quick to identify Christian faith with American values and their commitment to "positive thinking" owed more to cultural optimism than to Christian hope.[4]

Toward the end of the century, after the social and political upheavals of the 1960s and 1970s, however, it was easier to make a theological argument that Christian identity has its own integrity, not only different from that of the wider society but also incommensurable with it. The task of the church is to form a community shaped by virtues and values that the world cannot grasp. That theology looked back to the traditions of the Radical Reformation, but it was being taken up with particular effect in theological circles by Stanley Hauerwas, whose roots were in Texas Methodism, who formulated his theology while teaching with a Mennonite colleague at Notre Dame, and who informed generations of students at Duke Divinity School. In this "ecumenical sectarianism," the Christian community is not so much sociologically as conceptually separated from the larger society. Any of its central affirmations "cannot help but appear a 'confessional' assertion that is unintelligible for anyone who is not already a Christian."[5]

This theological development accentuates the declining influence of mainline Protestantism in American culture and the demographic changes that have reduced its membership and participation along with its visibility. A more inward-looking ecclesiology fits the circumstances, as congregations increasingly concentrate on solving internal problems, meeting the individual needs of those who still show up at worship, and holding larger social questions at enough distance to avoid alienating any more of the members they cannot afford to lose. Prophetic witness is hard to achieve when no one is listening, and residual ideas about a Christian

---

4. Andrew Finstuen, *Original Sin and Everyday Protestants* (Chapel Hill: University of North Carolina Press, 2009).

5. Stanley Hauerwas, *With the Grain of the Universe* (Grand Rapids: Brazos Press, 2001), 15.

society whose preachers articulate the best version of a set of shared values are dispelled when they enter what Richard John Neuhaus called "the naked public square."[6] If the voice of the church can no longer be heard outside its walls, perhaps the task is to make sure that the message is at least audible to those who are still trying to understand it.

For clergy who must respond to these changes, the appeal of an admonition to give primary attention to Christian identity and theological integrity is understandable. It suggests a program of worship, education, and formation that engages the available participants, welcomes growth, but does not expect it, and does not open the door to divisive questions from outside. Perhaps it also suggests that if people find us unintelligible, we must be doing something right.

But the focus on Christian identity and theological integrity also conveys a misleading impression that the church's problems are unique. Rather than supposing that secularization has rendered the Christian idea of God, grace, and human nature incomprehensible, we might notice that all shared ideas about human purposes—not just the religious ideas—have been driven to the margins of our public life. This larger problem ties the fragility of the church to the fragmentation of society and draws Christians back into the public square, whether or not they want to take responsibility for what goes on there. We cannot understand the problems that trouble us in the life of the church unless we understand how widely they are shared beyond it.

The most obvious example is our current political polarization. Here, the divisions are so entrenched that any terms we might use to begin a discussion of shared problems are already the property of one side or the other. "Freedom," "responsibility," "rights," "duties," and "choice," have all been built into catchphrases and acquired connotations that identify the politics of those who use the words. Even "life" itself is suspect until the speaker identifies which lives are meant. This makes it easy to Tweet about what you already believe, but almost impossible to discuss what the human good is in relation to specific political choices that we actually face. Before we begin, our choice of words assigns us a position. Those who are on the other side find us as unintelligible as Hauerwas expects to be when we are discussing the Trinity. The only values that remain available for general use are economic efficiency and national security. If it costs less or makes us more safe, we may be able to agree on it. Other questions are difficult even to engage. Answers remain elusive and blame is easily assigned to those who are shouting other slogans.

The result is the loss of moral vocabulary in our public life, and the loss is not confined to politics. Increasingly, our public forums are organized to meet expectations, not to challenge them; to satisfy desires, not to raise aspirations. The task is not to inform or persuade, but to convince the audience as quickly as possible that you are offering what they already want. Not only businesses, but

---

6. Richard John Neuhaus, *The Naked Public Square: Religion and Democracy in America* (Grand Rapids: William B. Eerdmans, 1984).

universities, charities, arts groups, and community organizations are concerned about survival measured in market share. As a result, all of these social settings lose sight of their distinctive goods in a race to adapt for their own uses behavioral models that were pioneered by marketing experts and electoral strategists.

Across a range of social settings and demographics, people have lost connection with activities and places that once gave them a sense of identity and purpose, the institutions that built what Robert Putnam calls "social capital."[7] His best-known example is the bowling league, which has largely disappeared, but his concern extends to a whole range of institutions and organizations that used to be centers of community life, but now attract consumers, rather than members—if they still exist at all. We have experienced a devastating loss of social capital in the places that used to be best at creating it. If mainline Protestant churches have become culturally isolated, this is not so much a unique result of the secularization of the public square as it is another example of social fragmentation and political polarization. In this context, the sectarian ideal of a community of believers sharing a common faith and separated from the world can be both illuminating and misleading.

Formation

The sectarian ideal is illuminating because it reminds congregations and denominations of how difficult it is to form a community with distinctive values and virtues. In today's world, as we have noted, our public forums are increasingly adapted to the models of the marketplace. Our society treats virtues and values like consumer goods—easily available on demand, requiring little maintenance, and quickly exchanged when they begin to show signs of wear.

That is unrealistic for values that really make a difference in the lives of those who carry them, and it certainly does not fit the Gospel accounts of what it means to follow Jesus by taking up the cross and being willing to lose your life in order to find it (Luke 9:23-25). But churches, too, have adapted to a consumer model of what it means to have an identity. Those who follow mass media or show up at popular venues expect to hear things that will make them feel good about themselves for being there, and they tend to carry that expectation with them wherever they go, including when they go to church. Pastors ignore that at their own risk. Books and sermons about faith, hope, and love slip easily into the idioms of self-help manuals. That advice may still be good in everyday, practical terms, especially for people with self-defeating habits who urgently need the help. But self-improvement is not quite the same thing as understanding all things in relationship to the Triune God. It is not only to those who are outside the church

---

7. Robert Putnam, *Bowling Alone: The Collapse and Revival of American Community* (New York: Simon and Schuster, 2000).

that a theocentric view of reality may seem unusual or even incomprehensible.[8] The opportunities to present a Christian understanding of reality in an hour or two on Sunday morning are limited, and the pressures to restate it in self-centered terms that are already familiar are considerable.

It is at this point that the sectarian ideal becomes most appealing. We cannot assume that even those who are regular participants in the life of a congregation will have a framework in which to construe their Christian identity apart from a fragmented consumer culture in which they are told again and again that what is most important is what they want and warned over and over against threats posed by those who have different identities and loyalties. It may seem impossible to listen for the Word of God without separating from this overwhelming social conflict and withdrawing into an alternative community in which a very different truth can be heard and understood. Even those who are active, committed church members may need a community of formation to become conscious of the distinctive meaning of their faith and bring it to effective expression in action.

This withdrawal from the culture has surprising appeal among mainline Protestants today, but others have grasped the lesson before them. The Black churches in America have long understood the importance of a community of faith that supports dignity and identity which are denied in the wider society.[9] Catholic thinkers have begun recently to speak of a "Benedict option" for contemporary Christians,[10] that is, a way of drawing on the monastic model of a community of life and faith that could exist apart from the disordered world around it. Protestants can find historical models in the Radical Reformation, but they are drawn today to more recent examples of resistance to totalitarianism, especially the Confessing Church in Nazi Germany. Dietrich Bonhoeffer's *Life Together* provides a compelling account of how a community of faith achieves unity and maintains its integrity against an idolatry of the nation and its leader.[11]

The situation of the Confessing Church, however, is not quite our situation. Bonhoeffer was trying to sustain his church at a point in history where an all-powerful state sought to define all legitimate social options. To proclaim God as the ultimate reality was, in itself, an act of resistance. In our world, the public square is more like a vacant space. Instead of a unified totalitarian force, the church faces a world in which competing moral languages retreat into their own sect-like spaces, each setting itself against itself against the others.

---

8. James M. Gustafson, *Ethics from a Theocentric Perspective, Vol. 1: Theology and Ethics* (Chicago: University of Chicago Press, 1981).

9. Howard Thurman, *Jesus and the Disinherited* (New York: Abingdon-Cokesbury, 1949).

10. Rod Dreher, *The Benedict Option: A Strategy for Christians in a Post-Christian Nation* (New York: Sentinel, 2017).

11. Dietrich Bonhoeffer, *Life Together* (Minneapolis: Fortress Press, 1996); see also J. Deotis Roberts, *Bonhoeffer and King: Speaking Truth to Power* (Louisville: Westminster John Knox Press, 2005).

In this social context, the work of formation within the church must be undertaken with the awareness that withdrawal into an alternative community may end up contributing to the fragmentation. This is especially important because unlike Bonhoeffer's community or a Benedictine monastery, the participants in our congregations go about the rest of their lives in the midst of this world of consumer culture, polarized politics, and a multiplicity of "ultimate" truths. A distinctive way of Christian formation in these settings cannot begin by setting boundaries or defining identities. Everyone is doing that. It begins with the delicate task of raising questions and encouraging discontent without naming and making enemies. Small groups with fluid memberships and short duration may serve this purpose better than well-defined intentional communities, especially if they are followed up with pastoral concern for those who may be left with unanswered questions or who may want to take the next steps.

Polarization and the Penultimate

Churches need a different way to define themselves. Fortunately, Bonhoeffer himself suggests how we might do this in the way that he focused the formation of his community on the details of ordinary life. The seminarians he describes in *Life Together* prepared themselves for ministry, not just by practicing sermons, but by living together. They shared their prayers and their problems, ordered the hours for work and study, provided for meals, and learned to serve one another in ways that respected both those who gave and those who received. The way they did this was unusual, living in community and apart from the rest of society, but the things they were concerned with are part of ordinary life for everyone—for people in the churches where they would preach, and for us today.

Bonhoeffer would later call these needs that we all encounter in daily life "the things before the last" (*die vorletzten Dinge*). His translators have usually turned to a more obscure English word, *penultimate*. The word has Latin roots that refer to what is just before the last thing in a series. In both German and English, the word is ordinarily an adjective, referring to particular things that come before the last things; but in theological terms, it can become a noun, *the* penultimate, referring to the whole complex of things that are part of ordinary experience, things which clearly are not ultimate, and yet which have a definite relationship to God as Ultimate Reality. To speak truly and clearly about the ultimate, we must also understand what is penultimate, both in how we act toward it and in how we speak of it. Bonhoeffer included a whole chapter on this in the ethics text he began to write in 1939.[12]

In a time of demonstrative patriotism, extreme nationalism, and glorification of the nation's *Fuehrer*, theologians often emphasized God's transcendence and called into question any effort to find a point of contact between human purposes

---

12. Dietrich Bonhoeffer, *Ethics* (Minneapolis: Fortress Press, 2005), 146–70.

and ultimate reality. As Karl Barth put it, "The Word of God becomes knowable by making itself knowable."[13] Hearing the Word is an event in which the Word creates its own hearing, and analogies and connections between that Word and other claims to meaning and value can only be misleading.

Bonhoeffer shared that concern especially in that moment in the life of the church, but he saw that in a larger view of the Christian witness, relating the concerns of human life to the reality of God is a risk that must be run. God gives significance to these penultimate realities as we build our lives around work, home, worship, friends, and family. As people of faith, we experience their connection to the ultimate, and when these things are missing, everyone feels their absence.[14] Bonhoeffer understood that while we must be careful not to confuse ultimate and penultimate things in our politics, we cannot eliminate the connection between them in our theology.

Our time, too, has a problem with ultimate and penultimate things, though it is not exactly like the totalitarian focus on nation, race, and leader that Bonhoeffer and his contemporaries faced. Our political idolatries are more polytheistic. Our polarized politics has multiple competing centers of loyalty. Or if you prefer, there are only two poles—ours, and everybody else's. Everyone interprets penultimate things in ways that tie them to one of the poles, and the space in between is emptied of meaning. Health, housing, employment, safety, and even faith and family must all belong to my party, and they are all put at risk by the other side—take your pick as to whom you want to tell the tale.

We need not suppose either of these contemporary parties has the totalitarian ambitions that Bonhoeffer faced. But what happens when penultimate goods are put in service of polarized politics is much the same as what happened in the middle of the twentieth century. Health, housing, employment, safety, faith, and family lose their concrete reality and have significance only in relation to a political identity that secures them against the forces that are said to be poised to destroy them. We lose the capacity even to talk about penultimate things in shared, public terms, because they have all become connected to a political ideal that sets itself in opposition to any but its own way of thinking about them. Ironically, this also has the result that the more we depend on a polarized political identity to give us our orientation to these penultimate goods, the less our political leaders need to tell us about how they will deliver them to us. Policy proposals no longer receive critical scrutiny and policy positions become increasingly vague. The important thing is not how the leaders of our party will deal with the penultimate things that make up the details of our lives. The important thing is that they will protect those things from the other guys.

What Bonhoeffer finally decided was that the theological task is not only to maintain the distinction between the ultimate and the penultimate but also to take the penultimate seriously on its own terms. That is what prevents the penultimate

---

13. Karl Barth, *Church Dogmatics*, I/1 (Edinburgh: T&T Clark, 1936), 282.
14. Bonhoeffer, *Ethics*, 98–102.

things that make up daily life from being absorbed into an idolatrous ultimate, whether there is only one available idol, as in Hitler's Germany, or two, as in our polarized politics, or more. The theological and pastoral problem of maintaining the importance of the penultimate against a self-proclaimed political ultimate remains much the same.

The penultimate is where human life is lived. It is diminished when it is not related to the ultimate, but it is distorted when it is prematurely absorbed into an ultimate, even when that ultimate is the genuine ultimate reality of God. Christian theology takes the penultimate seriously because Jesus entered into it and used its familiar elements as parables of the Kingdom. But the need for the penultimate is obvious in more ordinary terms, as Bonhoeffer understood:

> The hungry person needs bread, the homeless person needs shelter, the one deprived of rights needs justice, the lonely person needs community, the undisciplined one needs order, and the slave needs freedom. . . . To give the hungry bread is not yet to proclaim to them the grace of God and justification, and to have received bread does not yet mean to stand in faith. But for the one who does something penultimate for the sake of the ultimate, this penultimate thing is related to the ultimate.[15]

What becomes clear here is that in relation to what is truly ultimate, the penultimate will always retain its own integrity. Only leaders who seek to raise their own importance in history to the level of a false ultimate need to diminish the penultimate by absorbing it into their own purposes. We feed the hungry not to make America great again or as a first step in a program of economic equality, but because the hungry person needs bread. The church insists that penultimate things are already related to God and to each other as parts of God's creation. They do not need a political program to give them their significance.

From Formation to Vocation

Understanding penultimate things in relation to God frees us to see them in their own terms, rather than as part of someone else's Tweets or slogans. In relating to the penultimate, we bring things into relationship with one another, and we relate to other people. We take on roles and duties toward them. Together, we form organizations and institutions, and societies that relate us and the people we live with to others we do not know and will never meet. These relations quickly take us outside our community of formation and beyond intimate connections to family and friends and into a sphere of *vocation* or *calling* where we engage in common tasks and create possibilities that could not exist without this web of connections.

---

15. Ibid., 163.

Often what is at the center of these webs is a job, but to call it a vocation is a reminder that it includes responsibilities taken up by family members or by volunteers, responsibilities that center on caring for a family, or building up neighborhoods and communities, or providing comfort and companionship in hospitals, nursing homes, and other care facilities. Calling this a vocation is also a reminder that these tasks are where we actively build connections not just with things and people but also between God and the world. We are *called* to these tasks because it is in particular, concrete details that we begin to see all things in relation to God.[16] Without these penultimate things, the theocentric view of reality would remain an abstraction, something vaguely remembered from a verse in a hymn or a passing reference in a Sunday sermon.

Clearly, however, most of the opportunities to make these connections come while we are not immediately thinking about theology. We are immersed in the penultimate. We have deadlines, budgets, and production quotas to meet. We have a doctor's appointment for the baby and a parents' group that is meeting with the elementary school principal. We have promises to keep, choices to make, and a departmental "mission statement" tacked to the bulletin board to consider. These are the things that will occupy most of our attention.

Still, it makes sense to understand the results of these efforts as penultimate "goods." By that we mean not just material goods, such as furniture or face masks, but a good in the sense of a goal, sought because it is part of a good life for ourselves and others. This idea is ancient. The first systematic text on ethics in Western philosophy begins, "Every art and every inquiry, and similarly every action and choice, is thought to aim at some good."[17] We are happy to take home a paycheck, and we give much attention to the particular products or services we have to provide, but the satisfaction we gain from work derives from a conviction that what we do results in genuine goods. What we mean by that is not just what we, in particular, will produce today, but the way in which those concrete goods become part of a larger structure that allows them to continue. Pharmaceuticals and bed linens go to a hospital that provides a setting for the work of doctors and nurses, and that particular organization functions as part of a larger social structure of insurance, incentives, and regulation that makes health care affordable and widely available. Or at least it is supposed to. That is what we think we are doing when we work at a calling.

This is different from understanding what a thing is good *for*, in terms of the use we might make of it, or how we might market it in a consumer society. Whether the thing is as simple as a bedsheet or as complex as a health system, the point is to understand what is necessary for it to come together and continue in existence as a good. To understand a concrete good, we cannot grasp it without

---

16. James M. Gustafson, *Ethics from a Theocentric Perspective, Vol. 2: Ethics and Theology* (Chicago: University of Chicago Press, 1984).

17. Aristotle, *Nicomachean Ethics*, trans. W. D. Ross (Indianapolis: Hackett Publishing, 2014), 1094a.

considering other things and other people. We participate in cooperative activities and extended discussions about the various goods that are necessary to bring *this* good into being and about the various goods that become possible when it successfully does what it is meant to do. To fully understand these relationships, we must also know what penultimate goods cost, not in abstract terms of dollars and cents, but in terms of the other goods we must be prepared to give up, delay, or diminish to have this concrete good, now.

One way to describe a vocation, then, is to say that it is where we develop a detailed knowledge of how penultimate goods are created and an understanding of the institutions and social structures by which they are maintained. For Christians, this way of understanding the world is an important accompaniment to the formation that goes on in the community of faith. It cannot be done by proclamation alone, any more than we can say to a person who lacks food and clothing, "'Go in peace, be warmed and filled,' without giving them the things needed for the body" (James 2:16).

From Vocation to Politics

There are many ways to meet penultimate needs, including individual acts of kindness and charity through civic and religious institutions. But in the modern world, the maintenance and distribution of penultimate goods are also important matters of public, political discussion. The calculation of what a penultimate good is *worth*, as opposed to its mere monetary value, takes place at many levels, but it certainly extends beyond persons and corporations into politics. This modern reality reshapes the way we connect the proclamation of the Gospel to actually providing the penultimate needs of life. The social teaching of Christian churches in the modern world has understood the importance of formulating the Gospel's radical demands in terms that can be addressed by political means.[18]

Bonhoeffer's discussion of the penultimate is part of this larger theological concern. We remember his commitment to a church that could resist totalitarianism, but his ethical writings were also about the importance of maintaining the integrity of the penultimate when the world could return to ordinary politics.[19] The hungry person needs bread, as Bonhoeffer wrote, and also the other penultimate goods like freedom, order, shelter, and justice. Christian ethics cannot abandon concern for the neighbor's needs, even under conditions of tyranny or anarchy. It would be strange, then, to withdraw from this responsibility in a historical setting where politics is possible. Bread, freedom, order, shelter, and justice require attention to

---

18. Christine Firer Hinze, *Radical Sufficiency: Work, Livelihood, and a U.S. Catholic Economic Ethic* (Washington: Georgetown University Press, 2021), 17–49.

19. Joshua Mauldin, *Barth, Bonhoeffer, and Modern Politics* (Oxford: Oxford University Press, 2021), 92–109; Jens Zimmermann, *Dietrich Bonhoeffer's Christian Humanism* (Oxford: Oxford University Press, 2019), 291–330.

food banks, criminal justice, public safety, housing policy, and the courts. Christian ethics must enter fully into the discourse in which those needs are defined and met, even if the discourse itself does not entirely live up to our expectations.

That is to say, we cannot proclaim the relationship between ultimate and penultimate things without joining in a discussion with all sorts of people who can help us understand what is required to hold concrete goods together in meaningful lives. The skeptical, secular liberal who insists on keeping attention focused on the penultimate has something to contribute. So, too, does the political philosopher who has a "thin"[20] theory of the good that may identify some goods that are part of everyone's search, even if they are not quite all of the goods we need. The effort by which Christian ethics understands the penultimate includes persons of other faiths, and persons of no faith whose practical wisdom and depth of commitment to their neighbors speaks to us of God, even if it does not speak in that way to them.[21]

Our moral lives largely consist of the choices we make between competing penultimate goods. Most often, we create and maintain the goods we have chosen by daily decisions that get things done—effectively, efficiently, and with respect for the people around us. But sometimes the choices reach beyond the spheres of our vocations and raise urgent or persistent questions about the social consequences of the choices we have made as a whole society. At that point, understanding penultimate things requires the re-creation of a public discourse that is now missing from the contemporary realities of polarization.[22]

The Protestant problem of church or sect, engagement or withdrawal, remains with us. The faithful answer depends on circumstances and has to be reformulated for each generation, perhaps for each congregation. Few general rules are available to guide that task, but Bonhoeffer's suggestion that we think in terms of penultimate goods may help. Where a political community and its leaders are satisfied that they already have the answers right, and especially when they want to bring the church into line with what they have decided, the church does well to focus attention on the integrity of its own life and proclamation. But where politics is confused, leadership is ineffective, and the space between the scattered assertions of certainty seems like a moral vacuum, the church cannot simply proclaim the importance of bread, shelter, freedom, order, and justice. Christians must engage in their vocations to provide what politics has not. We do so with the hope that their formation will have adequately prepared them for what their callings mean in our circumstances.

20. John Rawls, *A Theory of Justice* (Cambridge, MA: Harvard University Press, 1971), 395–9.

21. Jens Zimmermann, "The Cultural Context for Re-Envisioning Christian Humanism," in *Re-Envisioning Christian Humanism*, ed. Jens Zimmermann (Oxford: Oxford University Press, 2017), 137–60.

22. Robert Putnam, *Upswing: How America Came Together a Century Ago and How We Can Do It Again* (New York: Simon and Schuster, 2020).

Chapter 6

BODY MATTERS

SOME BRIEF REMARKS IN PRAISE OF JERRY MCKENNY

Stanley Hauerwas

I turned eighty while I was working on this chapter. I have said and written a great deal in the time that I have been given. I am not sure I have anything new to say. Indeed, I am not even sure I know what I have said. That I am not sure what I have said has, in turn, led me to revisit what I have said over the years. I am writing a biography of my books in order to remind myself how one book led to the next book. I hope that by showing the connections others and I will be better able to understand what I have written.

I mention my own project because I had just arrived at *Suffering Presence: Theological Reflections on Medicine, the Mentally Handicapped, and the Church* when it came time to write this chapter honoring Gerald McKenny.[1] *Suffering Presence* was a book that was published in 1986. Like many of my books, this one fell stillborn from the press. I am sure there were many reasons for this, but one is surely because I did not share what most people in the emerging field of bioethics understood ethics to be.[2]

I remember a conference in medical ethics around this time where I delivered a chapter from the book as a lecture, with Bob Veatch responding. Veatch savaged the lecture as giving a far too positive account of medicine, as well as being unclear about what normative alternative I represented. His response confirmed my own judgment that I would never be a player in the field of bioethics. I was not particularly bothered by that, however, since I already had doubts about the wisdom of the very existence of such a field.

I would like to use this occasion to make explicit one of the things that I was trying to do in *Suffering Presence*, which was left largely implicit in the text itself. I

---

1. Stanley Hauerwas, *Suffering Presence: Theological Reflections on Medicine, the Mentally Handicapped, and the Church* (Notre Dame: University of Notre Dame Press, 1986).

2. For some further reflections on *Suffering Presence*, see Stanley Hauerwas, "Suffering Presence: Twenty-Five Years Later," in *Approaching the End: Eschatological Reflections on Church, Politics, and Life* (Grand Rapids: Eerdmans, 2013), 176–91.

thought that book was one way to do a form of natural law ethics. This is a claim that I suspect many of my critics as well as friends (and, of course, critics can often be friends) may find puzzling. After all, I am often considered the "Christ alone" ethicist. But I hope to show how attending to McKenny's first book makes how I worked in *Suffering Presence* seem not quite so odd.

McKenny published *To Relieve the Human Condition: Bioethics, Technology, and the Body* in 1997.[3] At the time I had thought the book was a game changer. The book had a rare clarity, while also developing an alternative way to think about the ethics of medicine, in a way which was sorely needed at the time. McKenny developed his account of medicine as a moral tradition by drawing on the work of James Gustafson, Leon Kass, Drew Leder, and Richard Zaner, among others. He also used my own work in a critical but constructive way to develop his account.[4] In McKenny's account, the task of bioethics is to reflect on the moral significance of the body as it is expressed in the discourses and practices of religious traditions. And medicine attends to and supports this moral significance of the body through its office of care.

In his reading of my work, McKenny understood that calling attention to the mentally handicapped was not simply a sentimental gesture, but a crucial test case for illuminating the moral character of medicine as such.[5] That the physician is to care for the patient even when they cannot find a cure is a commitment at the very heart of medicine. This commitment is further expressed in the presumption that a physician is to care for the patient in a way that prescinds all considerations except what must be done to respond to what makes the body of the patient sick. So understood, medicine is the ongoing bodily wisdom that physicians learn from the ill.[6]

Accordingly, medicine does not need an ethicist telling doctors what ethic they should use to make decisions because medicine is itself a moral tradition. The ethicist intent on helping agents of medicine articulate the moral convictions that shape their lives and practices are more like anthropologists than philosophers. Of course, that contrast depends on what kind of philosophy or anthropology is being assumed.

McKenny worried that my account of medicine as a moral tradition may not sufficiently attend to the perversion of medicine by technological utopianism. Yet, his account of my attempt to describe the moral commitments that make medicine ethically impressive is the best description of how I have used the engagement with medicine to make constructive theological claims.

---

3. Gerald McKenny, *To Relive the Human Condition: Bioethics, Technology, and the Body* (New York: SUNY, 1997).

4. See Ibid., 147–83.

5. Ibid., 182–3.

6. On this, see Stanley Hauerwas and Gerald McKenny, "The Strength to be Patient," *Christian Bioethics* 22, no. 1 (2016): 5–20.

I suspect that McKenny understands my work so well because he has absorbed both Alasdair MacIntyre and Michel Foucault.[7] In particular, he too recognizes how the ethical and political are inseparable. McKenny's own astute and critical identification of the Baconian project reflects his broad knowledge of the moral sources that liberal social orders provide. The projects to eliminate suffering and expand the realm of human choice, therefore, are the very conditions necessary to legitimate liberal regimes.

I suspect that McKenny also learned from Foucault that the liberal attempt to expand the realm of freedom can result in forms of self-inflicted slavery. McKenny's account and use of Foucault is a masterpiece of making sense of that profound but elusive mind. He quite rightly draws on Foucault to illumine how my account of medicine entails a politics that makes the church more than an afterthought.

Some may wonder why I never responded to Jerry's book at the time, and in particular to his criticisms of my account of medicine.[8] After all, he made criticisms of my work that I could have at least tried to answer. After providing an insightful account of my work, not only about medicine but also about my approach more generally, he makes three critical observations: (1) that I provide a far too uncritical account of modern medicine; (2) that my church must actually be what I say it has to be if medicine is to be sustained as a practice of presence; and (3) that I have not really freed myself from theodical accounts of pointless suffering.

The final criticism is the most important because it goes to the heart of the matter. The heart of the matter turns out to be the body (which is not surprising if you remember the heart is itself flesh). I later returned to and engaged this question of pointless suffering in *Naming the Silences: God, Medicine, and the Problem of Suffering*.[9] Here I argued that the very presumption that all suffering is pointless legitimates something like what McKenny calls the "Baconian project." Against this view, I argued that our bodies are gifts that provide us with possibilities and purpose. And that this, in turn, makes suffering bearable and allows us to draw moral insights from the body.

I should like to think that emphasis is something that McKenny and I share. Put simply, we both think the body *matters*. Indeed, I not only think the body matters, but I also believe we *are* our bodies, in ways that makes instrumental accounts of the body profoundly misleading. We do not *have* bodies but *are* bodies.[10] *Suffering*

---

7. See also McKenny's later engagement with MacIntyre on natural law. McKenny, "Moral Disagreement and the Limits of Reason: Reflections on MacIntyre and Ratzinger," in *Intractable Disputes About the Natural Law*, ed. Lawrence Cunningham (Notre Dame: University of Notre Dame Press, 2009), 195–226.

8. For these criticisms, see McKenny, *To Relieve the Human Condition*, 174–779.

9. Stanley Hauerwas, *Naming the Silences: God, Medicine, and the Problem of Suffering* (London: Continuum, 2004).

10. As Bonhoeffer writes, "A human being does not 'have' a body or 'have' a soul; instead a human being 'is' body and soul." Dietrich Bonhoeffer, *Creation and Fall: A Theological*

Presence was an early attempt to give an account of the body as the condition for the discovery of shared goods.

From my own perspective, the challenge is how one avoids abstract natural law theories in the interest of sustaining concrete moral judgments. When natural law is understood in this way, physicians can too easily become moral technicians who act from principles that are in turn derived from general presumptions. What is lost is the habituation of the body by diverse practices that make us who we are. These practices are the habits that have been learned from the care of one another through the office of medicine.

Accordingly, medicine is a practice that reflects the limits and possibilities of the body. But what I am calling the body here is itself partly constituted by the interventions we call medicine. To be sure, doctors and others who intervene in the body do so in order to care for that body. But the very authority to intervene in this way requires a form of authority that exists prior to any intervention. From this perspective, medicine represents and expresses the ongoing historical tradition of the care for the body that has been learned and passed on from one generation to the next. In short, medicine is a moral enterprise that can be understood as one way in which natural law is made historically concrete.

Because our understanding of the body differs depending on which history and tradition we inhabit, we should not be surprised that medicine itself will differ from one context to the next. This is not a formula for relativism. The exact opposite is the case: that natural law works in this way means we are continually discovering good and bad ways to stay healthy. In other words, arguments are possible between different medical traditions, in ways which may not finally be able to be resolved.[11]

McKenny, I think, would be in substantial agreement with what I am trying to claim about the significance of the body for the discovery of the goods that shape moral commitments in medicine. As suggested earlier, I think this can be an exemplification of what in the wider tradition has been called natural law. I have no particular investment in the word "natural," so long as this word is not used to avoid the importance of everyday caring for one another.[12]

This way of conceiving natural law is an attempt to avoid accounts of natural law that seem to come from nowhere. Advocates of natural law often try to avoid something called relativism by abstracting principles from contingent judgments

---

Exposition of Genesis 1–3, ed. John de Gruchy, trans. Douglas Stephen Bax (Minneapolis: Fortress Press, 1997), 77; Bonhoeffer, *Creation and Fall, DBWE 3*, 139.

11. For some broader reflections, see the collection of essays edited by Lawrence Cunningham, *Intractable Disputes About the Natural Law*.

12. On this question of how to understand natural law, see my critical engagement with Jean Porter in Hauerwas, *Approaching the End: Eschatological Reflections on Church, Politics and Life* (Grand Rapids: Eerdmans, 2013), 13–21. See also comments in Brian Brock and Stanley Hauerwas, *Beginnings: Interrogating Hauerwas*, ed. Kevin Hargaden (London: T&T Clark Bloomsbury, 2017), 144–45.

of a tradition discovered through time. Against this approach, I understand wisdom as being gained through time and passed from one generation to the next through training and formation. The training entails learning to see bodies with the complexity that comes with the habits that make life possible.[13] We do not live merely in order to survive, but rather our survival is constitutive of, and necessary for, more determinative ends: the wonder of friendship, for example. Natural law so understood turns out to be anything but an ethic of minimal duties. Rather, it is about the ongoing discovery of the shared commitments that make us human.

This perspective on natural law may seem at some distance from Aquinas' own account in the *Summa*, although I am very sympathetic to his understanding of natural law. It is important to note, however, that his account of natural law is not a treatise called "natural law" but is, rather, part of a "Treatise on Law."[14] The natural law as a fundamental inclination to do good and avoid evil will not get far without a more concrete exemplification of how the pursuit of the good is found in the law. This is broadly the move I am trying to make by calling attention to the goods discovered in our care of one another through the office of medicine.

Medicine conceived as a moral tradition brings together doctors, nurses, assistants, and patients in the common practice of care of the body.[15] The doctor-patient relationship is a particularly intimate relation. This is why, like all such relationships, it is one that can at times be frightening. There are too many ways in which the care of one another can go wrong, especially when medicine is understood and practiced in isolation from a wider community.

In his lovely book, *Attending Others: A Doctor's Education in Bodies and Words*, Brian Volck observes, "physicians work with bodies, with lives, until both are perfectly understood."[16] This indicates why medicine is an art requiring judgments about matters that fall outside of the practice of medicine itself. Doctors have to make judgments about suffering bodies in conditions of uncertainty. Even when practicing the very best medicine, doctors can still end up hurting a patient. Because the body matters, there is always a risk for those who undertake the practice of medicine. We cannot forget the lesson that McKenny so urgently teaches us: we are bodily creatures whose vulnerable bodies make illness and death a given.

---

13. On this need to be trained to see our bodies rightly by communities, see Brian Brock, "Discipline, Sport, and the Religion of Winners: Paul on Running to Win the Prize, 1 Corinthians 9:24–27," *Studies in Christian Ethics* 25, no. 1 (2012): 4–19.

14. Thomas Aquinas, *Summa Theologica I-II*, questions 90–108.

15. On the virtues specific to patients, see Hauerwas and McKenny, "The Strength to be Patient," 5–20.

16. Brian Volck, *Attending Others: A Doctor's Education in Bodies and Words* (Eugene: Cascade, 2020), 23.

Chapter 7

"THE WORD BECAME FLESH"

WHAT ARE THE IMPLICATIONS OF AN AUGUSTINIAN INCARNATIONAL ECONOMY FOR BIOTECHNOLOGY?

Travis Kroeker

Gerald McKenny has provided significant and influential contributions to the field of Christian ethics, especially in the areas of Karl Barth's moral theology and Christian ethics and biotechnology. In his recent field-defining work, *Biotechnology, Human Nature, and Christian Ethics* (2018), Jerry shows again why he is one of the very best students of our (and the "our" includes many influential Christian ethicists!) shared *Doktorvater* Jim Gustafson: he is a gifted, astute practitioner of a challenging Weberian genre that remains invaluable for ethical thinking—"ideal typology." Ideal types are not rooted in "idealist" philosophical projects but are, rather, the representation of iconic "ideas" as conceptual images or paradigmatic figures that enable us to better compare and test divergent complex approaches to important social questions and problems, and that do so in relation to empirical, philosophical issues with both descriptive and normative implications. Scholars who enact such comparative engagements well must above all be subtle thinkers attuned to complex claims and their contrasting theoretical and practical implications in the "real" world—a world that is not simplified through reductive or controlling ideologies, but "opened up" for dialectical exploration through outstanding, indeed iconic, "map-making."

Every *magister/magistra ludi* of this conceptual approach has an argument to make: ideal types are not intended to be neutral descriptions. So it's no surprise to discover that McKenny's preferred "ideal type" for thinking through the questions of biotechnology and ethics for Christian conceptions of normative human nature is one called *imago dei*. What kind of human nature is implied here? I shall not rehearse McKenny's arguments, which take up the accounts of two contemporary theologians, Kathryn Tanner and Karl Barth—though I'll attempt to engage some of the central aspects of this "type," especially in Tanner, for reasons that will become clear. I shall argue that a truly "Augustinian" account of *imago dei* comes closer to an understanding of "incarnational economy" in the service of a more critical engagement with biotechnology than is often recognized. In doing so I shall also aim to show that the "ideal type" McKenny identifies as Augustinian, human nature as "given" and therefore "completed" in a manner not to be "tampered with" technologically,[1] is not the only possible account of Augustine's *imago dei*. To the contrary, I shall argue that Augustine's messianic, apocalyptic account of *imago dei*, which also affirms the open-ended "*progressus*" (which does not imply "progressivism"!) of *imago dei* in time and space, is able to engage the language of "deification" without translating this into either a notion of "otherworldly" transcendence or "this-worldly" visions of transhumanist salvation, but, rather, offers resources for a critique of both in ways that are relevant to current debates about human nature and biotechnology in the Anthropocene. In other words, I want to add Augustine into the mix of McKenny's preferred *imago dei* anthropology in ways that complicate his representation of this ideal type. I undertake this exploration as a friendly "*contretemps*" in the service of better shared vision, which is how I've always, profoundly, experienced the meaning of friendship in my long friendship with Jerry.

Imago dei *and Human Nature*

McKenny argues that, in keeping with the biblical vision, human nature in Christian ethics is best understood as "made in the image of God" (Gen. 1-2:4, esp. 1:26-27). The "most common way" to understand the language of *imago dei* is related to the special dignity that human beings enjoy, which is also related to the human power to "hold sway" over the creatures of earthly creation.[2] For McKenny this dignity grounds certain moral requirements in which human nature is recognized as having responsibility for earthly creation that demands attention to "both the vulnerability of human biological nature and the interdependence of human beings in their vulnerability"—and these entail the "standard bioethical principles" of autonomy (responsibility), safety (vulnerability), and fairness (interdependence) (150).[3]

---

1. See Gerald McKenny, *Biotechnology, Human Nature, and Christian Ethics* (Cambridge: Cambridge University Press), chap. 2: the primary Christian ethicist identified with this position is Oliver O'Donovan, with his emphasis on "created order," sharply to be differentiated from "eschatological transformation."

2. McKenny, *Biotechnology, Human Nature, and Christian Ethics*, 149. I take this translation, "hold sway," from Robert Alter for the Hebrew *radah*; it is not the normal Hebrew verb depicting "rule" or "governance" or "dominion" (as in the "two great lights" of 1:16). It may be closer to "subdue" or "master" via creaturely agency in a more fleshly form of influence that is also highly passionate. Hence, even in the first creation narrative, the human existential passions are present. Robert Alter, *The Hebrew Bible, Vol. 1: The Five Books of Moses: A Translation with Commentary* (New York: W. W. Norton, 2019).

3. See also McKenny's development of these principles in his more recent article "Human Nature and Biotechnological Enhancement: Some Theological Considerations," *Studies in Christian Ethics* 32, no. 2 (2019): 229–40.

Yet, there is a second understanding of *imago dei* that is specifically Christian, deeply rooted in the New Testament and in patristic theology, that claims that Jesus Christ is the image of God in the most proper sense (McKenny cites the Pauline texts Rom. 8:29; 2 Cor. 4:4; Col. 1:15) and that to act in keeping with the divine image requires conformity to Christ via "union," or "imitation," or "witness" (150). In keeping with the theologians Karl Barth and Kathryn Tanner, McKenny considers this second understanding as the key to interpreting the first, namely, that the special dignity of human creatures made in God's image is definitively revealed in "the Word [that] became flesh" in whom the divine glory (or life or light) is "made known" in human form via "the only Son from the Father" (John 1:1-18). While McKenny doesn't cite this passage, which draws us into a Trinitarian consideration of the meaning of *imago dei* for Christian ethics, I argue that it is crucial to do so, and furthermore that Augustine helps us understand why—in ways that are deeply important for biotechnology. Above all, John 1 entails the claim that when the divine Word of creation takes on human flesh, it is revealed "in the form of the servant." The revelation of the Logos who displays divine glory in human form does so by way of the cross (John 12)—hence, the consistent pairing in Augustine's interpretation of the incarnational economy (which Paul calls the *mysterion* of salvation) of the Johannine Logos with the Pauline "kenotic" Christ (Phil 2). Furthermore, such a consideration requires us to move away from architectonic doctrinal formulations of the meaning of human nature or creatureliness, or, as McKenny puts it, from attempts "to adjudicate debates over the ethics of biotechnology by direct appeal to a metanarrative about creation and eschatology" (151). I suggest it will also require us to move beyond the "standard bioethical principles" of autonomy/freedom/responsibility, safety/security/protection, and fairness/equity/access as being adequate ethically to address the challenges biotechnology raises with regard to human enhancement, well-being and, indeed, "perfection." It will require us to pay more attention to the existential meaning of the human vocation to "hold sway" in the ordering of creation (in the enfleshed, passional fierceness of our created embodiment) with reference to the measure given in Jesus' most famous "teaching," the Sermon on the Mount: "you must be perfect [*teleios*], as your heavenly Father is perfect" (Matt. 5:48), namely, the completion of divine love, humanly embodied as mortal, sacrificially self-giving love in daily life on earth. Such perfection as the transfiguring process of "deification" images the kenotic serving love that reconciles "all things" to God through sacramental or sacrificial divine—human exchange rather than an anthropocentric model of agency as dominating control.

It is for this reason that I choose to engage more significantly Kathryn Tanner's account of human nature as *imago dei*, precisely because of her use of the language of "deification" as the human destiny "in Christ"—which Augustine also uses (albeit infrequently)[4] and which McKenny, following Barth, resists. While

---

4. The classic essay remains Gerald Bonner, "Augustine's Conception of Deification," *Journal of Theological Studies* 37, no. 2 (1986): 369–86. This process is not only an individual

McKenny approves of Tanner's emphasis on "plasticity" (Greek, *plastikos*: fit for moulding or shaping) insofar as human nature is "made" by God in a manner that reflects divine freedom and indeterminacy or "open-endedness" in ways that take human beings "beyond what is natural" so as to be made "fitting" for life with God, he is wary of the language of deification precisely because it suggests that human beings will "become divine" or fully "deified"—in other words, divine *rather than* human (i.e., no longer "creaturely"). I will return to this resistance later, since it entails a crucial critique of the project of "transhumanism" that increasingly inflects biotechnology as an aspirational project of "human" and humanly enacted technological enhancement that also includes immortality (and perhaps also virtual omnipotence, omniscience, and omnipresence), namely, disincarnate perfection. It is also the case that Augustine has been overtly called "transhumanist" in a recent interpretation of his account of human nature, Andrea Nightingale's *Once Out of Nature: Augustine on Time and the Body*.[5] For McKenny and Barth, there is a stronger "human" sense of the *imago dei* that is accepting of creaturely finitude that does not need to be "worked over" in order to be "perfected" in union with Christ so as to enjoy life with God. I argue that Augustine accepts this sense, while at the same time reworking the discourse of "deification" in important ways both theological and ethical that render it less technocratic and more relational, integrating natural human creatureliness into the Trinitarian economy of divine love. Such reworking challenges the discourses of biotechnological control, security, responsibility, and success by placing human aspirations into an alternative "messianic" economy.

For now I want to return to Tanner's claim that the "state of perfection" (and one wonders what it might mean to call it a "state," but it is a term used both by McKenny and by Tanner) "has determinately Christian love as its norm" (154), a substantive norm that goes beyond vague principles of liberation or progress to specify the form of life for which human nature has been created. This is, of course, in keeping with Augustine's well-known formulation that life "in Christ" is a life that is being conformed to the "power of love" and not the "love of power" (the latter of which Augustine identifies with the fallen desires of "anti-Christ"[6]). For Augustine this account of love that conforms human nature "to the divine image" has certain distinctively human characteristics displayed above all in the "Word made flesh" who reveals the glory of God (John 1) in suffering love (John 12), and in the kenotic Christ who "emptied himself, taking the form of a servant" rather

renewal of the image (*Trinity* 14.25), but it is an ecclesial and sacramental process in which the personal character of the *imago dei* is a fully social and relational character. See also David Vincent Meconi, *The One Christ: St. Augustine's Theology of Deification* (Washington: Catholic University of America Press, 2013).

5. Andrea Nightingale, *Once Out of Nature: Augustine on Time and the Body* (Chicago: University of Chicago Press, 2011).

6. Among other places, see Augustine, *The Trinity*, trans. Edmund Hill (New York: New City Press, 1991), 12.14–17; 13.17–18. We'll return to this later.

than grasping equality of God (Philippians 2) as a thing to be grasped.[7] These characteristics display the "justice of humility" as the property of the "good will" that loves itself and the world in a manner oriented toward divine perfection—in a way that despises neither embodiment and the fragilities of finitude nor the devastations of sin and injustice that cannot destroy the power of goodness itself so revealed in suffering love. These are radical claims that, I suggest, have significant consequences for the ethics of biotechnology.

Tanner's Trinitarian theological claims for *imago dei* and deification are related to Augustine's, but also rendered somewhat differently. Like Augustine, and, according to McKenny, unlike Barth, Tanner identifies the "true," or "strong," or "proper" image of God with Christ in Trinitarian terms as "the second person of the Trinity," *rather than*, as with Barth, "the firstborn of all creation" (Col. 1:15; cf. 2:9).[8] Thus, for Barth and McKenny, Christ in his humanity (and not only "in the form of God") represents the strong or proper sense of the divine image and is thus able to communicate this "relationally" to his fellow human beings. I suggest this distinction between the human and the divine, which results in two different "rather than's" in the case of Tanner (a denial of the "strong" or "proper" mediation of *imago dei* in finite human nature) and Barth/McKenny (a denial of the language of "deification" as proper to the completion of human creatures), is differently articulated in the case of Augustine in a manner that reconciles a (more Platonic) reading of Johannine incarnation and the kenotic "form of the servant" displayed in the suffering love of Jesus—and thereby shows a greater figural malleability and plasticity than either of these readings manages on its own, a reconciliation that I suggest has more radical implications for the critique of biotechnology than that ascribed to either Tanner or Barth. It can do so only through an openness to the apocalyptic "contingency" of divine providence understood as love, as the cosmic principle of dynamic spiritual motion in a creation that cannot sharply or "absolutely" divide (even as it distinguishes) spirit and matter, eternal and temporal, immortal and mortal.[9] This entails greater attention to the incarnational economy of *imago dei* that may be confidently translated neither into a fixed or "completed" creational "ontology" (O'Donovan) nor into the perfection of the human as a "transhuman" state (whether so defined by Tanner or by Nightingale).

---

7. See Matthew Drever's apt claim that Augustine's accounts of *imago dei* and "deification" are rooted in two main sources: the Johannine divine Logos narrative and the Pauline kenotic Christology, *Image, Identity, and the Forming of the Augustinian Soul* (Oxford: Oxford University Press, 2013), chap 6. See also Matthew Drever, "Entertaining Violence: Augustine on the Cross of Christ and the Commercialization of Suffering," *The Journal of Religion* 92, no. 3 (2012): 331–61.

8. McKenny, *Biotechnology, Human Nature, and Christian Ethics*, 164.

9. For my more elaborated account of Augustine's apocalyptic providentialism, see "Augustine's Messianic Political Theology: An Apocalyptic Critique of Political Augustinianism," *Messianic Political Theology and Diaspora Ethics* (Eugene: Cascade Books, 2017), chap. 3.

It entails, rather, an "iconic imagination" in which the "deification" of human beings is a transformation of sinful human nature that seeks to secure itself via the possessive, controlling diminishment of "all things" created by God, so as to become "like God" in those ways that only God may "perfect" or complete.[10] This is, I contend, both a material and a spiritual process in which "immortalization" is not a diminishment but rather the transformative apocalyptic completion of "incarnation" (in all its finite brokenness and suffering).

To see this more fully, consider Tanner's account of Augustine's *De trinitate* in *Christ the Key*, where she states that Augustine's attempt to find analogies for the Trinitarian relations within human nature in Books 8–11 has the effect of making "human nature seem a self-contained image of God in and of itself" through conscious "self-knowledge."[11] While she suggests that Augustine "undoes" this impression in subsequent books, his mistake is to want to identify the image with all three persons of the trinity, rather than only the "second person" of the trinity with whom the language of *imago dei* is singularly identified.[12] It is the "imaging process" of the second person of the trinity that properly represents the meaning of "image" wherever it is to be found, but especially so in the human because it is the "second person" of the trinity that, as the "Word" in which all things are made, "became flesh" and mediates *imago dei* in the created world, and hence in a "radically inferior" medium, namely "finitude."[13] Thus, while Tanner objects (like Barth) to Augustine's Trinitarian consideration of the great Platonic philosophical principle of human consciousness, namely "self-knowledge," as a vestigial "psychological" analogue of the divine image (*Trinity* 10.7), she will at the same time accept the Platonic formulation (rejected by Augustine) that the unlikeness of the human with the divine is rooted in finitude even more primordially than by sin. That is, human unlikeness to the divine is rooted in an ontological logic of identity in which, as Plato's *Symposium* 203A has it, "*nullus deus miscetur homini*";[14] like Plato, Tanner does not suggest that the light of the human intellect

---

10. For an excellent account of "iconic imagination," see Part II, "The Iconic Economy" in Marie-José Mondzain, *Image, Icon, Economy: The Byzantine Origins of the Contemporary Imaginary*, trans. Rico Franses (Stanford: Stanford University Press, 2005); the connections between *kenosis* and incarnation are richly articulated, 92–6.

11. Kathryn Tanner, *Christ the Key* (Cambridge: Cambridge University Press, 2010), 3.

12. Ibid., 5.

13. Ibid., 7.

14. This is, of course, Augustine's Latin translation of "*Theos de anthropo ou mignutai*"— "God with human does not mingle," and hence an "intermediary" principle of mediation, *eros*, is required who resides "between" (*metaxu*, *Symposium* 201E)—in Augustine's critique of the logic of Platonic mediation, in *City of God* 8.18–27. Augustine rejects this principle in his delineation of the incarnation of the messianic economy of divine providence whose salvific agency remains mysterious and may not be resolved through "ontological logics," but believed only by faith—a rule of interpretation Augustine also establishes at the very beginning of *Trinity*. This requires constant attention to the dramatic display of revealed

is its own possession or property, but, rather, is received via participation in a divine light beyond human nature and, indeed, "beyond being, exceeding it in dignity and power" (*Republic* 509B). Of course, Augustine would not reject this difference, since he agrees with Plato that the human soul or *psyche* is ordered toward the divine good, wisdom, truth. What is "alien" to the human participation as "likeness" to the divine good is human sin rooted in disordered love, and it is this unlikeness that must be, as Tanner puts it, "made over according to the Word's own wisdom in imitation of it."[15]

But note, here is where Tanner's account of this imitation seems more formal or abstract and both less embodied and temporal, and also less "inner" and existentially psychological than Augustine's—and perhaps also Barth's (at least on the former point).[16] For example, Tanner suggests that "Jesus Christ, the perfect human image of God because the perfect divine image, brings human life in himself back to its perfect beginning—the perfect beginning that in a sense never was—so that it might be achieved in a way not susceptible of loss."[17] The "created capacities" in human nature that enable human beings to receive the divine image and to be "made over" in imitation of it turn out to be precisely those traits of radical ontological openness and plasticity that are amenable to the "transhumanist" project: "Human beings must not only be changeable but susceptible to radical transformation beyond the limits of their own—or any—created nature. Human beings through divine power become what they are not and have no capacity of being by themselves: human versions of the divine image itself."[18] These claims are intensified in Tanner's following discussion of nature and grace:

> The problem that stands in the way of our being strong images of God and that grace remedies primarily has to do with human nature and not sin. We cannot receive the highest good that God wants to give us, the good of God's own life, while remaining creatures.... If God wants to give it to humans, they have to be

divine "missions" into the lived human world narrated in scripture as the starting point for messianic theology.

15. Tanner, *Christ the Key*, 23; also 28–9.

16. Bruce McCormack suggests that Barth resists "deification" language because it implies a metaphysical or ontological "indwelling" that fails to recognize the fully incarnate "historical" exaltation of the human through the imitation of Christ in the apocalyptic "event" of the Word made flesh that entails both the humiliation of God in a kenotic divine "giving" and the exaltation of the human who receives this gift in the "actualization" or "making real" of the divine-human relation in a "new creation." McCormack, "Participation in God, Yes; Deification, No: Two Modern Responses to an Ancient Question," in *Orthodox and Modern: Studies in the Theology of Karl Barth* (Grand Rapids: Baker Academic, 2008), chap. 9.

17. Tanner, *Christ the Key*, 35.

18. Ibid., 40. Elsewhere Tanner states, "Humans have a nature that imitates God only by not having, one might say, a clearly delimited nature" (49).

elevated beyond what they are themselves as creatures. In short, humans have to be given God *in addition to being given themselves.*[19]

I'm sure that I am not doing justice to the nuances of Tanner's full position here, but I have said enough, I think, to indicate that if this is also Augustine's position (I'm arguing that it is not), then Andrea Nightingale's account of it as "transhuman" is not far off the mark, at least in the sense that human beings seek a life beyond time and temporal nature, in a second Eden that overcomes the limitations of embodied human and creaturely existence in a mortal world from which we long to be liberated.

Human Nature, Deification, and Transhumanism

Before turning to Nightingale's account of Augustine, it might be useful to point out that biotechnological transhumanism may be described not only with reference to the myths of Prometheus and/or Epimetheus[20] but also, perhaps much more tellingly, with reference to the myths of creation and Fall in Genesis. That is, the desire of human beings to escape the limits of their mortal nature through divine knowledge (the tree of "knowledge of good and evil" that is also in close proximity to the tree of life and potential immortality in the primordial garden) seems built into their created nature as made in the divine image. That the primordial human couple were banished from the garden of Eden due to their successful "becoming like one of us, knowing good and evil," and so as to prevent their possible success in eating also of the tree of life and living forever (Gen. 3:22-24), has ever after become the second great divine prohibition tempting human desire for immortal life that is so closely tethered to the divine image. How might humankind liberate itself from the conditions of "fallenness" and the "burdens" of nature, including human nature? In his recent study of transhumanist movements, *To Be a Machine*, Mark O'Connell suggests that the biblical and Christian narrative of "the Fall" and redemption tells us a great deal about the motivations and aspirations of the biotechnological revolution and transhumanism in particular, tied as these are to

---

19. Tanner, *Christ the Key*, 60 (my emphasis). She spells this out further: "in some sense human nature considered in and of itself is already in a broken condition—broken in the sense of both being inoperable by itself and broken open or emptied" (61). These are evocative even if abstract characterizations of human nature. Sin, according to Tanner, simply makes a broken situation worse: "What makes us totally corrupt is the loss of something that we are not—divinity—and therefore our human nature is not essentially changed for the worse in losing it" (65). From an Augustinian perspective of the incarnational economy this is a shocking claim!

20. See Bernard Stiegler, *Technics and Time, 1: The Fault of Epimetheus*, trans. Richard Beardsworth and George Collins (Stanford: Stanford University Press, 1998).

Western conceptions of progress.[21] We could as well turn to Ivan Illich's apocalyptic messianic critique of the biotechnological and anti-incarnational systems of institutional salvation of Western modernity, which he reads with reference to

> the old Latin phrase: *corruptio optimi quae est pessima* [the corruption of the best is the worst]—the historical progression in which God's Incarnation is turned topsy-turvy, inside out . . . the mysterious darkness that envelops our world, the demonic night paradoxically resulting from the world's equally mysterious vocation to glory. My subject is a mystery of faith, a mystery whose depth of evil could not have come to be without the greatness of the truth revealed to us.[22]

The demonic perversion of the true reality of creation is not simply or primarily a violation of the ontological laws of reality but a personal turning away from the intimate revelation of divine reality in whose image human beings are made. Its correlative act is a turning in worship toward a false substitute, the apostatic *mysterium iniquitatis* Paul speaks of in 2 Thessalonians 2 that results in powerful deception.[23] This is the personal, intimate character of sin that also has pervasive social and political consequences—the substitution of other-regarding personal love revealed in the Word made flesh by self-securing institutional powers of technological wonder-working.[24]

These are large claims, and I can't pursue them in detail here. What I shall try to do is to show how a misunderstanding of the Augustinian account may ironically authorize a "transhumanist" account of human nature simply by ignoring the centrality of Augustine's incarnational economy rooted in a biblical theology of *imago dei*. Andrea Nightingale translates Augustine's term *peregrinati* as "resident aliens" on earth: "exiled from Eden, and 'deformed' by sin, they must

---

21. Mark O'Connell, *To Be a Machine: Adventures Among Cyborgs, Utopians, Hackers, and the Futurists Solving the Modest Problem of Death* (London: Granta Books, 2017).

22. Ivan Illich, *The Rivers North of the Future: The Testament of Ivan Illich as Told to David Cayley* (Toronto: House of Anansi Press, 2005), 29. I have argued for the compatibility between Illich and Augustine in "Augustine's Messianic Political Theology," and "Technology as Principality: The Elimination of Incarnation," *Messianic Political Theology and Diaspora Ethics*, chaps. 3 and 15, respectively.

23. See Augustine's analysis of this passage in *City of God* 20.19, tying it to the "whole body" of the Antichrist deceived by the "love of power" delusion, in contrast to the *totus Christus* whose judgment is shaped by the parable of Matthew 25 (*City of God* 20.5) where divine glory is mediated in service to the least.

24. This iconic messianic drama and its political and biotechnological implications are vividly anticipated in Fyodor Dostoevsky's Grand Inquisitor; see Travis Kroeker and Bruce Ward, *Remembering the End: Dostoevsky as Prophet to Modernity* (Boulder: Westview, 2001; New York: Routledge, 2019), chaps. 4 and 6.

toil on this earthly journey toward a final resting place in heaven."²⁵ Augustine's term, for Nightingale, depicts his disparagement of earthly life, the natural human condition in a fallen world; for Augustine, human beings are "extraterrestrials" who have fallen to earth as a "place of unbelonging" and a mortal condition of "psychic dispersion and bodily deterioration." There are three implications of this interpretation of Augustine's vision of human nature that are relevant to Tanner's depiction of *imago dei* and to McKenny's discussion of their relevance for biotechnology. The first is the construal of human nature as "in" but not "of" the embodied natural world. That is, human beings like Adam and Eve in Eden and the resurrected saints in heaven are made for a life "out of nature"²⁶—their nature, as Tanner puts it, is to "image" or "reflect" that which is "alien" or "utterly other," indeed, "exterior" to themselves, namely God. This is what gives both "plasticity" to human nature, including embodied human rationality to imagine the alterations to nature, including human nature, of which human beings are capable, and the seemingly innate human dissatisfaction in simply being "themselves," since they are made for transhuman deification—becoming "other" than themselves.²⁷ For both Nightingale's and Tanner's accounts, human beings as *imago dei* are distinct from all other creatures (and in some sense from "creation" itself, therefore) in this regard. In this regard one might note that the possibilities both for exceptional good and for exceptional evil are present within human agency and technological power.

The second implication follows from the first, namely, that embodied human life in the finite creaturely world is an "inferior" life not to be valued or "enjoyed" in and of itself. The Augustinian love of the world is, indeed, finally a refusal of the embodied earthly realm, since the "true dwelling" of humans is not the mortal world of finite flesh (the "food chain" as Nightingale likes to call it, and she suggests that Augustinian Christian asceticism seeks liberation from precisely this) but is, rather, the "transhuman" life of God in a "perfect, unearthly body" outside time and nature.²⁸ Even while in the "exile" of sin both bodily (they are now condemned to mortal existence, i.e., "death") and psychically (they are unable to live in the eternal presence and so condemned to inhabit the temporal "distentions" of birth, aging, and death of all creaturely organisms), humans nevertheless retain the awareness that they do not "belong" there. In this sense Nightingale's Augustine agrees with Tanner's "normative" depiction of *imago dei*: rational human "dominion" over the earth is rooted in their being made in the divine image "beyond" and "above"

---

25. Nightingale, *Once Out of Nature*, 3. For an alternative account of *peregrinatio* in Augustine, see Sarah Stewart-Kroeker, *Pilgrimage as Moral and Aesthetic Formation in Augustine's Thought* (Oxford: Oxford University Press, 2017), esp. 1–82.

26. Nightingale, *Once Out of Nature*, 4.

27. This is the theological argument of Tanner, *Christ the Key*, chap. 1, citing Augustine and others in support.

28. Nightingale, *Once Out of Nature*, 6–7. These claims are exegetically developed and theorized in chap. 1 ("Edenic and Resurrected Transhumans") and 5 ("Unearthly Bodies").

the natural world. This is what gives human beings their freedom to remake the world according to images and ideas not literally depicted therein, but that are suggestible in speech, the divine Logos to which they are uniquely attuned.[29] Here is how Tanner characterizes human nature over against "every other creature":

> Humans seem to have an underlying concern for what is absolutely good per se—for God—for what is not merely good in certain respects but fully good in a perfectly unlimited way. They want in some sense to *be* that absolute good rather than any particular sort of thing, rather than the specific sort of creature they are, by being formed in and through a relationship with the absolute good.[30]

Here we are back at the "rather than" we have already seen earlier that worries McKenny and Barth, and, indeed, Nightingale (for non-theological reasons)—and yet, for Tanner it is precisely the ground for hope in the mediation of divine redemption of bodies and the embodied world by being incorporated into the Body of Christ, the second person of the trinity. We will return to this important point later, namely, the *how* of incorporation as "deification," since it is precisely Augustine's characterization of this process as the kenotic economy of the incarnation of the divine word that Nightingale avoids[31] and Tanner resists and recasts.

The third related claim has to do with Augustine's vision of salvation, which is characterized by Nightingale as God taking Christians "out of the food chain, offering them denaturalized, transhuman bodies that will live eternally in the City of God"—"free of desire, pain, disintegration, and death."[32] The difference, Nightingale tellingly asserts, is that, unlike Adam and Eve, redeemed states will live in an eternal city rather than an Edenic garden. This may be related to her comment that in Augustine's view the resurrected body "will look a bit like the Pompidou Center, with the inner organs on view."[33] No doubt this is more revealing of Nightingale's contemporary aesthetics than Augustine's.[34] The Pompidou Center

---

29. Tanner, *Christ the Key*, 50. See also Kathryn Tanner, "In the Image of the Invisible," in *Apophatic Bodies: Negative Theology, Incarnation, and Relationality*, ed. Chris Boesel and Catherine Keller (New York: Fordham University Press, 2009), 117–34.

30. Tanner, "In the Image of the Invisible," 122.

31. See her astonishing footnote (fn.30), after stating the intention to "honor the literary, philosophical, and theological aspects" of "Augustine's conception of human embodiment": "I will not examine the incarnation of Christ and the church as the 'body of God' since my focus is on human embodiment." Nightingale, *Once Out of Nature*, 14.

32. Nightingale, *Once Out of Nature*, 25–6.

33. Ibid., 48.

34. Indeed, my own university, McMaster, constructed a "high-tech" ("structural expressionist") version of the Pompidou Center in its "world-class" medical school and hospital in the early 1970s—architecture characterized by flexibility, malleability, and the capacity not only for "expansion" but also for the integration of "interior/exterior" elements

is, of course, famous for its modern/postmodern arts, while the contemporary medical arts are their own self-evident justification, at the forefront of the most benevolent therapeutic and enhancement bio-engineering enterprises of our time (in my university the "world-class" medical center replaced expansive regional gardens and very quickly became the iconic center of McMaster University's aspirational identity, not least in relation to biotechnology). We'll return to the question of resurrection bodies in Augustine, but I want to call attention first to images of embodiment, including artistic and human embodiment, in our own time and place that are tellingly used to represent Augustine's salvific "images" of the human *imago dei* that make it more amenable to being made over in the image of transhumanist fantasies.

Nightingale cites Caroline Walker Bynum's work on early Christian accounts of bodily resurrection to argue that Augustine's and the Christian doctrine of the resurrection are "grounded in a rejection of time and nature,"[35] shifting from biological metaphors to metaphors of "assemblage" whereby human "liberation" from bondage to a mortal nature characterized by change and decay leads to "salvation as the crystalline hardness not only of stasis but of the impossibility of non-stasis."[36] The resurrected body is more like a statue recast by the divine Maker that recovers all scattered "bits" of one's embodied earthly identity—like so many relics recovered from martyred bodies—so as to perfect it in incorruptible, immortal bodies able at rest to truly image the profundity of eternal divine glory. Now it is true that in his famous Book 22 of *City of God*, Augustine uses the image of the clay pot and the remaking of a flawed statue by the divine Artist (22.19) and that he does so with special reference to the reconstituted bodies of the "blessed martyrs" that, like Christ's body, display the glory of their wounds. It is also the case that he waxes eloquent on the hellish miseries of mortal human life in a fallen natural world characterized by disease, deformity, and any number of horrific accidental misfortunes (22.22), to say nothing of the unending human struggles against temptations and the vices that grotesquely deform human souls and further deform the common nature of a world full of conflict, violence, pain, and death (22.23). Nevertheless, Augustine is equally eloquent about the many goods that remain present to a sinful and punitive world—goods closely related, he says, to the "original good" of creation: propagation and conformation (22.24). Here we see a good deal of the seminal language of natural causation,

and indoor/outdoor spaces, all of which are oriented toward the built technological environment and its functional requirements and interests of human control and management. I suggest this, too, is an element of the non-iconic imagination (in terms of the messianic economy of incarnation) behind biotechnology.

35. Nightingale, *Once Out of Nature*, 44.

36. Caroline Walker Bynum, *The Resurrection of the Body in Western Christianity, 200–1336* (New York: Columbia University Press, 1995), 97.

both hidden and invisible as well as the visible forms of beauty we behold.[37] This is tied to the creation mandate of procreation but also to the human freedom for conformation—the technical arts of human ingenuity divinely implanted in humans not only *in semine* but also *in ratione* that represent the remarkable *coaptatio* ("togetherness") and *harmonia* of the living being. There is also in this meditation on the resurrection of the body an eloquent account of technology in relation to aesthetics, the medical arts, agriculture, industry, and philosophy that by no means ignores the diverse uses and beauties of the natural created order, which is, after all, a divine miracle that therefore by faith one may believe will be perfected by the one who has fashioned it and sustains it in ongoing creation *ex nihilo*—a redemptive process in which human beings participate in their embodied practices (*technê*).

Yet for all of this, the most important image related to the resurrection of bodies and to the process that may be called "deification" with which Book 22 and the entire *City of God* ends, the "face to face" vision of I Corinthians 13, has to do with the existential, enigmatic completion of divine love beyond knowledge. Here as elsewhere Augustine is careful to distinguish worship of God from veneration of the martyrs: "our martyrs are not gods; for we know only one God, Who is the God both of us and of the martyrs" (22.10). Miracles done at the shrines of the martyrs are not the same as the "*Euhemerization*" process of Roman civil religious deification for heroic individual earthly immortality (6.7-9), since they are intended to give praise to the hidden power of divine goodness. For Augustine this is not unrelated to the eucharistic sacrifice of the Body of Christ—which is not offered *to* the body, but, rather, to the God of sacrificial love "because they themselves are that body" (22.10; cf. 10.6 & 20). That is, it is related to the incarnational economy of the Word made flesh who takes the form of the servant. What is the "measure" of embodiment by which to represent the resurrected body? Augustine cites Eph. 4:13, the "measure of the age of the fullness [*plenitudine/pleroma*] of Christ" (22.15f.), which is "conformity" not to "this age [*saeculum*]" but to the mind of Christ (Rom. 12:2). The perfection of human life is to be found in the "building up" of the messianic body through love of God and neighbor. Overcoming the evils of the world happens through death, "by dying" (22.9)— not simply by consenting to the death of the mortal body but also by dying to the desire to wish to dominate or conquer the world through god-like power to remake it in the human image. Indeed, only such an apocalyptic imagination of the incarnational economy is able to envision the suffered, embodied "wounds" of the martyrs as beautiful displays "in the body but not of the body" (22.19), of the sacrifices of compassion that also image Christ's suffering, which will be retained

---

37. See Augustine's seminal account of providential causation in *City of God* 5.11, which precedes his critical analysis of Roman love of glory rooted in earthly domination and love of human praise for heroic deeds.

and not "transcended" or annihilated in the final restoration and reconciliation of "all things" in the bodily resurrection.[38]

Exemplum *and* Sacramentum: *Incarnational Economy and Biotechnology*

I have been arguing in this chapter for a broadening of the language of *imago dei* and the incarnational economy to which it belongs—both narratively in relation to biblical theology and naturally in relation to the apocalyptic display of providential divine causality—so as to move from more fixed doctrinal "logics" (whether theological or scientific) toward dynamic and figural, iconic accounts of the real that require us to situate the Christian ethics of biotechnology more broadly within the messianic mystery of the divine economy: a creation destined for "deification" being remade messianically for divine dwelling.[39] This mystery or *sacramentum* that underlies the movement and relations of the incarnational economy is displayed in the mediation of its Logos in the human model of imitation that appears "in the form of the servant" (Phil. 2:7, the kenotic Christ)—the form that Christ as our neighbor (Matthew 25) also takes in the iconic "final" judgment.[40] The form of the servant is exalted as the non-clinging, dispossessive "form of God" that, as self-emptying abundance or "fullness," shares its gifted possessions with all in common. This form is also, in keeping with Paul's account of the "one mind" (Phil. 2:2-11; cf. Rom. 12:1-2), the *exemplum* to be imitated in the building up of the messianic body on earth and in the world—a body characterized by pilgrimage, not possessiveness; martyrdom, not domination. This is a theme established in *City of God* 1.1 that carries through to the end in deification, in a reversal of the meaning given by the tempter ("You shall be as gods")—that is, the divine perfection that completes and fills the "all in all" of creation is accomplished in the completion of sacrificial other-regarding divine love, not the possessive knowledge of good and evil. For Augustine, then, the "day of judgment" is not just the "last day" but an ongoing dynamic journey characterizing the whole created order in nature and history. The punishment for sins of pride and envy (the "evil eye" of privative, possessive desire)[41] is immediate and leads to hells of our own making: the violence and devastation of rivalry rooted in the objectifying, possessive gaze that loves the power to dominate and leads to the breakdown of trust and community. By contrast the messianic mind follows Christ both as embodied *exemplum* and hidden *sacramentum* via the mystical anointing

---

38. I'm indebted here to Sarah Stewart-Kroeker, "Love of and for the Martyrs: Resurrected Wounds and the 'Order' of Restoration," *Studia Patristica* 116 (2021): 91–8.
39. I have tried to give an orienting account of this in *Messianic Political Theology and Diaspora Ethics*; see the Introduction and Part 1.
40. *City of God* 20.29: "He humbled himself to become our neighbour." See fn. 23 earlier.
41. Ibid., 14.3&11.

that makes such humans all "priests" and "Christs"[42] in the community of sacrifice that offers itself to the transformation, the "making new" of "all things" through the *technê* of humble love.[43]

In such an economy, "heaven," figuratively speaking, is not a "place" or an "other world" but, rather, an invisible divine presence that is in continuity with the visible temporal world ("your will be done on earth as it is in heaven"). As Augustine makes clear, the divinely given spiritual motion of incarnation and transformation/regeneration by which God comes to dwell in God's own creation is not some form of space and time travel—God comes to where God already is.[44] The point of continuity, however, is consistently the cross. If one is to speak of an economy of glory it must be related to the ignominious death of the Messiah crucified by all forms of worldly authority, the "principalities and powers." In the crucial Book 10 of *City of God*, Augustine cites Rom. 12:1-2 to formulate the embodiment of the "living sacrifice" in the world in conformity with the "form of the servant" offered in the crucified Messiah.[45] There is no radical division between "being" and "acting," between "theology" and "ethics" in this messianic enactment of the mysterious reconciliation of "all things" in Christ. As Henri de Lubac puts it in his Augustinian *Corpus Mysticum*, this is the sacramental heart of the mystical Body of Christ, where "mystical" means more than "moral," but may not—because embodied and enacted in the everyday life of the world—be taken as "invisible"; it is visible to those with "eyes to see," the eyes of the heart.[46] Augustine's theology of the sacrificial messianic economy is nicely articulated by Joshua Nunziato as one that effectively "negotiates the limits of embodiment" as "occasions of parting without loss" such that "sacrifice can take the form of openheartedness: attention to others that recognizes our common good through exchange."[47] This enables us to recognize the limits of our shared mortal flesh without regarding those limits through the paradigm of a tragic burden that requires us to resist death and eliminate all suffering as evil. Such possessive human desire to overcome all given

---

42. Ibid., 20.9.

43. Ibid., 20.14. All of this is part of Augustine's exegesis of Revelation 20 with reference to the apocalyptic eschatology that completes creation via its "transformation," not its "destruction": "It is, then, the figure, not the nature, that passes away" (cf. I Cor. 7:31f.).

44. Augustine, *Teaching Christianity* 1.12–13, 34; *Trinity* 2.7.

45. Augustine, *City of God* 10.6 & 20. Cf. *Trinity* 14.22 where this same transformative process according to the form of the servant is related to Rom 12.

46. Henri de Lubac, *Corpus Mysticum: The Eucharist and the Church in the Middle Ages*, trans. G. Simmonds with R. Price and C. Stephens, ed. L. P. Hemming and S. F. Parsons (Notre Dame: University of Notre Dame Press, 2006), chap. 3, esp. 248–56.

47. Joshua Nunziato, *Augustine and the Economy of Sacrifice: Ancient and Modern Perspectives* (Cambridge: Cambridge University Press, 2019), 12; see esp. chap. 5.

natural limits through technological domination, indeed, imposes tragic sacrifices rather than eliminating them.[48]

I have argued in this chapter that the Augustinian account of the meaning of *imago dei* is not accurately or adequately represented in McKenny's placement of it into his NS1-type that reads it in terms of "human nature" and, indeed, the created order as architectonically "given." Rather, it should be interpreted within the larger theological context of the "incarnational economy" that also has implications for the ethics pertaining to biotechnology in the Anthropocene. I have argued that Augustine's account of divine providence and human deification is situated in a more apocalyptic, contingent, and dynamic theology of creation *ex nihilo* that relates "all that is"—the very *principium* of creation—to the transformative incarnational *principium*, the other-regarding movement of divine love mediated in the crucified and resurrected Christ. This also expands the scope of relevant "bioethical principles" from the more anthropocentric principles of human autonomy, safety, and fairness toward a more figural or iconic imagination of the *imago dei* in all creation in which human beings are participants. Such an iconic imagination, rooted in the economy of messianic mystery that situates the *imago dei* within the kenotic drama of humble self-giving love, is able to resource critiques both of escapist other-worldly transcendence (since this drama is simultaneously in heaven and on earth) and of this-worldly transhumanist visions of salvation (that take the transfiguration of the burdens of finite, mortal life out of the realm of the Word made flesh toward immortal invulnerability). To spell out the considerable implications of this for the ethics of biotechnology is a task for another time and place. We are in Jerry McKenny's debt for providing us with compelling typologies that situate this necessary work, and I have here only attempted to be of service in the critical clarification of the Augustinian *imago dei*.

Coda

Elizabeth Kolbert's Pulitzer Prize-winning account of the "event" that is upon us biologically and technologically right now she calls *The Sixth Extinction: An Unnatural History*, and by this she means to signal the age of the Anthropocene in which human beings have taken over a global project of remaking nature in the human image. It is not a felicitous image in terms of the sacrifices it entails, and I will simply characterize this in my own words. When Jerry and I were born in the late 1950s, the population on earth was 2.8 billion, only 32 percent of which were urban dwellers (a "density rating" of 19). I myself was born in southern Manitoba on my grandparents' farm and for the first four years of my life spoke the low German dialect (*Plautdietsch*) that my Mennonite ancestors had brought

---

48. Citing the WWF *Living Planet Report—2018: Aiming Higher*, which documents the sacrifice of 60 percent of vertebrate life on earth in the past fifty years, Nunziato nicely points out: "Today's economic culture has not eliminated the ancient rites of animal sacrifice: it has globalized them." Nunziato, *Augustine and the Economy of Sacrifice*, 28.

with them in their diaspora journey from the northern European lowlands to Prussia, Russia, and then Manitoba in 1874. In 2020, the human population on earth is 7.8 billion, 56 percent urban (and rapidly growing, with a density rating of 52). Since 1970, 60 percent of the world's wildlife species have disappeared, we are losing 150 plant and animal species per day, with a million at risk (and this, of course, includes human beings). Only livestock populations are growing, due to industrial farming and a boom of domestic animals, including pets (especially during Covid!). We are currently losing one human language every few weeks (the numbers vary), and some projections estimate that up to 90 percent of currently spoken languages will disappear this century, leaving us with about seven remaining "dominant" language groups. Related to this has been a huge process of biological and cultural displacement, not only outside but also inside the so-called first world that humans inhabit, with the attendant natural and cultural human "traumas": poverty, disease, addictions, violence, mental illness, suicide, and the list goes on, with the so-called "1 percent" shrinking to the ".01 percent" even while its share of the wealth grows. That is, even as we've witnessed tremendous technological advances globally, animal species and human cultures have been extinguished, and our world is showing very real signs of the dramatic extinction of many and perhaps all life-forms. And yet, what is the solution envisioned by this shrinking dominant global population? Technotopia! Even now we are being assured that while technology may have created some of our problems, only humanly contrived technological solutions will address and resolve them, thereby "saving" the planet—or perhaps at least the human species, or some version of the transhuman replication of anthropocentric life even if not on Planet Earth itself. This is an idolatry that an Augustinian account of the Word made flesh might help Christians to resist in their embodied sacrificial witness.

While the preceding paragraph (and perhaps not it alone) may strike many as hyperbolic—and so baldly stated, perhaps it is—my main point has been to argue that we cannot discuss the Christian ethics of human nature and biotechnology without considering this apocalyptic range of its significance. I have argued that Augustine did so in his own context, with the resources of biblical theology at his disposal in rethinking the ethical implications of *imago dei* in the context of a messianic incarnational economy of creation. That vision remains no less relevant to the challenges of the age of the sixth extinction in the *saeculum* of the Anthropocene than it did in the moribund decay of the Roman empire in late antiquity.

Chapter 8

THE NORMATIVE STATUS OF HUMAN NATURE

BARTHIAN AND THOMISTIC CONVERGENCES

Stephen J. Pope

James M. Gustafson considered Thomas Aquinas and Karl Barth the two most systematic and comprehensive thinkers in the history of Christianity.[1] While these immensely influential theologians represent radically different, and strongly opposed, ways of conceiving of Christian faith and life, over the course of the past several decades Thomists and Barthians have adopted a more appreciative stance toward one another's traditions.[2] Working in this vein, this chapter explores possible points of contact between Barthian and Thomistic ethics as represented, respectively, by the accomplished Barth scholar Gerard P. McKenny,[3] author of *Biotechnology, Human Nature, and Ethics*,[4] and his distinguished colleague at Notre

---

1. See James M. Gustafson, *Ethics from a Theocentric Perspective: Vol. 1., Theology and Ethics* (Chicago: University of Chicago Press, 1981).

2. In theology, for example, see Tyler R. Wittman, *God and Creation in the Theology of Thomas Aquinas and Karl Barth* (New York: Cambridge University Press, 2018); *Thomas Aquinas and Karl Barth: An Unofficial Dialogue*, ed. Bruce McCormack and Thomas Joseph White (Grand Rapids: Eerdmans, 2013); Eugene F. Rogers, *Thomas Aquinas and Karl Barth: Sacred Doctrine and the Natural Knowledge of God* (Notre Dame: University of Notre Dame Press, 1995). In the 1920s, Barth engaged neo-Thomists Erich Przywara and Erik Peterson. Catholic theologians Hans Urs von Balthasar and Hans Küng sought common ground with Barth in the 1950s and 1960s. See Amy Marga, "Barth and Roman Catholicism," in *The Wiley Blackwell Companion to Karl Barth: Barth in Dialogue*, ed. George Hunsinger and Keith L. Johnson, Vol. 2 (Hoboken: Wiley-Blackwell, 2020), 845–55.

3. See, especially, Gerald McKenny, *The Analogy of Grace: Barth's Moral Theology* (New York: Oxford University Press, 2010) and *Karl Barth's Moral Thought* (New York: Oxford University Press, 2021).

4. Gerald McKenny, *Biotechnology, Human Nature and Christian Ethics* (New York: Cambridge University Press, 2018).

Dame, Jean Porter, particularly her monograph *Nature as Reason: A Thomistic Theory of Natural Law*.[5]

Biotechnology, Human Nature, and Ethics offers a helpful typology of contemporary ethical positions on technological enhancement of human nature. McKenny traces four ways of understanding the normative significance of human nature in relation to biotechnological enhancement: human nature as given and morally unalterable ("NS1"), human nature as the ground of the human good and correlative rights ("NS2"), human nature as susceptible to intervention for the sake of progress ("NS3"), and human nature as the condition for imaging God ("NS4"). McKenny argues that NS2 is relatively superior to NS1 and NS3 and that NS4 is relatively superior to NS2. He proposes that we consider human nature as normatively significant to the extent to which it can help us "live with God." Seen in this light, biotechnological enhancement can be considered ethically legitimate when it can be used to serve this purpose.

First, in order to provide some context for the chapter's argument we begin with a brief sketch of the main themes of McKenny's *Biotechnology, Human Nature, and Ethics*. Second, we will examine the normative status of human nature in Jean Porter's theory of natural law. Third, we turn to Thomas Aquinas' theocentric account of normativity as the context within which he understands the moral significance of human nature. Here I argue that the Christian theological framework of Thomistic natural law does not fall prey to the problems of moral sufficiency, autonomy, and sovereignty that McKenny finds in secular versions of ethical naturalism (NS2). Fourth, I argue that if the previous analysis is correct, McKenny ought to expand his classification of properly theocentric conceptions of the normative significance of human nature (NS4) to include Thomas Aquinas alongside Barth and those influenced by him. The final section of this chapter explores ways in which these theocentric traditions, for all their differences, offer complementary views of how moral decision making must for Christians be construed most fundamentally in terms of fidelity to God's loving will.

---

5. Jean Porter, *Nature as Reason: A Thomistic Theory of Natural Law* (Grand Rapids: Eerdmans, 2005). The first four chapters of *Nature as Reason* concentrate on ethical naturalism, natural law, acquired virtues, and temporal happiness, but the fifth chapter offers a sketch of how she understands natural law interpreted from within theological ethics. Complete human happiness is attained only in the beatific vision and this "cannot be attained except through a transformative act through which God bestows new principles of knowledge and love into the created intellect and will" (Porter, *Nature as Reason*, 381). This chapter concentrates on *Nature as Reason* rather than taking into account the entirety of her published works. This is an important qualification because her other writings take up theological concerns that are not relevant to the theoretical agenda of this book.

Summary and Initial Assessment of the Four Positions

Biotechnology, Human Nature, and Christian Ethics begins with a central philosophical question: What is the "ground" of moral obligation? This metaphor is a way of describing the obligatory force, or the "oughtness," of moral injunctions. Immanuel Kant identified the distinguishing mark of competing moral theories according to the respective ways in which they attempt to justify their accounts of moral obligation. In the Kantian schema, moral philosophers base moral obligation either in some internal feature of agents (such as good character or some desirable feeling state) or in some criterion external to them (such as the divine law). Internalists base obligation in either subjective (as in moral sense theories) or objective grounds (as in Aristotle's *eudaimonia*). Externalists include those who appeal either to a subjective ground (as in appeals to traditional community standards) or an objective ground (such as the will of God).[6]

Kant, of course, opposed moral sense theories because he denied they can account for the universally and unconditionally binding character of the moral law. The objective, internal ground of Kantian obligation lies in the autonomy of the rational agent. Moral obligation is internal because unconditionally binding on the rational will rather than conditioned upon obtaining some external end and it is objective because it morally compels all similarly situated rational beings regardless of their subjective desires.[7]

McKenny, following Barth, regards moral normativity as grounded in the will of God; expressed in Kantian terms, he regards God as the objective, external ground of normativity. In McKenny's typology, NS4 alone acknowledges the divine ground of moral obligation. Alternatives locate the ground of normativity in human feelings, desires, decisions, autonomous reasoning, or some other feature of human nature. As McKenny reads it, NS2, which includes the natural law tradition, attempts to ground moral obligation in human nature rather than in God. This chapter argues that McKenny's criticisms apply to some versions of natural law but not to Thomas'.

Before discussing Porter and Thomas, however, we will briefly examine McKenny's fourfold typology. The first position, NS1 (shorthand for "normative significance"), is occupied by ethicists who believe nature is normative and ought not to be subjected to biotechnological enhancement. Figures as diverse as Jürgen Habermas, Michael Sandel, C. S. Lewis, and Oliver O'Donovan approve of the use of biotechnology to heal and restore but not to improve nature. They believe respect for equal human dignity is undercut when we conceive of persons as objects to be reshaped by some kind of scientific manipulation.

---

6. This typology is taken from Eric Entrican Wilson and Lara Denis, "Kant and Hume on Morality," *Stanford Encyclopedia of Philosophy*, Available online: https://plato.stanford.edu/entries/kant-hume-morality/ (accessed May 31, 2021).

7. See Immanuel Kant, *Groundwork of the Metaphysics of Morals*, trans. and ed. Mary Gregor (New York: Cambridge University Press, 1997), Sections I and II, 7–51.

Theologically based proponents of NS1 are sometimes mistakenly assumed to hold that genetic enhancement is illegitimate because they believe nature is sacred. The biblical distinction between Creator and creation, however, broke with the ancient pagan sacralization of nature and in so doing put in motion a cultural innovation that eventually made possible the modern scientific investigation of the natural world. Theological proponents of NS1, working with what McKenny calls a "nature-regarding but not nature-centered conviction,"[8] argue that using technology to improve human nature is offensive to the Creator and specifically a violation of the dignity of creatures made in the image of God. They tend to follow an Augustinian understanding of creation as a complete and finished work whose eschatological fulfillment cannot be advanced by human achievements (however noble or impressive in their own right). Advocates of NS1 object to the modern prideful temptation to strive for god-like mastery over creation. As seen in his first book, *To Relieve the Human Condition: Biology, Technology, and the Body*,[9] McKenny is sympathetic to the critique of modern hubris but instead of declaring human nature inviolable he suggests we ought to distinguish morally acceptable from unacceptable uses of biotechnology.

The second normative position, NS2, understands what is good for people as the appropriate fulfillment of natural human desires, needs, and inclinations. McKenny here examines a collection of secular thinkers like Leon Kass, Francis Fukuyama, and Martha Nussbaum; Jean Porter is the only representative of NS2 who does not treat the human good within an "immanent frame."[10] These moral theorists regard ethical normativity as having an internal objective source rather than being imposed upon human nature from some external authority. Their appreciation of ways in which biological and cultural evolution has brought about past variation and change in human nature gives them an openness to some kinds of technologically induced enhancements as long as they do not go so far as to alter human nature in ways that would threaten the goods enjoyed in our current state. Generally open to technological extension of capacities that are already features of human nature, advocates of NS2 promote deliberation over whether particular kinds of proposed interventions either promote or undermine human flourishing.[11]

NS2 is both more discriminating than the prohibitive NS1 and more cautious than NS3. McKenny suggests, however, that in the future advocates of NS2 will

---

8. McKenny, *Biotechnology, Human Nature, and Christian Ethics*, 9. See Michael Sandel, *The Case against Perfection: Ethics in the Age of Genetic Engineering* (Cambridge, MA: Harvard University Press, 2007).

9. Gerald McKenny, *To Relieve the Human Condition: Biology, Technology, and the Body* (Binghamton: SUNY, 1997), 9.

10. See Charles Taylor, "The Immanent Frame," in *A Secular Age* (Cambridge: Harvard University Press, 2007), 539–93.

11. There is no clear line that is crossed when a modification moves from strong extension within kind to transformation of kind.

likely find themselves facing a conundrum: either to allow for the alteration of human nature for the sake of an otherwise unattainable future good or to forsake possible future goods produced by biotechnological enhancement out of respect for the intrinsic normativity of human nature. Whereas the first option effectively detaches normativity from human nature, the second retains the normativity of human nature at the expense of the future human good. Either option, McKenny argues, undercuts the core conviction of NS2 that human goods are good precisely because they fulfill our nature. Defenders of natural law, however, might counter that anything identified as a good has to be recognized, at least in some way, as fulfilling human nature as we experience it now or at least as we could conceive of it being fulfilled in the future; enhancement, after all, suggests improvement rather than wholesale replacement. While sharing NS2's commitment to the goodness and intelligibility of creation, McKenny does not believe human nature can bear the normative weight that its proponents place on it. Human nature, he writes, "does not reliably reflect the good for which we have been created and ... the good for which we have been created is not fully intelligible in terms of our creaturely nature."[12]

McKenny disputes NS2's various ways of justifying an immanent moral order on the grounds that God alone determines the human good and provides, in Jesus Christ, the exclusive basis of knowing that good. As McKenny writes in *The Analogy of Grace*: "Moral theology [for Barth] has to do not with a good which human beings find in themselves but with the relation of human beings to a good that has already been accomplished in Jesus Christ."[13] In McKenny's judgment, then, NS2 suffers from a fatal anthropocentrism that fails to acknowledge the sovereign Lordship of Jesus Christ.

If advocates of NS1 and NS2 defend the claim that human nature is intrinsically normative (albeit in different ways), the third position, NS3, finds normative significance only in the open-ended and "plastic" character of our nature. Its advocates refuse to resign themselves to the currents limits of human nature, particularly when biotechnological means for progress are available. Theologians as diverse as Karl Rahner, Philip Hefner, and Ted Peterson interpret our creation in the image of God as giving us a responsibility to do what we can to improve human nature so that we can more effectively promote the reign of God in this world.

While most supportive of biotechnological enhancement, proponents of NS3 suffer from some significant flaws. According to McKenny, they tend to be excessively open-ended, unrealistic ("the results do not justify the hype"[14]),

---

12. McKenny, *Biotechnology, Human Nature, and Christian Ethics*, 109.

13. McKenny, *The Analogy of Grace*, 7.

14. McKenny, *Biotechnology, Human Nature, and Christian Ethics*, 143. It should be noted that prior to Barth natural law had a significant role within the Reformed tradition. See Stephen J. Grabill, *Rediscovering the Natural Law in Reformed Theological Ethics* (Grand Rapids: Eerdmans, 2006). For recent research, see Neil Arner, "Precedents and Prospects

normatively vague, insufficiently appreciative of the dangers of unrestricted genetic enhancement, and liable to assimilate human nature to "later capitalist production [for the sake of] undirected progress and ... [the] maximal adaptability of bodies."[15] Theologically, NS3 fails to show an appropriate level of respect for the goodness and finished quality of creation in general and human nature in particular. This defect is aggravated by a tendency to identify the inbreaking of the reign of God with the technologically focused quest for human perfection. Biotechnology contributes to various kinds of genuine human progress, but Christian faith acknowledges that God alone brings about the eschatological transformation of the world and the ultimate fulfillment of human beings.

Finally, McKenny finds NS4 to be most persuasive. Exemplified in the work of Barth and Episcopal theologian Kathryn Tanner, this position envisions the Creator as working through the evolutionary process to equip us with an array of biological traits that can be used to help us live theocentrically. Biological nature has normative significance in that it gives us the wherewithal to lead, as McKenny puts it, a "certain form of life with God and with other human beings."[16]

Unlike McKenny, Kathryn Tanner describes the Christian life as most fundamentally growth in Christ, transformation in the image of the second person of the Trinity, and increased participation in the life of God. Our creaturely nature can be completed only if "reworked" by grace to manifest the goodness of God "beyond the limits of any created nature."[17] Tanner draws from Gregory of Nyssa and other classical Orthodox theologians to develop a theology of deification that in some ways resonates with the Thomistic theology of grace and sanctification. Yet, she moves in a more dialectical direction when she describes grace as empowering the person to act "*unnaturally*, in a divine rather than human way."[18] As grace seems to replace nature, so the "Holy Spirit remains ... the motor of all that we become, of both our new dispositions and what follows from them."[19] The exclusive theocentric normativity in Tanner and McKenny thus form the antitype to the radical autonomy of nature advocated by NS2 naturalists.

While NS4 shares with NS2 a strong affirmation of the goodness and finished quality of creation, it denies that human nature is *intrinsically* normative. The Christian moral life is grounded in grace, not in human nature, and Christians are simply called to act as faithful witnesses to that grace rather than seeking their happiness through union with God. Since God alone determines what counts as truly good or bad, moral obligation is not based on what we desire, however

---

for Incorporating Natural Law in Protestant Ethics," *Scottish Journal of Theology* 69, no. 4 (2016): 375–88.

15. Ibid., 123.
16. Ibid., 10.
17. Kathryn Tanner, *Christ the Key* (New York: Cambridge University Press, 2010), 43, 40.
18. Ibid., 62; emphasis added.
19. Ibid., 84.

legitimate and appropriate in its own terms, but, rather, in what God commands. McKenny puts this point rather starkly: "human beings are not responsible for determining the good or bringing it about."[20]

NS4 regards human nature as normatively significant, then, but only indirectly, when recruited to serve "life before God." We are created to lead life with God with the help of grace working in and through the created nature we now have. The Creator has already given us the characteristics that equip us to lead theocentric lives, so we can live in accord with our vocation without biotechnological enhancement. At the same time, since we are to be "for others," we must be open to using biotechnological means when doing so might genuinely promote the human good (theocentrically determined).

Jean Porter's Natural Law Theory

We now turn to Jean Porter's account of the normative significance of human nature, particularly as proposed in *Nature as Reason*.[21] In its primary meaning, natural law refers to the exercise of practical rationality in light of the natural inclinations (prerational as well as rational) to goods proper to human beings.[22] Characterizing her position as a kind of "ethical naturalism,"[23] Porter believes that

---

20. McKenny, *The Analogy of Grace*, 17.

21. For Porter's take on theological aspects of Thomas' ethic, and particularly regarding grace and the infused virtues, see her "Responsibility, Passion, and Sin: A Reassessment of Abelard's *Ethics*," *The Journal of Religious Ethics* 28, no. 3 (Fall 2000): 367–94; "Virtue Ethics and Its Significance for Spirituality: A Survey and Assessment of Recent Work," *The Way Supplement* 88 (1997): 26–35; "Virtue and Sin: The Connection of the Virtues and the Case of the Flawed Saint," *The Journal of Religion* 75, no. 4 (October 1995): 521–39; and "Moral Virtues, Charity, and Grace: Why the Infused and Acquired Virtues Cannot Co-Exist," *Journal of Moral Theology* 8, no. 2 (2019): 40–66.

22. Porter writes, "For most Catholics, in contrast [to Protestantism], the natural law is identified more or less straightforwardly with the deliverances of moral reasoning, which takes account of the regularities of nature, to be sure, but not in such a way as to be bound by them" (Porter, *Nature as Reason*, 44). More conservative advocates of natural law would argue on the contrary that we are bound to observe the inherent teleological purposes (as distinct from the "regularities") of our created nature. They argue that the norms that protect our pursuit of the human good are based in human nature per se and therefore not subject to legitimate moral variation.

23. McKenny, *Biotechnology, Human Nature, and Christian Ethics*, 109. Porter's theologically supported account of ethical naturalism places her at some distance from the anti-theistic ontological naturalism common in Western philosophical ethics today. For the latter, see John Kekes, *The Examined Life* (University Park: Pennsylvania State University Press, 1988) and Owen Flanagan, *The Really Hard Problem: Meaning in a Material World* (Cambridge, MA: MIT Press, 2007).

human acts are intelligible on their own terms and that we can come to significant knowledge of the human good without relying on divine revelation. Drawing on Thomas' appreciation of the integrity of nature, she holds that it would be at least theoretically possible for someone without grace to know the essential constituents of the human good and to exercise the acquired virtues, and so to attain some degree of natural human happiness in this life (see ST I-II, 5,5; 62,1).[24]

Porter's naturalism is rooted in the Aristotelian-Thomistic metaphysics of formal and final causality.[25] To have a nature (a form) is to have an inbuilt inclination to a set of goods (ends) the possession of which constitutes flourishing. Nature is normative (not necessarily in a moral sense) in that what is good for a particular organism depends on the natural teleology that is characteristic of the specific kind of living creature it is. An animal's nature includes norms proper to its own flourishing. We are members of a species who are typically drawn to certain kinds of goods because we perceive them (either explicitly or implicitly, rightly or wrongly) as contributing to what we take to be our ability to flourish. Just as we can make judgments about whether a particular animal is healthy or sick, thriving or languishing, mature or immature, so we can make judgments about whether particular human beings are thriving. An ideal of the virtuous life generates moral standards that promote our overall well-being and, conversely, ideals of human flourishing are also justified by the way they conform to culturally dominant conceptions of the virtues.

Porter's natural law theory is not meant to function as a full-blown ethic in its own right and so has to be interpreted in light of the particular historically located and culturally defined ideals of human flourishing, the virtues appropriate to them, and the cultural practices that transmit and sustain them.[26] Ethical naturalism is

---

24. Citations from the *Summa Theologiae* are placed in parentheses within the body of the text and according to part, question, and article in which they are found. Quotations from Thomas are taken from the *Summa Theologiae*, trans. Fathers of the English Dominican Province (Westminster: Christian Classics, 1981).

25. See *Nature as Reason*, 174. Porter understands human nature in terms of Aristotelian formal and final causality, which she persuasively argues is fully compatible with evolutionary theory; see Ibid., 82–103. It should be noted, though, that knowledge of evolutionary mechanisms challenges theologians to think carefully about the scholastic assumption that nature as a whole reflects the wisdom and benevolence of the Creator (Ibid., 136–7).

26. Porter believes her theory is "Thomistic, in the sense that it takes his theory of the natural law as a starting point and develops it in a way that is, I hope, faithful to his overall intent" (Porter, *Nature as Reason*, ix). Later she writes, "I believe my own theory of the natural law is in its essentials that of Aquinas, as developed and extended in a contemporary context, or at least that it is a development and extension of that theory within the spirit of his overall project" (Ibid., 46–7). One of the most important ways in which Porter's project echoes Thomas' is in her insistence that theological claims about nature are accountable to well-established non-theological accounts of nature (see 59).

on display in her understanding of the institution of morality as expressing social requirements built into human nature over the long course of biological and cultural evolution.[27] Human nature is such that our communities maintain internal solidarity through common adherence to moral conventions. Moral conventions typically support some implicit or explicit account of what constitutes human flourishing; ethical reflection explicitly asks whether a particular community's moral conventions actually promote its members' flourishing.[28]

Rather than directly dictating moral standards, natural inclinations inform us about the goods that must be ordered in some way or other if people in a given society are to attain some reasonable level of flourishing. Porter holds that human nature and the natural law norms related to it "underdetermine" morality. While natural law generates both some general moral norms such as non-maleficence and benevolence, and some even more specific moral norms of the sort seen in the second table of the Decalogue, they stand in need of greater degrees of specificity that can be provided only by the specific moral cultures of particular societies.

Particular moral cultures (e.g., Confucian, medieval Christian, nineteenth-century British) order these goods in their own distinctive ways according to their specific ideal of an overall well-ordered and excellent human life. A particular culture's mores of sexual conduct, marriage, and family, for example, order and guide the expression of our prerational natural inclinations to sex, pair bonding, parental care, and kin alliances. Porter argues that since particular moral codes constitute various kinds of "natural moralities," we ought to recognize that there are many natural law moralities and not just one.[29]

Porter's naturalistic approach to moral theory brings two major benefits. First, assigning a significant role to practical moral reasoning within natural law theory provides a way of correcting popular moralists and religious leaders who

---

27. As a result, Porter displays a heightened awareness of the pervasiveness of contingency, variation, and change within human nature that is not always appreciated in other theories of natural law. See Porter, *Nature as Reason*, 131. In contrast, see the "new natural law theory" exemplified in Germain Grisez, *The Way of the Lord Jesus: Vol. 1, Christian Moral Principles* (Chicago: Franciscan Herald Press, 1983) and John Finnis, *Natural Law and Natural Rights* (New York: Oxford University Press, 1980).

28. A paradigm of this use of natural law is found in Martin Luther King, Jr's "Letter from a Birmingham Jail." See Martin Luther King, Jr., *I Have a Dream: Speeches and Writings that Changed the World*, ed. James Melvin Washington (San Francisco: HarperSanFrancisco, 1992), chap. 10, 83–100.

29. Porter thus argues that her theory of natural law is compatible with many different historically and culturally situated moral codes, normative frameworks, and conceptions of human flourishing. In contrast, see the International Theological Commission's 2008 document, "In Search of a Universal Ethic: A New Look at the Natural Law," Available online: https://www.vatican.va/roman_curia/congregations/cfaith/cti_documents/rc_con_cfaith_doc_20090520_legge-naturale_en.html (accessed June 14, 2021).

claim divinely bestowed authorization for overriding all other relevant moral considerations. Alert to ways in which we all too easily identify our merely human judgment with God's, practical reason, shaped by humility and compassion, can help to resist the temptation to "tie up heavy, cumbersome loads and put them on other people's shoulders" without so much as lifting a finger to ease them (Mt. 23:4).[30]

Acknowledging the thoroughly human nature of moral values, reasoning, and judgment allows Thomists to give proper credence to communal deliberation, reasoning, and dialogue. It puts communities in position to rethink previously held moral norms in light of new evidence. Social practices that at one time were widely assumed to have been morally obligatory, and adamantly supported by religious authorities speaking in the name of God, were later rejected after having been subjected to fresh and sustained moral scrutiny in light of new information, moral ideals, and social pressures.

The uniqueness of Porter's project lies in its attempt to give a specifically *theological* justification for her ethical naturalism. Against critics who regard natural law as secularizing Christian morality,[31] she argues that there are theological reasons for Christians to affirm the intrinsic normativity of human nature—that is, to claim that moral obligation is built into human nature rather than superimposed upon it. Religious affirmation of the world as the creation of an omnibenevolent and omnipotent God supports a vision of nature as structured by a moral order rather than as normatively chaotic. Natural law receives special backing from the biblical vision of human beings as created in the image of God, bearing a special

---

30. Ibid., 136. McKenny would share Porter's warning that we not "divinize morality," and even more that we not "divinize ourselves." Porter does not explain what exactly she means by "divinizing" morality, but at the very least she would share McKenny's and the wider Reformed tradition's allergic reaction to self-idolatry. Thomas himself envisions a progressive graced participation in the divine likeness and activity that enables us to become partakers in the divine nature (2 Pet. 1:4); he attributes this process to divine rather than human causality. See ST I-II, 112, 1 and III, 16, 8. Katheryn Tanner, the other major inhabitant of NS4, provides a rich account of *theosis* that draws mainly from Gregory of Nyssa, Augustine, and other Patristic theologians but also Thomas. See her Tanner, *Christ the Key*.

31. This agenda is what led Stanley Hauerwas to criticize Porter's ethic as "essentially a baptized version of secular liberalism," by which he seems to have meant something like an ill-conceived attempt to give Christian legitimacy to secular liberalism rather than, as Porter might have it, a critical appropriation of valuable liberal insights with a contemporary Thomistic ethic. Stanley Hauerwas, *Approaching the End: Eschatological Reflections on Church, Politics, and Life* (Grand Rapids: Eerdmans, 2013) 18. Porter would raise important theological objections to Hauerwas's intention to base ethics "only on Jesus Christ" (Ibid., 16), but some Thomists find resonances with Hauerwas's ethic. See, for example, Paul J. Wadell, *Happiness and the Christian Moral Life: An Introduction to Christian Ethics* (Lanham: Rowman & Littlefield, 2012).

dignity, possessing capacities for rationality and self-determination, bound together by common bonds of solidarity, and called to exercise stewardship for one another and other creatures.

Critics will view Porter's natural law theory as standing on a fairly thin theological foundation. Theologians coming from a more confessional perspective will worry that making nature rather than grace the primary reference point leaves her with rather minimal biblical support for her account of the doctrine of creation. Confessional theologians will worry that the Creator depicted in *Nature as Reason* is not the "God who acts in history" to redeem the world. They will also argue that this theory's lack of connection to core Trinitarian and Christological convictions undercuts any distinctively Christian theological justification for natural law. In the final chapter of *Nature as Reason*, Porter herself provides an outline of what a distinctively Christian appropriation of her natural law theory would look like.

In addition to providing a theological justification for her natural law theory, Porter also wishes to suggest ways in which natural law can be critically appropriated from within a distinctively Christian perspective.[32] She describes this agenda in several ways—as providing a theologically informed interpretation of human morality, a theology of the moral life in relation to "other central Scriptural and doctrinal concerns,"[33] and an interpretation of natural law within a "more comprehensive theological framework."[34] Theological reflection can give "direction and shape" to Christian interpretations of human nature and the natural law and on this basis, she writes, develop "an adequate Christian ethic."[35] Natural law theory neither ignores nor replaces Christian particularity: "There are many ways of being human, and what we must do, in order to develop a theologically adequate account of the natural law, is to develop an account . . . of what it means to be human in a Christian way."[36]

Christian morality is centered on God's will, particularly as communicated through both natural law and revelation.[37] Conceiving natural law in the more comprehensive setting of revelation and the Christian doctrinal tradition shapes the significance it has for the Christian moral life. The Christian vision of both happiness as beatitude and the grace-infused virtues proportionate to that end is a reflection of distinctively Christian beliefs about God as Triune, God's self-communication in grace and revelation, human nature as not only created good

---

32. This is the burden of *Nature as Reason*, chap. 5.
33. Porter, *Nature as Reason*, 326.
34. Ibid., 328.
35. Ibid., 339.
36. Ibid.
37. In an earlier work, Porter shows the biblical roots of scholastic natural law theory in a way that helpfully dispels the simple identification of natural law with reason and divine law with biblical revelation. See Jean Porter, *Natural and Divine Law: Reclaiming the Tradition for Christian Ethics* (Grand Rapids: Eerdmans, 1999), chap. 3.

but seriously wounded by sin, the Incarnation of the Word in Jesus Christ, and the ongoing activity of the Holy Spirit to the church and the world.

Thomas Aquinas on Natural Law

Thomas himself developed his account of natural law with a profoundly theological context. His interpretation of natural law reflects his theology of creation, but it achieves its full meaning in his theology of grace.[38] The *Summa Theologiae* was written as a textbook for young Dominican friars preparing for religious life, prayer, and pastoral ministry.[39] Thomas laid out his account of the moral life not primarily in terms of obligations, duties, and norms but mainly according to the infused virtues exercised by believers on their journey toward God. His innovation lay in providing a rich and detailed theological framework (Part I and Part III) for his treatment of ethics (Part II). The first section of Part I (the *Prima secundae*) examines the anthropological presuppositions of the virtue ethics of the second section of Part II (the *Secunda secundae*). The *Prima secundae* ends with a careful analysis of vice and sin (I-II,71-89), law (90-108), and grace (109-114). Thomas devoted only one Question (I-II,94) to the natural law and three to the "new law" of the Gospel (I-II,106-108).

Respect for the integrity of created nature, human agency, and human intelligence led Thomas to acknowledge the positive value of practical reason, the acquired virtues, and earthly happiness. He was not reluctant to acknowledge the possibility of true pagan virtue (as opposed to "splendid vices"), but he believed in these are virtues only "in a restricted sense" because they attain only a proximate and partial good, rather than the final and complete union with God (I-II, 65, 2; II-II, 23, 7).

Thomas interprets natural law from within the drama of creation, sin, and redemption. We truly flourish to the extent to which we allow God to replace our hearts of stone with hearts of flesh (Ez. 11:19, 36:26; Jer. 31:33). Grace is healing, forgiving, purifying, and perfecting of our creaturely capacities. Indeed, Thomas

---

38. The *Prima secundae*'s treatment of law culminates in an examination of the new law of the Gospel (I-II, 106-8) which prepares the context for Thomas' rich analysis of the theology of grace (I-II, 109-14). The latter is the climax of the *Prima secundae* and sets the context for Thomas' treatment of the infused virtues, first the theological and then the moral infused virtues, throughout the *Secunda secundae*. On the role of grace, the New Law, and the gifts of the Holy Spirit in the theological ethics of Thomas, see Thomas F. O'Meara, O. P., "Virtues in the Theology of Thomas Aquinas," *Theological Studies* 58 (1997): 254–85; Servais Pinckaers, O. P., *The Sources of Christian Ethics*, trans. Sr. Mary Thomas Noble, O. P. (Washington: The Catholic University of America, 1995).

39. See Leonard E. Boyle, O. P., "The Setting of the *Summa Theologiae* of St. Thomas—Revisited," in *The Ethics of Aquinas*, ed. Stephen J. Pope (Washington: Georgetown University Press, 2001), 17–29.

went so far as to say that the good of grace in a human soul has greater value than the entire good of the whole order of nature (see ST I-II, 113, 9 ad 2). While entirely preserving our humanity, grace elevates and transforms the human person.[40] This transformative emphasis contrasts with McKenny's confidence that "human nature does not need to become anything other than what it is, as created by God, to enjoy life with God."[41] For Thomas, grace elevates the human person to make us partakers in the divine nature. This transformation makes us *more* human, and ennobles us, by actualizing all of our deepest potentialities for being and thereby forming into the human likeness of God (see ST I-II, 62, 3 ad 2).[42]

Thomas recognized that while we are created with a basic orientation to right and wrong, and drawn to what we perceive to be good and repelled by what we regard as evil, our capacities to know and to do what is right have been seriously damaged by sin. Out of care for humanity, and in light of our weakened condition, God directs us to the good not only through our natural inclinations and the wisdom accumulated in moral cultures but also explicitly through the medium of revealed divine law. Grace is the only remedy for our sinful alienation from God, but even if we had never sinned, grace would still have been necessary for us as finite creatures to attain the final end to which God calls us. If normativity is grounded in human flourishing, and if we have been created to flourish only in union with God, then normativity is grounded in God. Human nature can be understood only as having a derivative and secondary normative status. Even if, under the right internal and external circumstances, we attain some partial flourishing in this life, such "imperfect happiness" is not our telos (ST I-II, 5, 3).[43]

Returning to Porter, we can note that her concern with the acquired virtues necessary for "terrestrial happiness" is consistent with the modern turn away from eschatological fulfillment and toward treating "purely human goods" as the "highest goals of human beings, even in the sphere of religion."[44] Rather than focusing on the path to heaven, many contemporary theologians rightly spend their energy

---

40. On the importance of spirituality for Thomas' theology, see Jean-Pierre Torell, O. P., *Christ and Spiritualty in St. Thomas Aquinas* (Washington: Catholic University of America Press, 2011).

41. McKenny, *Biotechnology, Human Nature, and Christian Ethics*, 159. For Thomas' understanding of deification, see Bernhard Blankenhorn, O. P., *Mystery of Union with God: Dionysian Mysticism in St. Albert the Great and Thomas Aquinas* (Washington: Catholic University of America Press, 2015).

42. As McKenny points out Barth does not have much to say about what happens to human nature in its resurrected state or eschatological fulfillment; see *Biotechnology, Human Nature, and Christian Ethics*, 181.

43. According to Thomas, as the will is formally ordered toward the universal good, and the universal good subsists completely only in God, we can claim the will has a natural inclination for God. The human soul possesses an "obediential potency" that by the power of divine grace generates an elicited desire for supernatural beatitude.

44. Taylor, *Secular Age*, 261.

both denouncing the living "hell" caused by systematic exclusion, oppression, and violence and advocating for more just socioeconomic and politico-legal institutions. Porter's own professional contribution to this effort can be found in her scholarly work on justice, natural rights, and civil law.[45] Nonetheless, the focus Porter gives to terrestrial happiness in her theory of natural law does not take into account the Christian vision of our true and final end. Critics might worry that her purely natural framework confirms the modern tendency of "exclusive humanism" to reduce the significance of religion to ethics.[46]

Expanding NS4

If the analysis provided here so far has been accurate, then McKenny is right to characterize Porter's natural law theory as belonging to NS2, but ought to consider Thomas' theologically rich appropriation of natural law as a version of NS4. McKenny himself suggests that a theologically centered reading of Thomas that gives primacy to the role of grace in the Christian life and acknowledges the sole finality of our supernatural end avoids regarding human nature as normatively sufficient. The argument here is that Thomistic theological anthropology properly construed deserves to be seen not as an acceptable form of NS2 but, rather, as better categorized as a variety of the fully theocentric position, NS4.[47] The argument for Thomas' membership in NS4 rests on his view of ethical normativity as supported by both immanent and transcendent bases. Thomas regards genuine ethical normativity as always ultimately a reflection of the wisdom and benevolence of God. Thomistic theology beholds creation, including the natural law, with a

---

45. See Porter, *Natural and Divine Law*, chap. 5 and *Nature as Reason*, chap. 5, but also *Ministers of the Law: A Natural Law Theory of Legal Authority* (Grand Rapids: Eerdmans, 2010) and *Justice as a Virtue: A Thomistic Perspective* (Grand Rapids: Eerdmans, 2016), chap. 4.

46. Some other recent accounts of Thomistic natural law are less amenable to classification as NS2. Russell Hittinger's *The First Grace: Rediscovering Natural Law in a Post-Christian World* (Wilmington: ISI Books, 2003) understands natural law within the context of the doctrine of divine providence and revelation rather than ontologically "free floating with regard to authority." Hittinger would concur with Porter's attempt to recover the theological basis of natural law, but he understands the mind as ordering the creation in more determinative and normatively specific ways than does Porter. Another rival theorist of natural law, Martin Rhonheimer, argues that the normativity of practical reason is derived from divine authority. Rather than autonomy, he prefers to speak of "participated theonomy." *Natural Law and Practical Reason: A Thomist View of Moral Autonomy*, trans. Gerald Malsbary (New York: Fordham University Press, 2000). Both Hittinger and Rhonheimer would qualify as versions of McKenny's NS4.

47. See McKenny, *Biotechnology, Human Nature, and Christian Ethics*, 148.

sacramental imagination that regards the Creator of our nature as the source of human normativity.

Our created nature, the kinds of beings we are, determines what we are supposed to be, what defines human flourishing, and what will completely fulfill us. But the normativity of human nature is vertically integrated within and ordered to the normativity of grace; proximate and ultimate loci of normativity complement rather than compete with one another. The proximate natural base is ultimately grounded in God's wisdom and goodness. Just as grace perfects but transcends nature, so the infused virtues comply with but go beyond the demands of the natural law. The Christian life, then, respects the moral law but is fundamentally moved by love, marked by interior freedom, and manifested in the fruit of the Spirit (Gal. 5:22-23). *Caritas*, for example, not only complies with the natural law prohibition against the direct taking of innocent life but also strives to love, forgive, and reconcile with the enemy.

Viewing Thomas as belonging to NS4 helps to call attention to his resonance with Barth's theocentrism. As Christians, they agree that the Triune God is "for us," creates a good world, creates human beings in the image of God, elects to enter into covenant with Israel, becomes Word Incarnate in Jesus Christ, forms a community of disciples called the church, continues to be present as Holy Spirit within both the church and the world, and calls humanity to eschatological fulfillment and eternal union with God. Both theologians affirm the primacy of grace and acknowledge that grace transcends nature while embracing and properly directing it.

Both Barth and Thomas regard the Christian life as one that generates grateful, generous, and joyful love of God and neighbor (see ST II-II, 28).[48] Grace empowers Christians to love, trust, and obey God, who knows what is good for us infinitely better than we do. Grace fulfills us beyond what we can imagine, but our fulfillment is found in self-giving rather than self-seeking love. They agree that the point of the Christian moral life is not to attain "terrestrial happiness" but, rather, to live a "life with God" patterned on the obedience of Christ. Even the best life here pales in comparison to what God has prepared for those who love him (cf. 1 Cor. 2:9). Even if a desirable outcome of the Christian life, terrestrial happiness is not the reason for living it.

None of these resonances should prevent us from concluding that Barthians and Thomists clearly occupy distinct domains within NS4. Thomas envisions grace as working *through* nature whereas Barth envisions grace as working *from above* human nature and directing it to God's purposes. In the Kantian categories mentioned earlier, Barth grounds normativity in objective external grounds (the will of God) and Thomas grounds normativity in both objective internal grounds

---

48. McKenny examines Barth on gratitude (McKenny, *The Analogy of Grace*, 208–12) but not joy. Barth discusses joy in a number of places in the *Church Dogmatics*, notably in light of the perfections of God in *CD* II, as a dimension of "being in encounter" in *CD* III/2, and, in an understated way, as accompanying the Easter event in *CD* IV.

(human nature) and objective external grounds (the wisdom and goodness of God). For Thomas, as Servais Pinckaers, O. P. explains, the natural law is "not the work of a will external and foreign to us." As an expression of our natural inclinations, the natural law is an "inner law" that "penetrates to the heart of our freedom and personality to show us the demands of truth and goodness."[49]

Obedience, Conscience, and the Command of God

Whereas Thomas' sacramental imagination views nature in the service of grace, Barth's dialectical imagination seeks to affirm the unparalleled sovereignty of the utterly gracious God of Jesus Christ. Thomas and Barth thus offer very different descriptions of how Christians come to concrete moral decisions, but they are not completely discontinuous. Thomas' concrete normativity takes place in practical deliberation under the inspiration of the Holy Spirit that issues a judgment of conscience. As befits rational animals, Thomas would point out that we come to discover the content of our moral obligations by engaging in the personal and communal labors of human reasoning, deliberating, and judging. Because grace perfects rather than supplants nature, those exercising the infused virtues need to be as reasonable and reflective as those exercising the acquired virtues.[50]

Both Thomistic and Barthian theological traditions appreciate the significance of obedience within the Christian life, but they do not describe its function in the same way. Both understand the act of obedience as compliance with a command issued by a legitimate authority. Thomas was interested in the moral psychology of the agent as one whose decision about how to act follows from what he calls "counsel" (*consilium*), a wise judgment of practical reason about what ought to be done in a concrete situation. In Thomistic moral psychology, "precepts" (moral obligations) refer not primarily to the command of a ruler over a subject but to the individual agent commanding her own powers to do what her practical reason judges ought to be done. After her moral deliberation generates a practical judgment about what she ought to do (*consilium*), her will chooses to act accordingly and her reason commands (*imperat*) that it be done (see I-II,17,1).[51] In the order of intention, reason determines what ought to be done (*consilium*) and the will makes a choice (*electio*) to move the other powers of the soul to

---

49. Pinckaers, *The Sources of Christian Ethics*, 453.

50. This is not to deny the difference between infused and acquired prudence nor to underestimate the significance of the gift of counsel (ST II-II, 52) and the gift of wisdom (see ST II-II, 45).

51. Thomists have been engaged in a lengthy debate over Thomas' interpretation of two different terms translated into the English word "command"—*imperium* and *preceptum*—and particularly whether *imperium* is primarily an act of reason or of will. Thomas is clear that the act of command involves the will's choice (*electio*) to move the other powers of the soul to act according to the judgment of reason.

perform the appropriate external acts; in the order of execution, the will moves the other powers of the soul to fulfill the command (*imperium*) issued by reason. The interdependent roles of reasoning and willing acknowledge the essentially reasonable nature of obedience, an emphasis also found in Thomas' definition of law as an ordinance of reason (see I-II, 90, 4).

Thomas understands moral obedience in terms of either the individual agent's compliance with the legitimate command of a superior or as the intrapersonal compliance of the agent's will and external acts with her judgment of practical reason. Though they function in different ways, both divine law and natural law reflect divine wisdom. We are morally obliged to obey the divine law because it has been issued by a divine lawgiver who is also the human good without qualification. We are morally obliged to obey the natural law because doing so is necessary for the attainment of our final end; normativity is intrinsic to the Thomistic view of human nature because only obedience to the precepts of natural law is consistent with movement toward our final end. Complying with moral obligations—whether communicated through natural law, or divine law, or both—always also constitutes obedience to God. Firmly convinced that God cannot command anything that contradicts divine goodness, Thomas would have disagreed with radically voluntarist theories that maintain that God can command anything whatsoever, for example, to hate rather than to love God.

Barth holds that we know what is good only through the revelation of Jesus Christ, so we know the true meaning of obedience only from Jesus' obedience to the Father. This obedience brings true freedom for life in God.[52] We are not to submit divine commands to the standard of human moral reasoning because to do so is to subject God's decisions to our standards of goodness. But we are to use all the intellectual and affective resources at our disposal to do the best we can to hear and obey the divine summons.

From a Thomistic standpoint, though, one would think we need some criterion, perhaps biblical, to distinguish what is authentically a command of God from what is not. While Barth rejects the attempt to proceed from a philosophical theory of the human good to Christian ethics, he does want us to move from the command of God to moral inquiry. Ethical inquiry and especially biblical narratives prepare us for hearing the command of God in our own lives—as McKenny puts it, they comprise a kind of "instruction by which we can arrive at a close approximation to what God will command."[53] Barth argues that divine commands will always come from God's being for us in Christ[54] and that our encounter with the Word of God in any given situation should be broadly continuous with what God has commanded

---

52. See Karl Barth *Church Dogmatics, II/2: The Doctrine of God*, trans. G. W. Bromiley et al. (Edinburgh: T&T Clark, 2010), 552.

53. McKenny, *The Analogy of Grace*, 247.

54. Locating divine commands within the covenant of grace and its Christocentric identity leads McKenny to argue that Barth avoids the arbitrariness associated with most divine command theories. See *The Analogy of Grace*, 267–9.

in the past. Moral inquiry, and, indeed, any feature of human experience or knowledge, might provide a context from within which we might encounter the command of God in any particular situation. The set of attitudes, dispositions, and patterns of behavior that facilitate hearing and obeying the command of God when encountered sound something like what Thomists would call virtues.

While Thomists find the language of command of God to be not only unfamiliar but also puzzling and obscure, it is important neither to oversimplify nor to mystify what this means. Normativity emerges in personal encounters that mediate distinct specific commands issued to concrete individuals. Rather than delivered to us as a kind of miraculous "bolt from above," the command of God is given to us in and through the concrete circumstances of our lives and most often through the words and deeds of particular people with whom we interact. Thus mediated, hearing the command of God does not require us simply to ignore all other sources of moral wisdom, including what we know from our prior experience, education, or surrounding culture.[55] As we have just seen, Barth conceives of the command of God as taking place within the context of our moral deliberation rather than as an alternative to it.[56]

Thomistic ethics gives a Christian's properly formed conscientious judgment a religious significance that is somewhat analogous to a Barthian command of God. The Roman Catholic tradition, essentially relying on Thomas, holds that a clear and definitive judgment of conscience must be obeyed without delay, equivocation, or compromise. Even if deeply mistaken, we please God when we do what we are subjectively convinced is right; conversely, if we fail to do so, God will hold us accountable. Rather than the decision of an autonomous conscience accountable to itself alone, a lively and informed conscience is the locus of divine self-communication; indeed, John Paul II went so far as to call the conscience "the witness of God himself."[57] In doing so he was merely following the teaching of the Second Vatican Council: "In the depths of our conscience, we detect a law which we do not impose upon ourselves, but which holds us to obedience."[58] This description connotes an external objective authority that should please a Barthian, albeit in tandem with the less pleasing accompanying depiction of the conscience as an internal norm. When it functions wisely, the judgment of conscience reflects the agent's discernment of what God requires us to do or not

---

55. McKenny offers a typically thorough and nuanced sketch of Barth's anti-rationalist but not necessarily voluntarist account of hearing the command of God, and how moral instruction and reasoning prepare the way for our encounter with the command of God, in *The Analogy of Grace*, chap. 6, 225–87.

56. On ethical reflection in Barth, see McKenny, *The Analogy of Grace*, 231–5; on preparing oneself for hearing the command of God, 247.

57. Pope John Paul II, *Veritatis Splendor*, 58, Available online: https://www.vatican.va/content/john-paul-ii/en/encyclicals/documents/hf_jp-ii_enc_06081993_veritatis-splendor.html (accessed June 28, 2021).

58. Vatican II, *Gaudium et spes*, 16.

do in a concrete situation. For Thomists as well as Barthians, then, the Christian life drives one to pray, "not what I will, but what you will" (Mark 14:36b, NRSV; Luke 22:42; Mt. 26:39).

Conclusion

This chapter has used McKenny's careful analysis of rival accounts of the normative significance of human nature to examine natural law ethics. While he correctly characterizes Porter's natural law theory as holding that nature is intrinsically normative, this description does not accurately capture the wider Thomistic tradition upon which Porter draws. This tradition regards the normativity of human nature to be secondary and derived from its primary ground, God. If this is correct, then the Thomistic approach to the normative status of human nature deserves a place alongside the Protestant inhabitants whom McKenny finds most theologically congenial. Thomists and Barthians might not be members of the same nuclear theological family, but they both belong to the wider extended theocentric family that is NS4.[59]

---

59. I would like to thank Arne Rasmusson of the University of Gothenburg, Sweden, for his careful reading of and insightful comments on a draft of this chapter.

Chapter 9

NATURE AND GRACE

A CONTRIBUTION TO A LONG CONVERSATION

Jean Porter

Is it possible to arrive at a defensible conception of human nature? And if so, to what extent and in what ways is human nature, thus understood, ethically and theologically relevant? Over the course of his distinguished career, Gerald McKenny has explored these questions from the standpoint of bioethics and biotechnology, on the one hand, and theological perspectives on creation and grace, on the other. While these may appear to be diverse perspectives, McKenny brings them together in creative and fruitful ways. In his recent book, *Biotechnology, Human Nature, and Christian Ethics*, he argues that for the Christian, at least, interventions in human nature should be evaluated by normative standards set by "human nature as that which suits or equips humans for a certain form of life with God and with other human beings."[1] Although the corresponding account is McKenny's own, it draws extensively on the account of nature and grace developed by Karl Barth, developed in conversation with the contemporary theologian Kathryn Tanner.

At the same time, he considers other options, including an Aristotelian/Thomistic account of the normative significance of nature defended by myself, among others. McKenny's attitude toward this account might best be described as appreciative, but not persuaded.[2] He offers a generous appraisal of the most recent versions of this and similar accounts of human nature, acknowledging that they are compatible with evolutionary science and can allow for the plasticity and developmental potential of human nature. Nonetheless, he questions whether an account of this kind can offer a coherent account of the normative status of human nature, in light of the unprecedented questions raised by biotechnologies

---

1. Gerald McKenny, *Biotechnology, Human Nature, and Christian Ethics* (Cambridge: Cambridge University Press, 2018), 10. An earlier statement of McKenny's account may be found in "Biotechnology and the Normative Significance of Human Nature: A Contribution from Theological Anthropology," *Studies in Christian Ethics* 26, no. 11 (2013): 18–36.

2. The following remarks summarize his appraisal of broadly Aristotelian accounts of the normative significance of human nature, including but by no means limited to my own, in McKenny, *Biotechnology, Human Nature, and Christian Ethics*, 70–110.

which promise to transform human nature itself. It is important to note that the issue here, as McKenny sees it, is not just that such an account cannot provide answers to specific normative questions pertaining to potential changes in human nature. Rather, he suggests that these questions challenge the very coherence of the account by calling into question the integral link between human nature and the goods proper to that nature. And while he does not say so in so many words, McKenny's treatment of Barth suggests a certain skepticism toward any attempt to develop an account of nature as it might be understood apart from grace.[3]

Even though McKenny's recent work on the normative significance of nature is developed within the context of bioethics, it clearly has implications that go beyond the normative questions that he raises, important though those are. At any rate, in this chapter, I will be bracketing questions of bioethics and biotechnology, except insofar as these pertain to the coherence of the Aristotelian/Thomistic conception of human nature. Rather, I will focus on the concept of human nature and the relation between nature and grace, two broad issues which, as we have seen, come together in McKenny's defense of a Barthian approach to human nature. More specifically, I hope to advance the conversation by offering a defense of Aquinas' accounts of both human nature and grace, developed in conversation with McKenny and responsive, I hope, to the actual or implied criticisms that he poses. In the first section, I offer a brief overview of Aquinas' account of human nature, and in the second section I defend the coherence of that account, over against the questions posed by the prospect of radical alterations of human nature. Next, I turn to Aquinas' account of grace, seen as a supernatural transformation of natural principles of action. Finally, I comment on Barth's criticism of Aquinas' approach, as McKenny presents it; I argue that this criticism misrepresents Aquinas' view in key ways, and misses what might be called the theological point of the account. My overall aim in all this is to bring out the theological significance of Aquinas' Aristotelian metaphysics, and more generally, to show that his approach to the perennial question of the relation of nature to grace is theologically cogent.

Nature, Form, and Aim

What does it mean to say that there really is something—not necessarily a thing, perhaps an idea, or a principle—answering to the expression, "human nature"? Aquinas answers this question, in key part if not entirely, in the Aristotelian terms of formal cause.[4] Human nature, thus understood, is the form proper to

---

3. See, for example, his positive assessment of Barth's account of nature and grace in McKenny, *Biotechnology, Human Nature, and Christian Ethics*, 157–8.

4. The Aristotelian account of the four causes—formal, final, efficient, and material—is fundamental to Aquinas' metaphysics, and runs throughout his writings. Within the *Summa theologiae*, key texts would include I 5.5, which lays out the relation between formal and final cause, and I 80.1, which lays out the relation of form to inclination and appetite. For a

humanity, that through which individual men and women are human beings and not some other kind of thing. Thus understood, human nature is a presupposition of individuation—each finite thing is some one kind of thing and not another—and also a principle of explanation—a human being, as such, is characterized by certain capacities to react to outside stimuli and to act in distinctive ways.

The Aristotelian conception of form is likely to strike contemporaries as artificial. In order to appreciate what is being said at this point, we need to take account of the context within which an Aristotelian conception of form has its place. That context is set by what in antiquity was characterized as the problem of motion, or as we might prefer to describe it, the problem of change and continuity. We experience the world as an array of things, which come into being, persist through time, and cease to exist. Over the span of their existence, these things undergo many changes, some of which are more consequential than others, without ceasing to exist. At the same time, some kinds of changes do seem to bring the existence of something to an end, while in the process bringing some other kind of thing into being. A statue can be chipped or defaced without its ceasing to exist as the statue that it is, but if someone takes a sledgehammer to it, it will cease to be, while a pile of marble stones will emerge in its place.

This example suggests a distinction between a thing, which persists over time and is the subject of changes, and those properties which exist only as characteristics of something else. In Aristotle's terms, the former is a substance, and its changeable properties are its accidents. This distinction implies, further, that a substance is not just a mass of matter—it instantiates a characteristic way of existing, which can be modified but not essentially changed. From an Aristotelian perspective, this characteristic way of existing is the form of something, which is not itself a further thing, but an ordered set of dynamic operations through which the entity exists over time.

Both Aristotle and Aquinas believe that the fundamental conception of substantial form can be applied to all creatures. But the clearest and most persuasive applications of this conception are to be found in the realm of living creatures. According to Aquinas, a living being is characterized by a capacity to move itself in some way, in accordance with the characteristic potentialities of its form (I 16.1).[5] Plants and the lower forms of animal life operate in accordance with internal principles, through active processes of taking nourishment, avoiding dangers, and the like. Nonetheless, these kinds of living creatures cannot be said to be active agents in their own processes of life and growth. They spontaneously grow and flourish in a predetermined way, and cannot be said to move themselves reflexively through these processes. The higher animals, in contrast, move themselves to act in response to inclinations elicited through sensate or (in our case) rational images

---

fuller analysis of the key concepts, see Aquinas' commentary on Aristotle's *Metaphysics*, In V Metaphysicae lect.2.

5. Unless otherwise noted, all references to Aquinas are taken from the *Summa theologiae*; translations are my own.

of desirable, noxious, or threatening objects. Hence, the higher animals can be said to take an active part in the expression and preservation of the form of existence that they embody, and the form of the living creature, correlatively, is nothing other than the dynamic matrix of species-specific operations, through which the living thing sustains and propagates its existence as a being of a certain kind.

So far, we have focused on phenomena of existence, change, and destruction considered in themselves. The example of living creatures illuminates a further aspect of form as Aristotle and Aquinas would have understood it. Not only are living creatures actively engaged with their environment; they also exhibit a series of changes over time, through which they pass from some kind of infancy, to maturity, and then decline and death. These cannot be described as examples of self-motion, but they are not just responses to the environment, either. On the contrary, the processes through which living things mature and then decay indicate the relative independence of the living creature from its environment in a distinctive way. Relative independence, certainly—no living thing can live, much less grow, without, at a minimum, access to food and shelter. But given certain basic necessities, a living creature undergoes a series of characteristic changes through which it not only persists over time but unfolds the capacities for dynamic operation that make it the kind of creature that it is.

The concept of form, as Aristotle and Aquinas understand it, can thus be understood as a way of affirming and offering a rational interpretation of the basic and universal tendency to apprehend things in the world as entities which persist over time, which in some instances undergo processes of development and decline, and in every case, eventually cease to exist. Thus understood, the concept of form does not imply that there is some separate entity, such as a Platonic idea, distinct from whatever it is that exhibits the form.[6] Rather, the idea of form presupposes that the categories under which things are sorted—or more exactly, some of them—reflect real qualities or aspects of the things in question, in virtue of which they count as the kinds of things that they are. By the same token, this view presupposes that the forms of things can be grasped through concepts, albeit imperfectly, and moreover that these concepts are genuinely explanatory—that is to say, they help us to make sense of the operations of natural things in ways that would otherwise be inaccessible to us.

In Aristotelian-Thomistic terms, these sorts of explanations are said to be appeals to the formal cause, but it is important not to be misled by this expression. A formal cause indicates the description under which something can be understood in terms of the kind of thing that it is. In this context, the language of "cause" does not necessarily imply efficient causality, but refers more broadly

---

6. The forms of things preexist as ideas in God, but as such, they are tantamount to God's knowledge of his own creative potential; they do not have separate existence, in the manner of Platonic forms; see I 15.1, 44.3. Aquinas considers, and following Aristotle, rejects the notion of separate forms at I 84.1; he goes on to explain that the intellect apprehends the form as embodied in some particular thing at I 84.7.

to any principle of intelligibility and explanation. Generally speaking, it is a kind of category mistake to think of the forms of living creatures as among the kinds of things that can have independent existence, prior to specification in some individual; they are instantiated, or they are not, and it is these instantiations, not the forms themselves, which come into being and pass away.[7] By the same token, the forms of living creatures do not exist apart from creatures in such a way as to exercise efficient causality on them. As James Lennox puts it, referring specifically to Aristotle's conception of the form of a living being, "the form of a living thing is its soul, and Aristotle considers soul to be a unified set of goal-ordered capacities—nutritive, reproductive, locomotive, and cognitive."[8] As such, the form is manifested in and through the modalities of efficient causality proper to the kind of creature in question.

In an earlier treatment of this subject, I made the remark that while species emerge and pass away through the processes of evolutionary change, the concept of a specific kind is timeless. McKenny objects that if this is so, our concept of a form will be falsified whenever something of a specific kind exhibits different norms of existence, as human beings sometimes do, in response to changing environmental or physical/psychic conditions.[9] I take the point, and I would now emphasize that even though our concept of a form is timeless—that is, it is not specified by reference to a particular time—it is, of course, not unchanging. On the contrary, our concepts of the forms of things change all the time, as we arrive at a better understanding of what it means to be an entity of this or that specific kind.

It is important in this connection to keep in mind that for Aristotle and Aquinas, the form is a principle of development, change, and causal interaction with the surrounding environment.

Correlatively, our understanding of the form of something depends on some grasp of its potential, both as a principle of existence and growth, and as a power to bring about changes in the world. It is probably fair to say that we do not have a comprehensive grasp of the potentialities of any kind of entity, and we certainly do not have a comprehensive grasp of our own potentialities for existence and

---

7. I do not mean to deny here that the human soul is a substantive form, of such a kind as to survive the death of the body. However, even the human soul cannot exist prior to its instantiation in a human body, nor can it ever be understood except by reference to its individuation in matter—which is not to say that it requires existence in matter at every point in order to continue to exist. For a helpful discussion of this point, see Robert Pasnau, *Thomas Aquinas on Human Nature: A Philosophical Study of Summa theologiae Ia 75–89* (Cambridge: Cambridge University Press, 2002), 45–57.

8. James Lennox, *Aristotle's Philosophy of Biology* (Cambridge: Cambridge University Press, 2001), 128; see, more generally, 127–30.

9. See "Biotechnology and the Normative Significance of Human Nature," 21–3. However, I am not sure that McKenny would continue to press this point; in *Biotechnology, Human Nature and Christian Ethics* he acknowledges that an Aristotelian account of human nature can allow for a considerable degree of indeterminacy and plasticity; see 74–5.

interaction with others. That is why we can be surprised by the new norms for living called forth by internal or external changes in our situation. It is also probably true that our conceptions of things are too general to capture the actual diversity of forms of life and existence. Abstract conceptions are clear and sharp, whereas reality is granular. But the open-ended and incomplete character of our concepts of the forms of things does not mean that things have no form. On the view that I am defending, each thing is something, that is to say, an entity informed by a specific way of existing and interacting with its surroundings.

Nature and the Goods of Nature

We are now in a position to evaluate the claim that the Aristotelian/Thomistic account of human nature cannot meet the challenges posed by contemporary biotechnology. The argument, as I understand it, goes as follows. Human nature, as Aristotelian and similar accounts present it, is normatively significant because it is the ground for goods and (perhaps) rights that we value and pursue. Up until very recently, human nature and human goods have been inextricably linked, but new biotechnologies raise the possibility that they may come apart in troubling and exciting ways. We may be able to secure, for our descendants at least, goods which are truly desirable and worth bringing about, yet incompatible with human nature as it now exists. If that is so, then we may find ourselves forced to choose between our good and our nature. As McKenny explains, under these circumstances, defenders of an Aristotelian option

> will have to decide whether normative status properly attaches (1) to human nature (in its current state) as the ground of the human good, in which case we must be willing to forgo some things we recognize as good and may be able to attain, or (2) to what we recognize as good, in which case we must be prepared to accept in principle the alteration of our biological functions and traits, perhaps even to a point where we may speak of a change to our nature or even a change of our nature into something else.... And with this forced choice, the two benefits of [this approach] for Christian ethics—that it accounts for the goodness of creation and the intelligibility of the good, and that it provides a basis for the ethical evaluation of biotechnological enhancements—are lost.[10]

This is a formidable objection. The Aristotelian/Thomistic account of human nature implies that the intelligibility of human nature and its normative status are inextricably linked. We can grasp what it means to be a human being, only insofar as we grasp what it means to flourish as a human being; and correlatively, the human desire for well-being and happiness is always informed by some conception,

---

10. McKenny, *Biotechnology, Human Nature, and Christian Ethics*, 86–7; for the full development of the argument, see 86–110.

however incomplete or distorted, of what counts as perfection or fulfillment, in accordance with one's self-understanding (I-II 1.4,6,7). If it is possible to drive a wedge between human nature and the goods proper to human nature, then these connections are defeasible, and the coherence of the overall account is called into question.

But, in fact, we cannot drive a wedge between human nature and the goods proper to that nature in the way just suggested. This line of argument presupposes that discrete goods can be identified as such—that is to say, as desirable and worth having—without reference to any wider context. But on closer examination, this assumption is untenable. It seems safe to say that if we are to judge some state of affairs, object, or activity to be good, then at a minimum we are committed to regarding it as desirable and worthy of pursuit. Our desires and pursuits, however, do not just come out of nowhere. Rather, they emerge out of an ongoing dynamic of needs and practices, some of them very closely linked to organic functions, others seemingly generated by social values or even abstract ideals. Within this framework, we can identify certain objects or states as goods, because they meet a need, or further some aim, or bring comfort or delight by their congruence with our innate preferences and sensibilities. So far, I have spoken in terms of our desires and pursuits, but the indexical reference is not crucial. The point I want to make is, rather, that we cannot meaningfully identify something as a good, without some kind of plausible conception of the good, globally considered and spelled out by reference to some coherent nexus of needs and interests—which in the nature of the case will be something's needs and interests. Otherwise, we will be unable to account for the desirability of the putative good—and, although I cannot explore this point here, we will also be unable to make practical comparative judgments about competing goods. "Bare goods" are no more plausible than "bare particulars."

These considerations bring us to a critical point. Our judgments about discrete goods depend on some account of the good, globally considered. This account need not be developed along Aristotelian lines, but the Aristotelian/Thomistic account of human nature does offer one such global conception of the good. As we have seen, this account depends on a conceptual link between the intelligibility of the form of the creature and its goodness, understood as its full development—that is, its perfection in accordance with the potentialities of that form. The key point here is that goodness inheres in the full development of the potentialities of the form taken as a whole, considered not as discrete goods, but as "a unified set of goal-ordered capacities." The link between the overall flourishing of the creature and its goods, and the priority of the former over the latter, are conceptual and not contingent. We cannot identify something as a good without some account of the form of the creature for which it is a good, and correlatively, some account of its fit, its dynamic relationship, with other goods that are proper to creatures of this kind.

The coherence of the Aristotelian/Thomistic account of human nature is thus not undermined by what we might call the biotechnological challenge. In order to even pose this challenge, the advocate for goods that are not proper to human nature would need to provide some account of the kind of creature for which these supposed "post-human" goods would really be goods. Hence, the challenge would not force a choice between human nature and desirable goods; rather, it would force a choice between one kind of nature, for which certain goods are desirable, and another kind of nature, for which other kinds of goods are desirable.

We might still ask whether the Aristotelian/Thomistic account of human nature would have the normative resources to address this kind of choice. I am not sure whether it would, or not; but at the very least, it offers a criterion for formulating a meaningful challenge. The relevant alternatives here are not human nature and goods that are not, currently, natural to us; rather, the only meaningful choice that we could entertain would be a choice between two kinds of natures, presented in terms of the "ordered sets of functions" and the attendant goods proper to each. I suspect that this would be rather difficult to do. It would involve imagining, and then discursively analyzing, a whole new species of living creatures, together with its proper environment. In order to carry out this task, we would need to envision the lives of these creatures in considerable detail. We would also need to make a series of hard philosophical choices. For example, a proposal to download our personalities into a very sophisticated computer will demand some reflection on the nature of cognition, and its dependence, or otherwise, on sense data. At any rate, we will not be in a position to choose whether to bring about another kind of creature, with all its attendant goods, until we can describe the proposed alternative in such a way as to enable a real, rational choice.

At this point, we turn to the relation between nature and grace.

Nature and Grace

Aquinas' appropriation of Aristotle's metaphysics yields a rich and persuasive way of interpreting our experiences of the world and its active, ever-changing creatures—or so I would argue. But what is its theological relevance? We could answer this question from a number of different perspectives, but at this point I want to consider the relevance of Aquinas' account of nature to his doctrine of grace.

On a first reading, Aquinas' account of grace and its relation to nature appears paradoxical. On the one hand, he insists that apart from grace, no human being—or for that matter, no angel—can attain the full union with the Triune God that constitutes the highest human happiness (I 12.4). Even the human soul of Christ would be incapable of full union with God, apart from the transforming effects of grace (III 7.1). What is more, he makes it clear that this is so, most fundamentally, because our natural faculties cannot extend, by themselves, to the kind of knowledge and love of God that constitutes salvation; that is to say, they are not proportioned to a supernatural fulfillment (I-II 51.4, I-II 109.5). In its uncorrupted state, human nature could attain a knowledge of God as the originating source of all finite existence, and could, accordingly, love him above all things as the ultimate end of creation (I-II 109.3). But this kind of knowledge and love falls infinitely short of the personal love generated through grace and the virtues infused with grace, especially charity, which is a kind of friendship arising out of God's communication of his happiness to us (II-II 23.1; cf. I-II 109.3 ad 1).

And yet, even though grace, understood in its most proper sense, is distinct from nature, it presupposes and mirrors, as it were, the natural form of the human creature, with its distinctive capacities for knowledge and action. This point comes out clearly at I-II 110.2, where Aquinas asks whether grace is a quality of the soul. He begins by observing that God can be said to aid someone gratuitously by moving him to some cognition, or volition, or action, and in this case, the effect of God's aid is a motion of the soul, rather than a quality. He goes on to say that

> in another way the human person is aided by the gratuitous will of God in such a way that some habitual gift is poured into the soul by God. And this indeed, because it is not appropriate that God should provide less for those whom he loves in such a way that they have supernatural goods, than he provides for creatures that he loves in such a way that they have natural goods. For he provides for natural creatures in such a way that he not only moves them to their natural acts, but he also bestows on them certain forms and powers, which are the principles of acts, so that they are themselves inclined to motions of this kind. And so the motion by which they are moved by God is made connatural and easy to creatures. . . . Much more, therefore, does he pour out certain forms or supernatural qualities on those whom he moves to attain the supernatural good of eternity, according to which they are moved by him sweetly and promptly to attain the good of eternity. And so the gift of grace is a certain quality. (I-II 110.2)

Clearly, Aquinas does not set aside the conceptual structure of his metaphysics of nature when he turns to the topic of grace. Just as we exist through a natural form of existence, operating through species-specific potencies and powers, so we attain the new life of grace through "certain forms and powers, which are the principles of acts," through which we are moved "sweetly and promptly" to attain everlasting life. Implicit here and stated explicitly elsewhere is the claim that grace perfects natural potentialities, albeit at a higher level than could be naturally attained (cf. I 1.8 ad 2).

Aquinas goes on to say that grace is a kind of accidental form (I-II 110.2 ad 2). More specifically, it is a kind of habit, that is to say, a stable disposition toward a characteristic kind of existence and operation. As an accidental form, grace does not change the essence of the soul, but it qualifies the way in which that essence is actualized. Considered within the context of the natural order, this kind of habitual disposition of the soul would be superfluous, since the soul is "the form completing the human nature." Nonetheless, "if we speak of a superior nature, in which the human person can share, nothing prohibits the existence of some habit in the soul according to its essence, that is, grace" (I-II 50.2).

In order to appreciate the point that Aquinas is making, we need to look more closely at another of his appropriations of Aristotelian natural philosophy, namely, the concept of habit. Aquinas identifies habit as one of two kinds of internal principles of human acts, the other being the potencies or faculties of the soul, including the powers of sensory and intellectual perception and the appetites (I-II 49, introduction). These principles are not unrelated, of course, since Aquinas goes on to argue that habits are best understood as stable dispositions of innate human faculties, particularly those which are immediately oriented toward action (I-II 49). As such, a habit properly so called reflects a kind of development or formation, through which the powers of the intellect and the appetites are oriented toward certain characteristic kinds of activities (I-II 49.3). Habits are therefore perfections, in Aquinas' characteristic metaphysical use of the term—that is to say, they are actualizations of the latent potencies of the form of a rational creature (I 4.1, 3; I 5.1, 3). More specifically, a habit is a kind of development of the rational creature's capacities for action, that is to say, faculties of intellect, the passions, or the will (I-II 49.3). Habits are therefore oriented toward action and defined by reference to the characteristic kinds of acts that they generate (I-II 54.2).

At this point, we are in a better position to appreciate the significance, and also the difficulty, of Aquinas' claim that grace is a habit of the soul itself.[11] The soul is the substantial form of the human person, and as such, it is oriented toward the fulfillment and flourishing of the individual's humanity, naturally and apart from any further disposition (I-II 50.2). Nonetheless, Aquinas argues, considered in relation to the supernatural fulfillment toward which it is oriented, the soul stands in need of a reorientation to divine life, through which every faculty of the human person is directed toward a higher level of perfection than would be naturally attainable. By the same token, the infusion of grace into the soul is the necessary precondition for the infusion of virtues and gifts, which are dispositions of the specific potencies of the soul:

> if however grace differs from virtue, it cannot be said that the potencies of the soul are subjects of grace because every perfection of a potency of the soul has the rational character of virtue.... Hence it follows that grace, just as it is prior to virtue, has as its subject that which is prior to the potencies of the soul, such that it is indeed in the essence of the soul. For just as through the intellectual potency the human person participates in divine cognition through the virtue of faith; and according to the potency of the will he participates in divine love through the virtue of charity; so also through the nature of the soul he participates, in accordance with a certain similitude, in the divine nature through which he is regenerated or recreated. (I-II 110.4)

---

11. Aquinas apparently changes his mind on this point. In the earlier treatise *De veritate*, he denies that grace is a habit, since it is not immediately oriented to action, even though he does assert that it is a created quality of the soul; see De Ver. 27. 2 ad 7; cf. De Ver. 27.1. In the ST, he has apparently dropped the requirement that a habit be immediately oriented toward action; there, he says that grace is a habit which orients the soul to participate in a higher nature than its own; see I-II 50.2.

This text exemplifies the robust realism of Aquinas' doctrine of grace. On his account, grace, understood in its most proper sense, is a disposition of the soul, expressed most immediately through further dispositions of faculties of cognition and desire, namely, the infused virtues and the gifts. Something really happens when a man or woman receives grace, and that something—the orientation toward union with God, culminating in salvation—shapes the individual's outlook and orientation in profound ways.

As Aquinas goes on to say, the habit of grace gives rise to habits of the intellect, the will, and the passions. These are the infused virtues and the gifts, through which the orientation of grace is actively expressed in the subject's thoughts, desires, and actions. This is an important point, because for him the formation of habits through grace is necessary in order for men and women to act freely, out of the new orientation that grace provides:

> He therefore acts freely who acts from himself. Now by the fact that a human person acts from a habit appropriate to his nature, he acts from himself, since habit inclines in the mode of nature.... Because therefore the grace of the Holy Spirit is just like an interior habit infused in us inclining us to right operations, we freely do those things which are appropriate to grace, and avoid those which are repugnant to grace. (I-II 108.1 ad 2; cf. I-II 113.3, 114.3,4; II-II 23.2)

This passage illustrates one of the key values underlying Aquinas' account of grace. That is, he is committed to offering an account of grace which preserves human freedom, and guarantees that the effects of grace—virtuous dispositions and actions worthy of an eternal reward—are truly the dispositions and acts of the graced individual who performs them. Correlatively, he rejects the view, handed on to him on the authority of Peter Lombard, according to which the theological virtue of charity is nothing other than the Holy Spirit indwelling in the soul, on the grounds that this position is inconsistent with the claim that the act of charitable love is a free act of the will itself (II-II 23.2). For Aquinas, grace and the infused virtues perfect the human agent with respect to what he or she most fundamentally is—a creature capable of moving itself through its powers of intellect and will, imitating God's providence by being provident for itself and others (I-II 91.2).

Grace without Nature?

At this point, we turn to Karl Barth's criticism of Aquinas' account of grace, as represented and partially endorsed by McKenny. Barth's own concept of grace is notoriously complex, and I will not attempt to examine it in any detail. Nonetheless, I do hope to say enough about that conception to indicate what is fundamentally at stake in the deep disagreements between these two classic theologians.

At an early point in his study of Barth's theological ethics, *The Analogy of Grace*, McKenny attempts to locate Barth's paradoxical approach to ethics within the context of his doctrine of grace.[12] As McKenny shows, Barth's account is shaped by his criticisms of Catholic and Pietist teachings on grace, on the one hand, and Lutheran approaches, on the other. Probably, Barth's engagement with Lutheran accounts of grace was more important for the shape of his own theology, but his critique of Catholic accounts is what concerns us here. McKenny summarizes this critique as follows:

> moral theology may fail to portray the good as that which God determines and brings about. Instead, the good is represented as attainable through human moral activity, though not without the work of divine grace. While it affirms the necessity of grace, what is decisive about this position in Barth's view is that the working of grace presupposes continuity, ultimately rooted in the analogy of being, between our moral activity and its final, transcendent end. On the basis of this continuity the moral life is portrayed in gradualist terms, as a transformation from sinfulness to perfection accomplished by the cooperation of human action with divine grace. Moral theology of this kind may make strong claims about the priority of grace, but in Barth's view it cannot sustain these claims. "Grace which has from the start to share its power [*Kraft*] with a force [*Vermögen*] of nature is no longer grace." Even when its necessity is acknowledged and its priority to human action asserted, grace in this scheme is compromised, assimilated to a process that occurs in the human subject. . . . In the end, this subject will acknowledge nothing beyond its own possibilities and limitations, and the good at which it aims will be one that is proportionate to its capability, its activity, its achievements.[13]

McKenny goes on to express reservations about this way of construing the Thomistic/Catholic understanding of grace, which on his view does not fit with our "best understandings" of either the Catholic tradition or its alternatives:

Consider in this context the version of a well-known Thomistic dictum quoted by Barth

> in a discussion of Catholic moral theology: *gratia sanans et elevans naturam* ("grace heals and elevates nature"). For Barth, this dictum, or at least its customary interpretation, binds grace to the possibilities inherent in nature, that is, to human capability. As we have seen, to understand grace in this way is, for Barth, to fail to take it seriously. . . . However, the dictum is better understood to mean that while our natural capacities are incapable of bringing us to our final end of union with God, which must rather be the work of grace, yet it is our natural capacities, and not some others, which are elevated and perfected in being brought to this end by grace. The continuity between our moral activity

---

12. Gerald McKenny, *The Analogy of Grace: Karl Barth's Moral Theology* (Oxford: Oxford University Press, 2013).

13. Ibid., 25–6.

and its final end resides in the active exercise of our capacities but not in our capability; in the latter respect, grace does not share its power with a force of nature. For Barth, as we have seen, grace accomplishes our good apart from our activity, actualizing it for us in Jesus Christ. Yet grace also summons and empowers us to participate in its accomplishment with all of our capacities, which were created precisely for this purpose. It is clear that the difference between the Thomist and the Barthian positions cannot be captured by a simple contrast between continuity and discontinuity of our moral activity with the ultimate good. Rather, it is the difference between a notion of grace as working in us to bring about a perfection of our natural capacities which they are incapable of accomplishing, on the one hand, and a notion of grace as bringing about our good apart from our activity and summoning us, from the site of its actualization, to active participation in it, on the other hand.[14]

This is an important corrective to Barth's misreading of the Thomstic/Catholic account of grace and, by implication, of Aquinas himself. At the beginning of the last section, we observed that for Aquinas, nature and grace stand in a paradoxical relationship of discontinuity and continuity. Barth reads the Thomistic doctrine of grace in terms of continuity alone, and he inevitably distorts it in the process. We see one indication of this distortion in the phrase McKenny quotes: "Grace which has to share its power with a force of nature is no longer grace." We are left with the impression that grace and nature are two distinct principles of action, which may compete or work together, the former complementing the latter and taking it to a higher plane of accomplishment. But as we have seen, this way of construing the relation of nature and grace rests on a profound misunderstanding of Aquinas' position. On his view, human nature, at least in its rational aspects, never does operate as a principle of action, apart from some kind of formation through which it is given a rational structure. Grace and the infused virtues represent one kind of formation, by means of which the faculties of the soul, and the soul itself, are oriented toward operations of a certain kind. In other words, grace and the infused virtues comprise a perfection of human nature. As McKenny says, grace perfects human nature, and not some other set of capabilities, but that does not mean that grace can be understood in terms of a kind of unfolding or development of natural powers. Rather, grace bestows capabilities to know and love the Triune God that are altogether beyond the natural powers of the rational, or for that matter, the angelic creature.

At the same time, Barth's critique of the Thomistic tradition is not just based on a misreading. There is at least one key respect in which Barth gets this tradition right, namely, the central place that it gives to the freedom of the human subject acting out of grace. Again, this point is familiar by now. Aquinas defends the claim that grace and the infused virtues are habits on the grounds that only in this way can we affirm that acts performed through grace are the agent's own free acts,

---

14. Ibid., 27–8.

Similarly, he rejects Lombard's claim that charity is the indwelling Holy Spirit, on the grounds that in that case, acts done out of charity would not be acts of the human subject. It would seem that in this respect, at least, Aquinas is vulnerable to Barth's criticism. But that way of framing a conclusion begs the question against Aquinas, because it presupposes that there is something theologically problematic about affirming human freedom in the operation of grace. And Aquinas would not accept this; on the contrary, he is at pains to affirm human freedom on theological grounds. Why is this affirmation so important to him? And what might he say to Barth's contrary position?

In order to understand the theological significance of human freedom for Aquinas, we need to return once again to his repeated claim that grace perfects nature. God's gracious transformation of his creature comes about in such a way that its fundamental formal structure and its faculties are preserved; otherwise, grace would have the effect of perverting or destroying, rather than perfecting the creature. This line of thought suggests that grace will be most evident in those aspects of human life which are most characteristic of the human creature. And as we have already seen, and as Aquinas repeatedly notes, the most characteristic feature of the human creature is her capacity to move herself to act through rationally informed volitions—in other words, her capacities for reason and will. Through her rational faculties, the rational creature is able to participate in God's providence in a distinctive way, "being provident for herself and others" (I-II 91.2) The human capacity for rational freedom represents the fundamental way in which the human person can be said to be in the image of God, and this Imaging of God at the natural level is the fundamental presupposition for the closer image attained through grace and glory (I 93.4).

No doubt, all this would strike Barth as deeply problematic. Once again, he would remind us that "grace which from the start has to share its power with a force of nature is no longer grace." This may seem to be a compelling critique, but I believe that Aquinas would question the terms in which it is framed. Barth speaks of a force of nature as if nature stood over against grace as an independent, potentially competing entity. But as we have already observed, it is a mistake to hypostasize nature in this way. The natural capacities of the rational creature have no effective power until they are informed by habits, whether through grace or through naturally attainable virtues or vices. More fundamentally, Barth's invocation of a force of nature standing over against grace raises questions about the provenance of this impetuous force. For Aquinas, the force of nature as such can never stand over against grace, because the order and casual power of creatures is a product of divine wisdom and creative love—just as grace is. Barth's contrast between grace and a force of nature suggests that the natural world, as such and apart from sin, is in some way separate from, and potentially hostile to, God.

Is Barth therefore a kind of dualist? His remarks on nature and grace, taken by themselves, may suggest as much, but I believe that McKenny would argue that this conclusion cannot ultimately be substantiated. On the contrary, Barth assimilates nature, or at least human nature to grace. God destined us from all eternity to union with Him and created us with the capacities necessary to fulfill our destiny: "Barth insists that human nature as created by God is already suited to the enjoyment of life with God and need not undergo any working over to be made fit for it."[15] On this account, there is no need and no room for a distinction between nature and grace. We might say that our existence is radically and without remainder God's gracious gift, or we might say that we are created in such a way as to be naturally suited to union with God.

How might Aquinas respond to this? The first thing to be said is that Aquinas acknowledges that it is legitimate to speak of grace in the way that Barth does, as God's gracious gift and favor to men and women (I-II 110.1). I believe he would also grant that God freely creates us and keeps us in being, and in this sense our existence, in all its dimensions, can be described as a kind of grace. Nonetheless, Aquinas would deny that because human nature is one of God's gracious gifts, therefore there is no place for a distinction between nature and grace. Human nature, as Aquinas understands it, simply cannot attain the kind of union with God to which we are called, because our natural powers are limited to the attainment of finite objects. That is why our natural powers, and our very selves, need to be perfected at a higher level in order to attain our predestined end of friendship and union with God.

It would be natural at this point to say that if this is the consequence of Aquinas' metaphysics, then so much the worse for it. But I believe that this response reflects a misunderstanding of Aquinas' overall project. The motivation for insisting on the distinction between nature and grace is theological, although his philosophy gives him a set of categories for formulating his account of nature and grace in a precise and persuasive way. Aquinas insists on the distinction between nature and grace, because he wants to hold together two seemingly contrary insights, namely, God's ungraspable distance from any created reality, and God's intimate union with those he has chosen to share in his very life. One might almost say that from Aquinas' standpoint, it is not enough to say that God takes up a favorable stance toward us. He wants to say that God has come to live in us and through us, through an intimate union that transforms every aspect of our lives.

This brings us to the point with which we began. An Aristotelian account of human nature plays a central role in Aquinas' overall theological synthesis. At the same time, he also insists that grace transforms the human person in a profound way, endowing her with new principles of knowledge, desire, and action. What are the theological advantages of this approach?

In order to answer this question fully, we would need to go beyond the scope of this chapter, to examine the many ways in which Aquinas draws on the Aristotelian account of nature in order to underscore and safeguard God's freedom as creator, the unqualified dependence of all things on God's existence, and the movement of all things back to God. Aristotelian natural philosophy fits well with a theological emphasis on the goodness and integrity of creation and the intelligibility of natural

---

15. McKenny, *Biotechnology, Human Nature, and Christian Ethics*, 157.

causes, all of these values that Aquinas shared with his scholastic forebears and contemporaries.

By the same token, Aquinas' account of human nature offers a way of bringing together two theologically foundational claims, namely, the goodness of the human person as God's creature, and the infinite gap between the created capacities of the human creature, or any creature, and the power and perfection of God. Grace is not just a remedy for sin, according to Aquinas, although given our current state, a remedy for sin is necessary. Nonetheless, Aquinas insists that even compared to the far-reaching and formidable powers of uncorrupted human nature, the capacities bestowed by grace are infinitely greater. Paradoxically, the life of grace as we experience it may well seem to be partial, incomplete, ambiguous, as we strive for and fall short of an ideal of charity that we cannot fully grasp, much less attain. This too is a reflection of the transformative life of grace, an indication that one is living on the basis of a fulfillment that cannot be imagined, much less attained in this life.

The point I want to underscore is that for Aquinas, grace is a disposition of the soul, and as such, it has tangible effects on our beliefs, desires, and capacities for action. It bestows a new set of purposes and a new freedom of action. Through grace we are enabled to share in God's happiness, even in this life, and on that basis we become friends of God. Aquinas' account of nature provides him with a framework for explaining how this transformation can come about, without in the process destroying the human creature, and that, I would suggest, gives him a powerful motive for affirming that account.

I conclude with a few comments on the relevance of Aquinas' account of nature and grace to McKenny's own ethical and theological project. As we have already noted, McKenny's comments on Aquinas and contemporary Thomists reflect a generous and nuanced appreciation of what we might call the Thomistic project. Nonetheless, I am quite sure that he would not identify himself as a Thomist, and I am tempted to ask why not. Of course, that is not a serious question. But it is worth pointing out that the theological approach to human nature that McKenny commends is closer to Aquinas' account than he perhaps realizes. So far as I can tell, at this point his only major objection to Aquinas' account is its supposed vulnerability to a forced choice between human nature, considered as a normative standard, and the goods proper to that nature. As we have seen, this is not a tenable objection.

More importantly, Aquinas' overall account of human nature fits within the approach to the normative significance of human nature that McKenny commends. Near the end of *Biotechnology, Human Nature and Christian Ethics*, he summarizes this approach as follows:

> to say that the ground of our good transcends our nature is not to say that it is realized apart from our nature and thus requires us to abandon our nature or change it into something different. The good that transcends our nature, namely, life with God, is fulfilled in Jesus Christ, who shares our nature, and we enjoy it in him by the grace of God working in or through our nature. It is as

creatures with this nature that God willed for us to enjoy life with God, which is to be realized *by* the work of grace, and whatever our eschatological fulfillment consists in, it will be the fulfillment of this creature with this nature.[16]

Aquinas could affirm everything in this summary statement. Of course, the same could be said of Barth, or the contemporary theologian Kathryn Tanner, whose work provides McKenny with another example of what he takes to be the most satisfactory approach to the normative significance of human nature. McKenny's statement is meant to identify the central features of a certain approach, rather than characterizing a specific theology. Nonetheless, it is worth pointing out that Aquinas, in his own distinctive way, affirms the kind of relation between nature and grace that McKenny regards as critical to a satisfactory treatment of the subject. Perhaps it is time for a reconsideration of Aquinas' account of nature and grace, not only for its historical interest but also as a powerful and attractive way of addressing contemporary questions.[17]

16. Ibid.,188.
17. I would like to thank Michael Mawson and Paul Martens for their helpful comments on earlier versions of this chapter. Needless to say, all mistakes and deficiencies are my own most grievous fault. And I'd like to take this occasion to thank Jerry and Toy most warmly for their many years of friendship. You both embody the best ideals of intellectual inquiry, comradeship, and Christian friendship. Let's hope and pray for more years to come!

Chapter 10

ENCOUNTERING GRACE AFTER THE FALL

THE NORMATIVITY OF NATURE IN PROTESTANT ETHICS[1]

Michael Mawson

In *Biotechnology, Human Nature, and Christian Ethics* (2018), Gerald McKenny explores the role and status of human nature for ongoing work in Christian and philosophical ethics. More specifically, he identifies and reflects upon four different ways in which Christians and others have understood nature as having normative significance, especially in relation to negotiating recent challenges presented by biotechnology and biotechnological enhancement. How should Christians understand and appeal to nature when responding to attempts to extend the human life span, for example? Or how should Christians respond to the emergence of other technologies and therapies that could significantly alter human nature or enhance abilities beyond the normal range?

In the first approach that McKenny outlines in *Biotechnology*, nature is understood as having normative significance simply in its givenness. Accordingly, this implies that what is natural should be respected rather than altered or enhanced through biotechnology. Labeling this position "NS1,"[2] McKenny identifies it with thinkers as diverse as Oliver O'Donovan, Michael Sandel, and Jürgen Habermas.[3] In the second approach, nature is normative as a ground for human flourishing and rights (NS2). Proponents of this view share a basic concern that the alteration of natural capacities and traits by means of biotechnology might imperil distinctively human goods and rights. Drawing upon Aristotelian philosophy, its advocates include Francis Fukuyama, Martha Nussbaum, and Leon Kass. In the third approach, nature is normative through its malleability or susceptibility to intervention and alteration (NS3). For those who take this approach, the very indeterminacy, open-endedness, and malleability of human nature invites and

---

1. Amy Erickson, Brandin Francabandera, and Paul Martens provided insightful comments on a draft of this chapter.

2. "NS" is McKenny's shorthand for "normative status."

3. Locating this position theologically, McKenny suggests that NS1 is in some respects anticipated by Augustine's theology. Gerald McKenny, *Biotechnology, Human Nature, and Christian Ethics* (Cambridge: Cambridge University Press), 34–6.

even requires ongoing enhancement. Unlike the previous positions, proponents of NS3 often embrace and advocate for the enhancement and alteration of human nature through biotechnology.[4] Fourth, and finally, nature has normative significance in that it equips or prepares us for life with God (NS4). "According to NS4," as McKenny summarizes, "our creaturely nature suits or equips us for a particular form of life with God that was God's purpose in creating us."[5] Each of these different ways of understanding the normative status of human nature facilitates a different response to the challenges presented by biotechnology.

In this chapter my interest is primarily in McKenny's presentation of NS4, his own preferred option, which he constructs through careful readings of Kathryn Tanner and Karl Barth.[6] In the first section I outline the main features of McKenny's NS4, remaining close to the relevant chapter of *Biotechnology*. I also review some weaknesses which McKenny himself identifies with Tanner's and Barth's versions of NS4.[7] In the second section, I set out Dietrich Bonhoeffer's reflections on human nature in his unfinished "Natural Life" manuscript, suggesting how "Natural Life" can be read as a version of NS4. Finally, I conclude by briefly reflecting on some advantages of this Bonhoefferian version of NS4, as compared with the versions found in Tanner and Barth.

McKenny's NS4: Human Nature as the Condition for Imaging God[8]

In McKenny's account, NS4 is the view that human nature has normative status because God has created and determined human beings with this particular nature in order to equip them for relationships with God and one another.[9]

---

4. Theologically, this position finds a precedent in Irenaeus and various Patristic theologians. Its modern subscribers include Ted Peters and Philip Hefner. In McKenny's account it also has resonances with some aspects of Kathryn Tanner's theology. *Biotechnology, Human Nature, and Christian Ethics*, 137–42.

5. McKenny, *Biotechnology, Human Nature, and Christian Ethics*, 147.

6. Others have begun to respond to McKenny's presentations of NS1–NS4 in *Biotechnology, Human Nature, and Christian Ethics*. In this volume, the chapter by Travis Kroeker challenges and expands McKenny's understanding of NS1; the chapter by Jean Porter responds to McKenny's account of NS2; and Stephen Pope's chapter expands McKenny's account of NS4 by relocating Aquinas' here (rather than in NS2).

7. In what follows I assume a level of familiarity with McKenny's work. My summary of his sophisticated presentation of NS4 is necessarily brief.

8. Of the four options that McKenny explores in *Biotechnology, Human Nature, and Christian Ethics*, NS4 is the most explicitly theological in that its point of departure is Christology. Indeed, at the end of his chapter McKenny suggests that this may, in fact, be a weakness of NS4, as I mention later.

9. As McKenny succinctly puts this, "Normative status therefore attaches to human nature (which with its present traits and powers is to be understood as in some sense the

Furthermore, this view implies that human nature as it stands is sufficient and good: "with respect to its status as God's creation, human nature is good insofar as it suits human beings for the life with God for which God has determined them."[10] If we have been created and determined by God as the particular creatures that we are, then this implies that there is no inherent need to pursue alterations or enhancements that fundamentally alter or enhance the nature that we have.

McKenny develops his account of NS4 using theological language of *imago dei*: "God created human beings to reflect something of God: life with God . . . is lived in that reflection; and their creaturely nature equips human beings to live with God in this way" (150). As beings created in God's image, humans have a "unique dignity" that extends to and encompasses their biological nature (149). Specifically, he follows Paul (citing Rom. 8:29; 2 Cor. 4:4; Col. 1:15) in opting for a Christological interpretation of *imago dei*: "to be in the image of God is in some way to conform to Jesus Christ" (150). Both of McKenny's two main interlocutors for constructing his account of NS4, Kathryn Tanner and Karl Barth, understand the *imago dei* in terms of this Pauline conformation to Christ.

For Tanner, this conformation is understood mainly in terms of the "plasticity" of human nature.[11] Human nature is normative or has ethical significance simply in its capacity to be reformed and remade. As McKenny summarizes, "[I]t is the almost unlimited capacity of human nature to be shaped by intentional human action . . . that equips humans to receive God's image and be remade by it" (152). It is because human beings have been created with a highly flexible or malleable nature that we are able to be remade into Christ's image through the work of the Spirit.

In terms of her Christology, Tanner understands Christ as God's image with reference to his divine nature, namely Christ as the second person of the Trinity. Christ "shares the divine nature and thus images God as 'the perfect manifestation of all that the first person is'" (152). We in turn attain or enter into this image, then, by being drawn into Christ's divinity. As McKenny summarizes, we "image God 'by participating in what we are not,' namely God" (153). This indicates the "deificationist orientation" of Tanner's Christology and related anthropology (157).

On this basis McKenny suggests there are continuities between Tanner's position and the view he outlined in an earlier chapter in *Biotechnology* as NS3 (that human nature has normative significance in its susceptibility to being transformed into something else entirely).[12] He suggests, however, that despite this

---

good and finished work of God) as the condition for the particular form of life with God for which God has created us." *Biotechnology, Human Nature, and Christian Ethics*, 148.

10. For the remainder of this section, all page numbers in brackets in the main text refer to McKenny's *Biotechnology, Human Nature, and Christian Ethics*.

11. McKenny's engagement focuses on Tanner's *Christ the Key* (Cambridge: Cambridge University Press, 2009).

12. Note that McKenny also discusses Tanner's theology in his chapter on NS3. *Biotechnology, Human Nature, and Christian Ethics*, 122–3.

proximity Tanner finally remains within the parameters of NS4: "Tanner's position . . . expresses the principle that our nature is equipped for enjoyment of life with God by virtue of the creaturely characteristics it now has, even as, by virtue of the plasticity of these characteristics and powers, it is susceptible to work of the Spirit, which takes our nature beyond what is natural to it" (154). Because our nature opens us to God's work in the Spirit "by virtue of the characteristics it now has," Tanner's position draws back from the view of nature entailed in NS3's pursuit of radical transformation.

In developing his account of NS4, McKenny gives more sustained attention to Karl Barth's theology.[13] While similarly holding that our nature equips and determines us for life with God, Barth is even clearer that "human nature as created by God is already suited to the enjoyment of life with God and need not undergo any working over to be made fit for it" (157). As compared with Tanner, he is even clearer that our nature is sufficient for this enjoyment as it stands. Following Barth, we are conformed to the image of God in Christ *in*—and not simply *through*—the nature we already possess as God's creatures.[14] This means that "for Barth, life with God does not take us beyond our created state" (172).

This difference relates to how Barth and Tanner each understand Christ as *imago dei*. Barth also holds that it is Christ who is the image of God in the true sense, and that we in our place image God in conformity to Christ.[15] In contrast to Tanner, however, he insists that "it is in his *humanity*, and thus in his *creaturely nature*, that Christ is the image of God" (emphasis added, 164). In his humanity or human nature, Christ repeats and reflects *ad extra* who God is in Godself. Specifically, Barth holds that Christ does this through his love for his fellow human beings: "What characterizes Jesus' humanity for Barth is his absolute and unconditional being for his fellow humans, which accomplishes in time God's absolute and unconditional being for humanity that is God's eternal resolve, and thereby fulfils the covenant of grace" (164).

This is also what gives human nature its normative status. For Barth, Christ's "being for his fellow humans . . . in time" presupposes and attests to the "natural characteristics that make it possible for Christ to be with us and for us" (174). In other words, these natural characteristics have significance because Christ's concrete love and service for others presupposes and requires them. This is Barth's

---

13. McKenny is focusing in particular on Barth's *The Church Dogmatics*, III/2, ed. G. W. Bromiley and T. F. Torrance (London: T&T Clark, 1960).

14. As McKenny clarifies, "Barth holds, in contrast to Tanner, that our nature participates in the image of God just as it is, without having to be worked over by the Holy Spirit in such a way that it is no longer natural with respect to its created state or condition." *Biotechnology, Human Nature, and Christian Ethics*, 162.

15. As McKenny summarizes, "Jesus Christ is the proper image of God: His is the one in whom God is God with and for humanity. Other human beings image God as those whom God is with and for in Jesus Christ." *Biotechnology, Human Nature, and Christian Ethics*, 170.

counterintuitive move in his anthropology: we are to understand the significance of human nature not directly or in itself, but by looking to Christ.[16] God from eternity has created all human beings with the particular nature that we have in service to Christ as God's image in time.

This creaturely nature also anticipates and makes possible our own conformity to Christ as God's image. As McKenny writes, it is what enables us to "live in a way that conforms to God's being with and for us in Christ" (165). In a more limited and conditional way, therefore, we too are able to express the same concrete love that Christ has for others. As beings created with the same human nature as Christ, we too can witness to God's image in Christ through acts of love and service.

In reflecting on this nature that is attested to in Christ, Barth largely refrains from speaking in terms of specific natural powers and capacities (i.e., reason, will, etc.). Instead, he presents our creaturely nature in terms of three aspects: "relationality, as a composite of body and soul, and as temporal" (160). God has created and determined humans as relational, integrated, and temporal beings in anticipation of Christ's concrete work of love. Furthermore, these broad aspects of human nature can be viewed as "signs" of how God has prepared us to participate in this work. Recognizing that God in Christ has embraced and works through human nature frees us to similarly embrace the aspects of the nature that we have been given.[17] Looking to Christ allows us to recognize, for example, that a bounded life span is one way that God frames and directs our concrete love and service to others.[18]

With respect to biotechnology, McKenny suggests that NS4 does not provide principled grounds for opposing enhancement and alteration. Even Barth's position, he reflects, "could accommodate . . . many of the possibilities that biotechnology might bring about" (174).[19] What NS4 does provide, however, is a place from which to evaluate specific technologies and their anticipated effects:

---

16. This is part of what sets NS4 apart from NS1. For Barth and Tanner, even as our nature attests to God's purposes, it is not intelligible in itself or directly. In other words, we are able to understand nature as normative only by seeing it in relation to God's work in Christ.

17. Nonetheless, at the end of his chapter McKenny suggests that a limitation with Barth's version of NS4 is that his three "characteristics of human nature (relationality, body-soul composition, and temporality)" remain at a general and abstract level (182), and that Barth himself provides little reflection on "the concrete functions or the rational, volitional and sensible capacities that are the "stuff" of human nature." As a result, McKenny observes, Barth leaves it "unclear how these concrete aspects of our concrete nature signify its meaning and purpose" (182).

18. That is, in a way that frees us from needing to resist or overcome a bounded life span through the pursuit of life-extending technologies and therapies.

19. And for McKenny it is conceivable that certain enhancements and alterations may even serve and enhance our creaturely relationality, integration, and temporality.

The crucial claim is that the point of our creaturely nature is to equip us to image God by attesting to God's being with and for us in actions as creatures. The question posed to biotechnology, then, is this: In acting to determine the possibilities of our creaturely nature, are we instantiating (in our creaturely nature as well as our actions toward it) that point or some other one? (176)

Following Barth, the question is whether a proposed alteration or enhancement will actually help us to better attest to God's image in Christ.

At the end of his presentation of NS4, McKenny draws attention to some limitations or "flaws" in the versions that he has drawn from Tanner and Barth.[20] On the one hand, he suggests that even while Tanner's version remains within the parameters of NS4, there is still an "insufficient affirmation of the goodness of our nature in its present state, with the possibilities that are inherent in it apart from the work of the Holy Spirit" (181). In other words, Tanner's version is limited due to the fact that "the normative significance of our creaturely nature consists entirely in its capacity to be transformed into something else" (180).

On the other hand, McKenny suggests that Barth's version "risks the opposite error" (181). Barth celebrates the goodness of human nature in its current condition in a way that leaves little room for the "eschatological transformation of our nature into the divine likeness" (180). As McKenny elaborates, Barth tends to understand the life to come, our resurrected nature, in terms of an affirmation or restoration of the nature that we already possess.[21] As McKenny succinctly states, Barth's view of resurrection "comes perilously close to the notion of resurrection as a kind of resuscitation" (181).[22]

Nonetheless, the very fact that NS4 can "accommodate positions with opposite shortcomings" means that, in McKenny's judgment, "the vices of these two positions do not nullify the virtues of NS4." McKenny concludes that NS4 itself is "broad enough to include the range of theological positions that fall between

---

20. See McKenny, *Biotechnology, Human Nature, and Christian Ethics*, 180–3.

21. For more on Barth's anthropology and understanding of resurrection, see the rich essay by Donald Wood, "*This* Ability: Barth on the Concrete Freedom of Human Life," in *Disability in the Christian Tradition: A Reader*, ed. Brian Brock and John Swinton (Grand Rapids: Eerdmans, 2012), 391–426.

22. McKenny also suggests that a limitation with NS4 (at least as compared with NS1, NS2, and NS3) is that the "Christological grounds appear to confine NS4 to those who accept that human nature is the creaturely condition for a form of life with God that is given to us in Jesus Christ" (183). Put differently, NS4 seems to exclude all those who lack specifically Christian convictions and commitments. Or at least he seems to render this version incomprehensible and inaccessible to those without such commitment. Yet, McKenny briefly reflects that even with its Christological grounds, NS4 is not "entirely esoteric." Without providing details, he speculates that those familiar with NS2 and NS3 may still be able to account for its differences in ways that "ignore" or "place less emphasis on" revelation (183).

Tanner's and Barth's positions" (183). Indeed, early in his account of NS4 he makes clear that his own use of Tanner and Barth is "exemplary" rather than exhaustive (152). This leaves space for reflecting and expanding upon McKenny's NS4 by drawing in other voices.

Bonhoeffer's "Natural Life"

In the winter of 1940, the Lutheran theologian Dietrich Bonhoeffer drafted a manuscript, "Natural Life" (*"Das natürliche Leben"*[23]), as part of an intended work on theological ethics (edited and published posthumously by Eberhard Bethge as *Ethics*).[24] Bonhoeffer worked on "Natural Life" while staying at Ettal Abbey in Bavaria, making use of the abbey's extensive library.[25] As with all of the *Ethics* manuscripts, he composed "Natural Life" in the context of National Socialism and during the Second World War.[26] He left Ettal in February of 1941, never finding an opportunity to return to and complete this text.

Running to fifty-five pages in the most recent German edition,[27] "Natural Life" is one of the longest manuscripts of *Ethics*. It contains reflections on how to situate and approach nature or natural life theologically, as well as detailed discussions of specific ethical topics, including euthanasia, suicide, marriage rights, birth control, and forced sterilization. In these discussions Bonhoeffer goes into a level of concrete detail that is notably absent from most of the other manuscripts of *Ethics*. Furthermore, it is not always clear how "Natural Life" fits with some of his wider claims and ideas,[28] even while fairly closely following and building upon

---

23. In this section, I follow the DBWE translators in rendering "Das natürliche Leben" as "natural life," but it might also perhaps be rendered as "natural *living*." This would capture the more dynamic sense of how God encounters and works with human beings in the midst of their everyday living.

24. Dietrich Bonhoeffer, *Ethics*, DBWE 6, ed. Clifford Green, trans. Reinhard Krauss, Charles West, and Douglas W. Stott (Minneapolis: Fortress Press, 2006). All page numbers in brackets in the main text of this section refer to Bonhoeffer's *Ethics*.

25. Dietrich Bonhoeffer, "52. To Hans-Werner Jensen," in *Conspiracy and Imprisonment, 1940–1945*, ed. Mark Brocker (Minneapolis: Fortress Press, 2006), 112.

26. Given the central concern with bodily life and natural rights, "Natural Life" can be read as partly responding to the racism and eugenic programs of the Nazi regime. See Bernd Wannenwetsch, "My Strength is Made Perfect in Weakness: Bonhoeffer and the War over Disabled Life," in *Disability in the Christian Tradition: A Reader*, ed. Brian Brock and John Swinton (Grand Rapids: Eerdmans, 2012), 354–60.

27. Dietrich Bonhoeffer, *Ethik*, DBW 6, ed. Isle Tödt, Heinz Eduard Tödt, Ernst Feil, and Clifford Green (München: Chr. Kaiser Verlag, 1992).

28. I first read Bonhoeffer's *Ethics* and the "Natural Life" manuscript in a doctoral seminar with McKenny at Notre Dame in 2007. There was rigorous discussion about whether and how Bonhoeffer's emphasis on reason in "Natural Life" relates to his more thoroughgoing

the preceding manuscript: "Ultimate and Penultimate Things." "Natural Life" ends abruptly with a few scattered remarks following a subheading: "The Natural Rights of the Life of the Spirit."

While there has been limited secondary scholarship on "Natural Life,"[29] one trend has been to read the manuscript as an attempted recovery of the natural law tradition.[30] In a rich essay, Jens Zimmermann has recently exemplified this approach; he positions Bonhoeffer as anticipating a subsequent Catholic (and now also Protestant)[31] return to natural law.[32] In Zimmermann's reading, Bonhoeffer "clearly assumes a 'natural order of the world', woven into the fabric of God's creation, to which human beings ought to conform."[33] Furthermore, he continues, "in granting fallen reason the power to discern creational directives for human flourishing, Bonhoeffer establishes the natural as common ground for public

---

critiques of reason elsewhere in his theology. See, for example, his negative comments about "human discernment" in the manuscript "God's Love and the Disintegration of the Word," *Ethics*, 323.

29. Some of the main engagements include Adam C. Clark, "The Creator Sovereign in Christ: Dietrich Bonhoeffer and Protestant Natural Law Retrieval," (PhD Dissertation. University of Notre Dame, 2017); William F. Connor, "The Natural Life of Man and its Laws: Conscience and Reason in the Theology of Dietrich Bonhoeffer," (PhD Dissertation. Vanderbilt University, 1973); Steven van den Heuvel, *Bonhoeffer's Christocentric Theology and Fundamental Debates in Environmental Ethics* (Eugene: Pickwick Publications, 2017), 22–72; Robert Vosloo, "Body and Health in the Light of the Theology of Dietrich Bonhoeffer," *Religion and Theology* 13, no. 1 (2006): 23–7; Heinz Eduard Tödt, *Authentic Faith: Bonhoeffer's Theological Ethics in Context* (Grand Rapids: Eerdmans, 2007), 142–50; essays in Ralf K. Wüstenberg, Stefan Heuser, and Ester Hornung, eds., *Bonhoeffer and the Biosciences: An Initial Exploration* (Pieterlen: Peter Lang, 2010); Jens Zimmermann, "Recovering the Natural for Politics: Bonhoeffer and the Natural Law Tradition," in *Dietrich Bonhoeffer, Theology and Political Resistance*, ed. Lori Brandt Hale and W. David Hall (Lanham: Lexington, 2020), 27–48.

30. This trend is partly in reaction to readings of Bonhoeffer that have emphasized his proximity to Barth. An example can be seen in Robin Lovin, *Christian Faith and Public Choices: The Social Ethics of Barth, Brunner, and Bonhoeffer* (Minneapolis: Fortress, 1984), 168–72. While not discussing "Natural Life" directly, Jordan Ballor has recently argued for a reading of Bonhoeffer as a natural theologian. Ballor, "Christ in Creation: Bonhoeffer's Orders of Preservation and Natural Theology," *Journal of Religion* 86, no. 1 (2006): 1–22.

31. Zimmermann mentions a "spate of publications" in the 1990s that "indicated a renewed interest among Protestants in natural law theory." Zimmermann, "Recovering the Natural for Politics," 28. As an example, he refers to Stephen J. Grabill, *Rediscovering the Natural Law in Reformed Theological Ethics* (Grand Rapids: Eerdmans, 2006).

32. In the conclusion to his essay, Zimmerman draws a parallel between Bonhoeffer and Jacques Maritain. Zimmermann, "Recovering the Natural for Politics," 42.

33. Zimmermann, "Recovering the Natural for Politics," 29.

moral reasoning."³⁴ Following this natural law reading, reason provides us with access to nature as a set of moral prescriptions or directives. For all that this kind of reading has to offer, approaching "Natural Life" as a version of NS4 provides insights into some less recognized aspects of Bonhoeffer's account of natural life.³⁵

Bonhoeffer begins his manuscript by positioning it as an attempt to recover a concept of nature or the natural for Protestants. He notes that the concept of the natural has "fallen into disrepute in Protestant ethics" (171), which has in turn led to a loss of the "relative differences within the human and the natural." The result, Bonhoeffer reflects, is that Protestant Christians no longer have the "ability to give clear guidance on the burning questions of natural life" (172). Bonhoeffer aims to recover a concept of nature, then, that might assist with negotiating these burning questions and providing concrete ethical guidance.

In recovering this concept, Bonhoeffer is clear that nature or natural life can properly be understood and approached only from God's revelation. Much like Tanner and Barth, he holds that nature or natural life is not intelligible and does not have normative significance in itself.³⁶ Rather, it has significance only because of who God is and what God has done: "The concept of the natural must be recovered from the Gospel" (173). For Bonhoeffer, we recognize and affirm nature as normative on the basis of God's Word.

Bonhoeffer, too, develops this claim Christologically: "Only through *Christ's* becoming human do we have the right to call people to natural life and to live it ourselves" (emphasis added, 174). In the incarnation, God has disclosed and affirmed human nature or natural life as a place of God's own presence and work. And this means that all those who follow Christ are called to attend to God's presence and work in natural life: "Because Jesus Christ is the reconciliation of God and the world," as one commentator recently put it, "one cannot look to Christ without looking to the natural life that he has taken upon himself."³⁷ Like Tanner and Barth, Bonhoeffer approaches nature or natural life from the standpoint of being conformed to Christ.

---

34. Ibid., 33.

35. Following McKenny's classification, Zimmermann is largely locating Bonhoeffer's "Natural Life" as a version of NS1 (nature has normative significance in its givenness prior to and apart from human action or intervention). While this reading captures important aspects of Bonhoeffer's position, I worry that it underplays what is at stake with Bonhoeffer's situating of nature as postlapsarian, as well as the fluid and dynamic ways in which he understands reason in relation to natural life. For a reading that comes closer to what I am proposing, see Adam C. Clark, "The Creator Sovereign in Christ: Dietrich Bonhoeffer and Protestant Natural Law Retrieval," (PhD Dissertation, University of Notre Dame, 2017).

36. That is, the position McKenny labels as NS1 in *Biotechnology, Human Nature, and Christian Ethics*.

37. Joel Banman, *Reading in the Presence of Christ* (London: T&T Clark Bloomsbury, 2021), 170.

It is significant, however, that at this point he avoids using language of *imago dei*. This indicates a major difference from the two versions of NS4 outlined by McKenny in *Biotechnology*. Even while holding that it is Christ who allows for recognizing and attending to natural life as normative, Bonhoeffer carefully distinguishes between this normativity and the goodness of God's creation. In contrast to Barth, he insists on keeping the normativity of nature separate from our status as God's creatures and covenant partners.[38]

This difference is most readily apparent in Bonhoeffer's consistent positioning of natural life as postlapsarian: "Through the fall, 'creation' became 'nature'. The unmediated relation to God of the true creation becomes the relative freedom of natural life."[39] In other words, because of the Fall we no longer possess the same kinds of relationships with God and one another that we had in the primal state. This is why language of *imago dei* can no longer accurately describe what we are as human beings.[40] Bonhoeffer is using the concept of nature or natural life only in relation to the *new* space or situation in which human beings live and exist after the Fall. Specifically, he uses this concept for describing how God continues to uphold and preserve (*erhalten*) human beings as fallen creatures.

In an earlier book, *Creation and Fall*, Bonhoeffer had provided detailed reflection on how God continues to care for the first human beings after the Fall. Here he reflects at length on how God continues to work with and care for a sinful humanity: "God accepts human beings for what they are, as fallen creatures. God affirms them in their fallenness . . . . God's action accompanies humankind on its way."[41] Accepting these first human beings as fallen creatures, God upholds and preserves Adam and Eve by ordering their lives: "By making cloaks for human beings God shows them that it is their wickedness that makes this necessary . . . God's way of acting to preserve the world is to affirm the sinful world and to show it its limits by means of order."[42]

This anticipates how Bonhoeffer understands and presents human nature or natural life as postlapsarian in *Ethics*. After the Fall, God acts to preserve and order human beings through the very form of natural, bodily existence itself: "God wills and gives life a form [*Gestalt*] in which it can live, because left to its own resources

---

38. Bonhoeffer, "We speak of the natural as distinct from the created, in order to include the fact of the fall into sin." *Ethics*, 173.

39. Bonhoeffer, *Ethics*, 173.

40. Reference to *imago dei* is almost entirely absent from *Ethics*. When it does appear, it is being used to draw a contrast with what human beings become after the Fall. See comments to this effect in the manuscript "God's Love and the Disintegration of the World," *Ethics*, 301.

41. Dietrich Bonhoeffer, *Creation and Fall*, DBWE 3, ed. John de Gruchy, trans. Douglas Stephen Bax (Minneapolis: Fortress Press, 1997), 139.

42. Bonhoeffer, *Creation and Fall*, 139.

it can only destroy itself" (178).⁴³ Accordingly, the concept of nature or natural life is naming a particular form of God's preserving work. It is describing one way in which God has chosen to impede and limit our continuing attempts to flee from God and one another.⁴⁴

With respect to Christ, this means that God's presence and preserving work in the form of natural life has a kind of "penultimate" (*vorletzten*) significance.⁴⁵ It is one way that God preserves and orders human life *for Christ*, without directly being part of God's ultimate work of reconciliation and redemption *in Christ*.⁴⁶ As Bonhoeffer himself writes, "the natural is that form of life preserved by God for the fallen world that is directed toward justification, salvation and renewal through Christ" (174). Natural life has a kind of anticipatory or preparatory status with respect to God's ultimate work of reconciliation, even while natural life is not itself necessary or foundational for this work.⁴⁷

---

43. Elsewhere in *Ethics* Bonhoeffer treats history as a way in which God works to order and preserve human beings. See, "Heritage and Decay," *Ethics*, 103–33.

44. Bonhoeffer holds that God preserves fallen human beings through a kind of impulse or "basic will" that is embedded in the very form of natural life: "Life itself tends toward the natural." *Ethics*, 176. For Bonhoeffer, this form of life thus provides guidance or exerts normative claims in ways that ultimately exceed our attempts to organize or understand them: "The natural cannot be organized but is simply there." *Ethics*, 177.

45. Hans Ulrich has observed that Bonhoeffer "understands the natural primarily in its directedness to Christ, and thus in the ways in which it is preserving and preparing shared human living for Christ." Ulrich, "The Form of Ethical Life," in *The Oxford Handbook of Dietrich Bonhoeffer*, ed. Michael Mawson and Philip G. Ziegler (Oxford: Oxford University Press, 2019), 302.

46. Bonhoeffer provides more detailed reflection on this relationship between God's penultimate and ultimate work in his preceding manuscript, "Ultimate and Penultimate Things." "From a Christian perspective," he writes, "the fallen world becomes understandable as the world preserved and maintained by God for the coming of Christ, a world in which we as human beings should live a 'good life' in given orders." *Ethics*, 165. As Christians we are called to recognize God's preserving work in these given orders, including in the form of natural life. We are called to embrace and attend to what God is providing in this place.

47. As Bonhoeffer writes, "The natural does not compel the coming of Christ, nor does the unnatural make it impossible; in both cases the real coming is an act of grace. Only through the coming of Christ is the natural confirmed in its character as penultimate and the unnatural definitively exposed as the destruction of the penultimate." *Ethics*, 173. At the same time, however, in *Ethics* Bonhoeffer also affirms the ways in which God's ultimate work in Christ takes up and affirms natural, bodily life: "Jesus Christ the human being— that means that God enters into created reality, that we may and should be human beings before God." *Ethics*, 157.

What does this mean for human thinking and action? Following the Fall, with their newfound knowledge of good and evil,[48] human beings now have a relative freedom to think and act in ways that either embrace or aim to overcome God's preserving work through natural life. Within the relative freedom of postlapsarian life, Bonhoeffer insists, "there is a difference between its right use and its misuse; there is therefore a relative openness and a relative closedness for Christ" (174). In other words, there is a difference between attending to God's preserving work in the form of nature and attempting to live and exist apart from this form. In "Natural Life" Bonhoeffer presents and develops these two alternatives as "the natural" and "the unnatural" (176).

Beginning with the latter, he identifies two unnatural ways of relating to life in particular: vitalism and mechanization (*Vitalismus und Mechanisierung*). He describes the former as a kind of "absolutizing of life" or treating it "as an end in itself" (179). Vitalism is an attempt to construe life or the pursuit of life as the ultimate good.[49] By contrast, Bonhoeffer describes mechanization as the construal of human life as simply a means to an end. Here natural life becomes sacrificed to something higher. As Bonhoeffer states (in the context of National Socialism), "the individual is understood only in terms of usefulness [*Nutzwert*] to the whole, the community only in terms of its use to an all-controlling institution, organization or idea" (179). In the case of mechanization, human life exists solely for the service of something beyond itself, and thus in a way that subverts and displaces natural life as God's chosen place of preserving work.

While Bonhoeffer construes vitalism and mechanization as unnatural, he nonetheless insists that they are both still based on partial truths. In the case of vitalism, "it arises from the false absolutizing of an insight that is essentially correct, that life, both individual and communal, is not only a means to an end, but an end in itself" (178). Theologically speaking, vitalism on some level still recognizes natural life as a place of God's presence, even while failing to attest to how it is preserving or preparing human beings for something else: for Christ. By contrast, mechanization tries too quickly to move beyond the given form of natural life to achieve something higher. Ultimately, Bonhoeffer suggests that vitalism and mechanization equally "express . . . despair about natural life, an enmity to life, a weariness of life, an incapacity for life" (179). On their own terms both these responses fail to attend to natural life as a place where God is upholding and preserving human beings.

---

48. On the knowledge of good and evil, see Bonhoeffer's manuscript, "God's Love and the Disintegration of the World," *Ethics*, 299–303.

49. In *Creation and Fall*, Bonhoeffer describes this as "essentially a desperate, an unquenchable, an eternal thirst that Adam feels for life." *Creation and Fall*, 143. Bonhoeffer's discussion of vitalism helpfully diagnoses the thirst underlying the more recent pursuit of technologies that might radically extend the human life span. See Mark O'Connell, *To Be A Machine: Adventures Among Cyborgs, Utopians, Hackers, and the Futurists Solving the Modest Problem of Death* (London: Granta, 2017), 179–93.

Against these unnatural responses, how are we to embrace and attend to natural life? "How is the natural recognized?" (174). On the one hand, Bonhoeffer maintains that in a "formal" sense (*formale Bestimmung*) the natural "can only be recognized by looking at Jesus Christ" (174).[50] As we have already seen, and in alignment with NS4, he holds that we can understand the purpose of natural life as a place of God's preserving work only with reference to Christ.[51]

On the other hand, Bonhoeffer suggests that we recognize specific claims or "content" of the natural (*die inhaltliche Bestimmung des Natürlichen*) in a different way: through reason.[52] "With respect to the content of natural life, human 'reason' (*Vernuft*) is the organ for recognizing the natural" (174). Bonhoeffer presents this use of reason as a kind of "grasping" (*erfassen*) or "perceiving" (*vernehmen*) of what has been naturally "given" (*Gegebene*) (174).[53] Here it is worth noting that this use of reason remains close to the ground. Contra the natural law reading of Bonhoeffer, as outlined earlier, reason is not a capacity for deriving prescriptions or directives from nature, which we then adhere to or enact.[54] Rather, reasoning is a more dynamic, open-ended grasping of the significance of natural life within a given situation.[55]

This leads to Bonhoeffer's detailed reflections on natural rights (*Rechte*). In his manuscript, he insists that using reason to grasp the content of natural life involves discerning and protecting the rights of natural life: "The natural . . . becomes rights

---

50. As Bonhoeffer continues, this is because "the natural is determined by the preserving will of God and by its orientation toward Jesus Christ" (174).

51. That is, what natural life is in its anticipation of and orientation to Christ's coming.

52. Bonhoeffer endorses reason as the means by which human beings are to discern natural life and its form. Nonetheless, he is also careful to insist that "reason is not a divine principle of cognition and order in human beings, superior to the natural. Rather, it is part of this preserved form of life" and "completely embedded in the natural." *Ethics*, 174. He is also clear that even while reason allows us to recognize the form of the natural (and also natural rights), it does not allow us to discern God's work in and through that form. Bonhoeffer, *Ethics*, 184.

53. It is worth noting that there is no specifically Christian ground for using reason in this way. For Bonhoeffer, *all* human beings are capable of discerning the content of God's preserving work in natural life, even when they do not name it as such.

54. Bonhoeffer's position is not an attempt to understand nature or creation as providing moral order, that is, in the sense of Oliver O'Donovan's *Resurrection and Moral Order*. McKenny engages O'Donovan in detail in the second chapter of *Biotechnology*, 25–69. For a penetrating critique of this aspect of O'Donovan's work, see Sam Tranter's *Oliver O'Donovan's Moral Theology* (London: T&T Clark Bloomsbury, 2020).

55. Of course, there are many understandings of natural law that are dynamic and open-ended in ways that resonate with this aspect of Bonhoeffer's approach. See, for example, Stephen Pope, "Reason and Natural Law," in *The Oxford Handbook of Theological Ethics*, ed. Gilbert Meilaender and William Werpehowski (Oxford: Oxford University Press, 2007), 148–67.

with respect to human beings. The rights of natural life are the glory of God the Creator in the midst of the fallen world."[56] Much of Bonhoeffer's manuscript is occupied with outlining specific rights, and then reflecting on how these can help with negotiating pressing ethical questions and challenges. We attest to God's presence and work in human nature by affirming and upholding the natural rights of others. These reflections on rights are integral to Bonhoeffer's specific version of NS4.[57]

When he first turns to considering rights, Bonhoeffer clarifies that they need to be held in tension with certain obligations or "duties" (*Pflichten*) that similarly proceed from natural life.[58] Indeed, it is by holding rights and duties together that natural life is concretely affirmed vis-à-vis the extremes of vitalism and mechanization: "In the context of natural life . . . life as an end in itself is expressed in rights [*Rechte*], and life as a means to an end is expressed in duties" (180).[59] Affirming both rights and duties is therefore a way of avoiding these unnatural responses. Nonetheless, Bonhoeffer suggests that procedurally rights should be given a certain priority over duties: what is "given to life" by God precedes the obligations that are then "demanded of it" (180).

If rights are about affirming and protecting natural life, this takes place as the protection of the bodily life of individuals.[60] Bonhoeffer is primarily interested in the rights of the specific, individual body over against attempted encroachments by collectives or institutions: "The most primordial right of natural life is the protection of the body from intentional injury, violation, and killing" (186). With echoes of Kant, he asserts that "the human body never becomes simply a thing that might fall under the unbounded power of another person, to be used only as a means to that person's end" (214). All of the natural rights that Bonhoeffer outlines proceed from this initial need to protect and preserve bodily living.

Furthermore, protecting and supporting the integrity of individual bodies involves making space for the "joys" and freedom of bodily life. Because God upholds and preserves the natural life of the individual person as an end in itself,

---

56. Bonhoeffer, *Ethics*, 180.

57. To some extent this emphasis on rights brings Bonhoeffer's version of NS4 into proximity with the position McKenny outlines as NS2 (that nature has normative significance as a ground for rights and human flourishing). However locating natural rights in terms of God's *preserving* work results in a more constrained and less teleological account of rights.

58. In an important essay, Michael DeJonge has emphasized the importance of duties for Bonhoeffer's approach, even while this aspect of his text is underdeveloped. DeJonge, "Respecting Rights and Fulfilling Duties: Bonhoeffer's *Formed Life* in Bioethical Perspective," in *Bonhoeffer and the Biosciences: An Initial Exploration*, ed. Ralph K. Wüstenberg, Stefan Heuser, and Ester Hornung (Pieterlen: Peter Lang, 2010), 109–22.

59. Put differently, it is by discerning and protecting natural rights that we avoid construing life either as an end in itself or as a means to an end.

60. As Bonhoeffer writes, "Each Individual Brings a Natural Right into the World at Birth." *Ethics*, 183.

"there is a right to bodily joys without subordinating them to a further, higher purpose" (186). This plays out in a number of Bonhoeffer's discussions of specific rights. He insists that a natural right to housing, for example, is not simply about "protection against bad weather and the night" but also facilitates and provides a "space in which human beings may enjoy the pleasures of personal life." (187).[61] Later he insists that a right to marriage is grounded in the bodily freedom or "free decision of each individual" over against all external factors or pressures (204). These and other rights attest to God's work as it preserves and upholds the integrity and freedom of human beings in their natural, everyday living.

In his account, Bonhoeffer outlines a number of rights when critiquing encroachments and affirming the joys and freedoms of natural life. In places he insists on a particular right unequivocally. Without mentioning the T4 Program explicitly, he opposes the idea of euthanasia simply in that it "comes from the false presupposition that life consists only in its social utility" (193). Against this presupposition, he is adamant that all "life created and preserved by God possesses an inherent right" irrespective of its usefulness (193).[62]

In most other cases, however, his discussions are more fluid and his judgments less definitive. Bonhoeffer's reasoning about natural rights displays a certain tentativeness. In an extended reflection on suicide (*Selbstmord*), he insists that the very freedom of bodily life is what makes this act possible, which means that it cannot be judged "before the forum of morality" but only by God.[63] Elsewhere he affirms the "right of developing life" while suggesting that responsible reason can support the use of contraception. Indeed, he suggests that limiting family size might itself be a kind of "natural" attempt to create a "sort of breathing space for human nature" within growing populations (208).[64]

The point here is that Bonhoeffer is not so much appealing to rights in the abstract or as absolute. Rather, he deploys natural rights language as part of his reasoning

---

61. What Bonhoeffer has in mind is perhaps evident in a later manuscript of *Ethics*, "The Christian and the Ethical as a Topic," in which he celebrates "eating, drinking, sleeping, as well as conscious decision making and acting, working and resting, serving a purpose and just being without purpose, meeting obligations and following inclinations, striving and playing, abstaining and rejoicing." *Ethics*, 365–6. Rights are about protecting and making space for this kind of natural, everyday living.

62. On similar grounds Bonhoeffer affirms the rights and dignity of disabled persons or "persons severely retarded from birth." *Ethics*, 195.

63. That is, judged as a failure of faith that life (even in extreme difficulties) is a place of God's work and preserving presence.

64. When discussing birth control, Bonhoeffer also acknowledges tensions between different natural rights: the right to bodily communion, the right to reproduction, and the right to control over one's own body. He finally concludes that "the facts here are not so clear" and that "we need to make room for the freedom of a conscience responsible to God." *Ethics*, 210. In other words, Bonhoeffer proceeds in a way that leaves significant room for differing, even conflicting opinions.

or discerning of the content and claims of natural life amid pressing challenges. Indeed, he allows his understanding of rights to itself be shaped by these challenges and contexts. In this sense his reasoning about rights involves a continual openness to what is being given through the form of nature in a specific context. If discerning and protecting natural rights is about attesting to God's preserving work in natural life, then this may look very different in different times and places.

This relates back to Bonhoeffer's fundamental framing of natural life and natural rights as postlapsarian. Because rights can only ever attest to nature or natural life as a place of God's preserving work (not to the goodness of creation per se), they are reflective of and "rooted in sin that is also at work in the natural" (182). Bonhoeffer is clear that rights and the freedoms they support have at best a "relative correctness" (182); they attest to God's work in ways that remain ambiguous and incomplete.

Conclusion: Assessing Bonhoeffer's Version of NS4

In "Natural Life" Bonhoeffer's central claim is that human nature or natural life has normative status because of how God preserves fallen human beings for Christ. After the fall, God uses the form of natural life to uphold and order human living in preparation for and anticipation of Christ. And we in our place attest to this preserving and ordering work by discerning and protecting natural rights.

Bonhoeffer's account of natural life clearly qualifies as a version of McKenny's NS4. As with the other two versions that McKenny outlines, Bonhoeffer holds that our human nature or natural life equips us for life with God, even if in a penultimate and less direct sense. Furthermore, Bonhoeffer holds that there is a certain sufficiency or adequacy of human nature or natural life for this task. Christ comes to and encounters us as fallen human beings, meaning that we do not need to strive to become more or other than what we are for this encounter.

Without needing to endorse every detail of Bonhoeffer's account, his understanding of human nature in terms of God's preserving work offers something distinctive as compared with the versions of NS4 drawn from Barth and Tanner. Bonhoeffer's version would seem to overcome or at least mitigate the two main shortcomings that McKenny identifies with these other versions. Bonhoeffer's positioning of natural life as a place of God's preserving work, as well as his attentiveness to the dangers of mechanization and vitalism (as making nature either a means to an end or an end in itself) allows him to stake out a "plausible" version of NS4 between Tanner and Barth's positions.[65]

On the one hand, Bonhoeffer's position seems to avoid Tanner's understanding of human nature as having normative status only in its capacity to be transformed into something else. By situating natural life as postlapsarian, he avoids the "deificationist orientation" of Tanner's theology (157). As we have seen, Bonhoeffer

---

65. McKenny, *Biotechnology, Human Nature, and Christian Ethics*, 181.

maintains a firm distinction between the normativity of nature (as penultimate) and God's ultimate and transformative work in Christ. He thereby distinguishes between our nature as fallen creatures and any transformation that we might undergo through God's work in Christ. As compared with Tanner, this means that he is better able to affirm the integrity and value of natural life as such. Natural life has integrity precisely as a place of God's preserving work.

On the other hand, by situating natural life as penultimate, Bonhoeffer avoids the main limitation McKenny associates with Barth's version of NS4. By understanding nature or natural life as a place of God's preserving work (not in terms of the goodness of creation per se), Bonhoeffer leaves more room for a final, eschatological transformation that will take us beyond our present state. In other words, he avoids coming so close to "the notion of resurrection as a kind of resuscitation."[66] By maintaining a distinction between natural life and our status as creatures and covenant partners, Bonhoeffer anticipates a more decisive break between this life and the life to come.[67]

Finally, what is at stake with Bonhoeffer's version of NS4 for negotiating and responding to challenges presented by biotechnology and enhancement? What does his specific account of nature or natural life have to offer with respect to these recent challenges? Without providing a basis for principled or outright opposition to the alteration or enhancement of nature, Bonhoeffer's version of NS4 arguably facilitates a more critical and cautious posture toward biotechnology.[68] Or at least his account of natural life encourages close, sustained attention to how the pursuit of alteration and enhancement may be bound up with continuing (unnatural) attempts to resist and overcome bodily life and its claims.[69] Against the desire to escape nature and become more or other than what we already are, Bonhoeffer's specific version of NS4 encourages us to attend closely to natural life as a place of God's presence. In particular, his theology presses us to discern and uphold natural rights as a way of affirming and protecting natural, bodily existence and living.

66. Ibid.

67. Similarly, Bonhoeffer's language of preservation leaves more room for acknowledging the presence of sin in the midst of nature or natural life as we experience it. As compared with Barth, he gives greater emphasis to the deep ambiguities and conflicts that rend human nature and natural living in the here and now.

68. Does McKenny's care and "even-handedness" when treating so many different positions in *Biotechnology, Human Nature, and Christian Ethics* lead him to a position on biotechnology that is too measured? See comments to this effect at the end of Robert Song's review of *Biotechnology, Human Nature, and Christian Ethics*. Song, "Review of Gerald McKenny's *Biotechnology, Human Nature and Christian Ethics*," *Theology* 123, no. 1 (2020): 46–7.

69. Whereas Barth encourages us to embrace aspects of our creaturely nature (relationality, integration, and temporality) as good, Bonhoeffer focuses on our continuing attempts to flee from God's presence and work in natural life. Put differently, Bonhoeffer's version of NS4 encourages more direct attention to the (unnatural) impulses that are driving the current pursuit of biotechnological enhancement and alteration.

Chapter 11

THE FULFILLMENT OF CREATURELY NATURE

Jennifer A. Herdt

"Should humans commit themselves to those moral norms and virtues and social and political arrangements that enable them to live rightly and well with their characteristic vulnerabilities and limitations?"[1] Or should we, instead, seek to *overcome* these vulnerabilities and limitations? And if divine grace, like virtuous human agency, fulfills rather than transforms our creaturely natures, what is the difference made by eschatological consummation? One of Gerald McKenny's most important contributions to theological ethics has been to develop a distinctive and attractive position on the relationship between nature and grace, rooted in Karl Barth's (oft neglected) theology of creation and articulated in conversation with the Thomistic alternative that McKenny portrays as its most compelling alternative. Most simply, this position understands grace as the fulfillment rather than the transcendence of our creaturely natures. In *Biotechnology, Human Nature, and Christian Ethics*, McKenny addresses these questions of human identity and destiny as they are raised by biotechnology. I seek in what follows to extend these reflections on the normative status of human nature into a terrain illuminated by evolutionary and comparative anthropology and psychology. I will suggest that evolutionary theories of social selection, which indicate that human beings have shaped their pro-social tendencies by way of their own endorsement and promotion of these pro-social tendencies, offer rich fodder for theological reflection on the dynamic relation of human beings to their own natures. This situates us to address what McKenny himself identifies as one of the major theological liabilities of the position he otherwise defends: that it renders unclear what it means to affirm the eschatological transformation of our nature into the divine likeness. While we can and should affirm that our natures, as they now are, are already suitable to the end of life with God, we should also attend to peculiar features of accountable agency that point to fuller realization of the form of life with God to which humankind is called. In human beings, we witness the universe waking up and becoming potentially conscious of itself as created, beloved by God, and summoned to eschatological consummation.

---

1. Gerald McKenny, *Biotechnology, Human Nature, and Christian Ethics* (Cambridge: Cambridge University Press, 2018), xv.

Human nature, as it is, is embraced and affirmed by the incarnation, but Jesus also proclaims and anticipates the inbreaking reign of God. To confirm what Jesus has accomplished, to image the image of God, is to anticipate this reign as one in which group solidarity is no longer reinforced by hoarding wealth and privilege, by hostility to out-groups, and by torment of those who refuse to adopt the markers of group identity.

Human Hyper-cooperativity

One way to get a handle on human nature is by way of features that distinguish human beings from their closest primate relatives. What particularly interests me here is what scholars characterize as human hyper-cooperativity.[2] Bringing together the results of primate studies and the results of infant and early childhood studies, comparative psychologists have highlighted the distinctive cooperativeness of human beings. Chimpanzees participating in a joint activity to obtain a reward simply cease cooperating if their own reward becomes available; young humans persist until both partners receive the reward. Further, human three-year-olds seek to divide rewards for a collaborative activity equally among participants; chimpanzees do not.[3] Great apes form societies, but they do not engage in cooperative childcare, seek to communicate to others information useful to those others, make group decisions, or, of course, create social norms, institutions, and conventional languages. All of these are expressions of the intensely cooperative character of human beings.

Evidence gathered from the present-day hunting-gathering societies that are thought best to preserve the forms of life of the earliest humans, those of the Pleistocene, suggests further that human societies were characterized by a fundamentally egalitarian social structure that sharply differentiated them from other great apes.[4] This egalitarian structure is exemplified most notably in equitable food sharing; successful hunters must give up their large game prey and share the bounty with the entire group. Human beings did not thereby eliminate tendencies

---

2. See, for example, Michael Tomasello, *A Natural History of Human Thinking* (Cambridge, MA: Harvard University Press, 2014); Christopher Boehm, *Moral Origins: The Evolution of Virtue, Altruism, and Shame* (New York: Basic Books, 2012); and S. Bowles and H. Gintis, *A Cooperative Species: Human Reciprocity and Its Evolution* (Princeton: Princeton University Press, 2011).

3. Tomasello, *A Natural History of Human Thinking*, 39–40. See also Julia R. Greenberg, Katharina Hamann, Felix Warneken, and Michael Tomasello, "Chimpanzee Helping in Collaborative and Noncollaborative Contexts," *Animal Behaviour* 80, no. 5 (2010): 873–80. Katharina Hamann, Felix Warneken, Julia R. Greenberg, and Michael Tomasello, "Collaboration Encourages Equal Sharing in Children but Not in Chimpanzees," *Nature* 476 (2011): 328–31.

4. Boehm, *Moral Origins*, 78–81.

toward hierarchical bands dominated by an alpha male, but their tendencies toward intensified cooperation were paired with a host of strategies for reigning in dominant individuals. One of the most powerful, argues Christopher Boehm, is the conscience, internalized moral standards with which human individuals emotionally identify and according to which they assess themselves.[5] Another are practices of "preaching," by which sharing and generosity are explicitly endorsed and actively taught and promoted.[6]

This does not mean that humans are not also competitive in ways fundamentally akin to our great ape neighbors. Indeed, it seems most likely that the development of culture, as this latest evolutionary expression of cooperativeness, was spurred by competition: "a loose pool of collaborators had to turn into a proper social group in order to protect their way of life from invaders."[7] It was, then, precisely the notion that "we" are distinct from, and threatened by, "you" that spurred heightened cooperation. As Michael Tomasello observes, "this means that group members were motivated to help one another, as they were all now clearly interdependent with one another at all times: 'we' must together compete with and protect ourselves from 'them.'"[8] Our great ape relatives think of members of other groups as strangers; we humans make strong in-group/out-group distinctions. We tend to identify strongly with our in-group affiliates, and regard members of out-groups as enemies.[9] Distinctive cultural practices serve as markers that allow us to distinguish easily between our own group-mates and outsiders. They allow us to know whom we can trust. Members of the in-group who fail to conform to the ways in which we walk, talk, eat, and dress are regarded as unreliable cooperators and left out of the game—shunned or punished. We typically anticipate how we are being perceived by others and experience guilt and shame when we fail to conform to the social norms of our group.[10] By the age of three, children tell others what they should and should not do even when they themselves are not affected by the others' actions; they actively seek to enforce social norms.[11] They have learned that there is a right way to do things; it is the way that *we* do things. Human cooperativeness and human tendencies to demonize deviants and members of out-groups are therefore two sides of the same coin, linked, scholars believe, in their evolutionary emergence.

---

5. Ibid., 19–32.
6. Ibid., 189–93.
7. Tomasello, *A Natural History of Human Thinking*, 82.
8. Ibid.
9. Ibid., 84.
10. Ibid., 89.
11. Ibid., 87; Marco F. H. Schmidt and Michael Tomasello, "Young Children Enforce Social Norms," *Current Directions in Pyschological Science* 21, no. 4 (2012): 232–6.

Social Selection and Human Nature

One burning question for evolutionary anthropologists has been how to account for forms of generosity and cooperation directed toward nonkin. Generosity toward kin is not difficult to account for, given that kin carry some of an individual's genes, so sharing with kin tends naturally to elevate an individual's "fitness," or success, in transmitting their own genes to the next generation. Generosity toward nonkin, in contrast, appears to come at a cost to fitness, and thus their persistence in the genetic pool is challenging to explain.[12] A host of hypotheses have been developed, but those that are gaining ground emphasize the importance of "social selection," that is, the ways in which the dispositions and behaviors favored by social groups enhance the fitness of those who display them due to various ways in which this social favoring (and disfavoring) affects fitness. For instance, once generous behavior was socially favored, generous behavior rendered individuals more attractive as mates.[13] The rest of the band is also more likely to cooperate with generous individuals, sharing food with them, which boosts their health and fitness. Furthermore, free riders who seek to benefit from others' generosity in purely selfish ways are also effectively dealt with insofar as they must either suppress their selfishness and thus act generously even if they lack generous inclinations, or be subjected to various forms of reputational disadvantaging by the group, with real costs to fitness.[14] "Selection by reputation" is thus capable of explaining how "costly traits involving self-sacrificial generosity" can persist and be amplified in populations.[15] Social selection does a better job of explaining generosity toward nonkin than does reciprocal altruism, which assumes precise tit-for-tat exchanges which are rare outside of lifelong marriage.[16] And it offers a better explanation of how the problem of free riders is addressed than do group selection models.[17] It does so, strikingly, without explaining generosity away; generous dispositions are socially rewarded even when the generous individual lacks resources to share.[18]

What I want to emphasize most about social selection is that it implies not just that human societies have been preaching generosity and cooperation for a very long time—as long as humans have existed, in fact—but also that it was patterns of behavior expressing social approval and disapproval *that themselves made it possible* for pro-social dispositions to take root and grow as a defining characteristic of the human genome. The preaching continues, since we are egoistic and nepotistic as well as altruistic, and the social group constantly works to pull us in the direction

---

12. Boehm, *Moral Origins*, 53–4.
13. See Ibid., 49–7. This approach was pioneered by Richard D. Alexander, *The Biology of Moral Systems* (London: Routledge, 1987) and is being developed by Boehm and others.
14. Boehm, *Moral Origins*, 65.
15. Ibid., 64.
16. Ibid., 60–1.
17. Ibid., 59–60.
18. Ibid., 296–7.

of the latter rather than the former tendencies. But these social forces do have genetically given dispositions to work with.

Let us now recall McKenny's driving question: "Should humans commit themselves to those moral norms and virtues and social and political arrangements that enable them to live rightly and well with their characteristic vulnerabilities and limitations, or to those that press them to overcome as many vulnerabilities and limitations as they can?"[19] McKenny recognizes that this is no simple either-or, even if some of the approaches he considers choose to take sides. He recognizes, too, that "human beings have always sought and found ways to intervene in their nature despite its alleged givenness."[20] If social selection theory is correct, human beings have been shaping their natures toward greater generosity and cooperativeness for as long as they have existed. Their very efforts to live rightly and well with their characteristic vulnerabilities and limitations (teaching children to share, praising generous adults and favoring them as partners, shunning and punishing the greedy and dominating) have shaped the genome, favoring the fitness of those who are more generous and cooperative, and thus the prevalence of those genes within the human gene pool. To be sure, even if our early human ancestors knew very well what they were doing on one level in teaching and preaching generosity—reinforcing the moral norms accepted by the group—they could not know that they were thereby shaping their very natures. What changes if we come to know this to be the case? At the immense timescales of natural evolution, one might argue, nothing changes at all—whereas with biotechnology on the scene, and the possibility of germ line genetic engineering, our natures rest like putty in our hands. I want to argue that knowledge of the historical role of human activity, of social selection, in the evolution of human nature itself constitutes a significantly new moment in human history. Reflecting on its significance can help orient us to the future.

Human Nature and Its End

Creation, fall, redemption, and eschatological consummation offer a flexible doctrinal envelope within which Christian reflection on human nature takes place. There are certain givens here: First, that creation is good, and with it, human nature as created. Second, that the world we experience is not the world in its created state, but is fallen, riven by sin and evil. Third, that the world in its created goodness is not the world as eschatologically consummated. The eschaton, moreover, is, like creation itself, not brought about by human, but by divine, agency. It is only very partially imaginable by humans, and anticipated only in a fragmented way by grace-filled persons and practices. These positive affirmations preclude judging (created) nature evil, while cautioning against identifying nature

---

19. McKenny, *Biotechnology, Human Nature, and Christian Ethics*, xv.
20. Ibid., xiv.

as observed with created nature, or with God's final intentions for humanity or for creation. Stances that reject any interventions in human nature on the grounds that human nature is a stable given often fail to distinguish between created and fallen nature. They also in some cases fail to acknowledge the interpenetration of nature and culture, and the fact that human activity has always been shaping human nature.[21] A stance that simply affirms what is and rejects all interventions into nature can thus be dismissed. Conversely, a stance that evacuates human nature of any significance and embraces transcendence of that nature as an end in itself can also be rejected on theological grounds. For this involves a refusal to acknowledge the goodness of creation, and may also assume for human agency responsibility for realizing the eschaton: "to attach normative status to human nature with respect to indeterminacy, open-endedness, and malleability alone," remarks McKenny, "is to imperil recognition of the goodness of our created nature as it now is."[22] At the same time, there is nothing obvious or transparent about the task of distinguishing created from fallen nature, or of delineating the appropriate scope for human agency.

Making further headway requires that we be able to say something about *ends*. For what end did God create? To what end does God redeem? To what end does God bring creation to eschatological consummation? What is "the good that God purposes for humans in bringing a creature of their nature into being and destining it for eschatological fulfillment"?[23] McKenny proposes that we understand that telos to be life with God. Normative status therefore attaches to human nature insofar as it is "the condition of life with God," rather than insofar as it is "the ground of human good or rights," or immune to "intentional human determination," or open-ended and malleable.[24] Life with God thus serves as the ultimate criterion against which human activity, including interventions into human nature, are to be assessed.

Importantly, this means that the goodness of human nature, and of creation as such, are not complete in themselves, but are fundamentally broken open, ecstatically oriented to God. The fundamental problem with approaches that affirm the goodness of creation as given without regarding creation specifically as ordered to life with God is that they regard creation as a complete, closed entity. Neo-Aristotelian approaches, meanwhile, that understand the good in terms of the natural flourishing of a given kind (and hence approach nature as the ground of the human good or rights) in their own way also regard this flourishing as

---

21. McKenny considers these as problems to which the position he designates as NS1, human nature as given, is prone. At the same time, he argues that the best versions of NS1 escape these objections, *Biotechnology, Human Nature, and Christian Ethics*, 28.

22. These are the tendencies which McKenny identifies in his NS3, human nature as susceptible to intervention, *Biotechnology, Human Nature, and Christian Ethics*, 145.

23. McKenny, *Biotechnology, Human Nature, and Christian Ethics*, 187.

24. Ibid., 193.

intelligible in itself.[25] And approaches that regard open-endedness and malleability as in themselves good have no criteria according to which to direct this ongoing process of formation. If creation is understood as directed specifically to life with God, its goodness, and the goodness of human nature, are to be understood neither as enclosed in themselves nor as proceeding in directionless self-transcendence.

Darwin and the Return of Teleology in Nature

Darwin, and his theory of evolution, have profoundly transformed human self-understanding. We have come to appreciate our intimate kinship with all of life. Not only do all living things on earth share the same double-helical DNA molecules, there is also a stunning overlap in our very genomic sequences, with 61 percent of human genes shared with fruit flies and 90 percent with domestic cats. Increasingly, we have freed ourselves from Cartesian illusions that framed nonhuman animals as machines and human beings as mind-body conglomerates. At the same time, however, Darwinism has alienated us from our natures. We have come to regard ourselves, and all living creatures, as animated by selfish genes.[26] Even when we remind ourselves of the absurdity of attributing selfishness to genes, which wholly lack intentionality and agency, we continue to be confronted by the moral blindness of natural selection. Genes that lend reproductive advantages become more common in populations. That's it; no rhyme or reason, just genes that are or are not perpetuated from one generation to the next. Social Darwinism, which drew direct lessons for intentional human behavior from the notion of survival of the fittest, has by and large been rejected as morally reprehensible. But we were left with moral impulses wholly unmoored from nature, red in tooth and claw. Final causality was rejected. The world was essentially matter; form, meaning, morality, are not to be found within but imposed from without, by us, in an essentially voluntarist project. As Christine Korsgaard puts it, "if the real and the good are no longer one, value must find its way into the world somehow. Form must be imposed on the world of matter. . . . [R]eason—which is form—isn't in the world, but is something that we impose upon it."[27] In important respects this sober modernist stance actually perpetuated in reformed guise a kind of Cartesian dualism.

While in many respects this remains the reigning dogma, hints of change are in the air. Teleology, long banned from philosophy of biology, or tolerated only as colorful anthropomorphism, has returned, together with neo-Aristotelian notions

---

25. These are the approaches that McKenny collects under the heading NS2, "human nature as ground of human goods and rights," 70.

26. As in Richard Dawkins' influential book, *The Selfish Gene*, 2nd ed. (Oxford: Oxford University Press, 1990).

27. Christine Korsgaard, *The Sources of Normativity* (Cambridge: Cambridge University Press, 1996), 5.

of what it is to flourish as an instance of a particular natural kind.[28] Teleology has begun to return, too, to natural history writ large. An important example of these developments is found in Thomas Nagel's nuanced argument for the failure of psychophysical reductionism, and with it of materialist accounts of the development of living organisms. Nagel concludes that "principles of a different kind are also at work in the history of nature, principles of the growth of order that are in their logical form teleological rather than mechanistic."[29] Not only is he convinced that teleological principles are needed to explain the growth of order in nature, he argues, further, that we have reason to think that it is not merely arbitrary that these teleological principles hold, but, rather, that "the value of certain outcomes can itself explain why the laws hold."[30] Prominent among these valuable outcomes, in his view, is the emergence of creatures capable of grasping value, "capable of thinking successfully about what is good and bad, right and wrong, and discovering moral and evaluative truths that do not depend on their own beliefs."[31] In other words, Nagel argues that final causes help to account for the emergence of creatures capable of assessing their own actions in relation to the bewildering complexity of the world in which they find themselves. "Each of our lives is a part of the lengthy process of the universe gradually waking up and becoming aware of itself."[32]

Nagel is staunchly resistant to any theological interpretation of this teleology.[33] However, there is certainly ample room for Christian thinkers to make common cause with his approach. Sarah Coakley's recent work on evolution and cooperation

---

28. Jennifer Frey, "Neo-Aristotelian Ethical Naturalism," in *The Cambridge Companion to Natural Law Ethics*, ed. Tom Angier (Cambridge: Cambridge University Press, 2019), 92. The material in this paragraph is drawn in part from my book *Assuming Responsibility* (Oxford: Oxford University Press, 2022), introduction and conclusion.

29. Thomas Nagel, *Mind and Cosmos* (Oxford: Oxford University Press, 2012). What Nagel has in mind are teleological laws expressing "principles of change" that over time tend "toward certain types of outcomes," pointing to John Hawthorne and Daniel Nolan's "What Would Teleological Causation Be?" in *Metaphysical Essays*, ed. John Hawthorne (Oxford: Oxford University Press, 2006), 265–83.

30. Nagel, *Mind and Cosmos*, 67.

31. Ibid., 106.

32. Ibid., 85.

33. Nagel argues that theism fails to shed light on the intelligibility of the natural order as such, since it "pushes the quest for intelligibility outside the world." "If God exists," he writes, "he is not part of the natural order but a free agent not governed by natural laws," *Mind and Cosmos*, 26. But this implies a contrastive notion of divine transcendence that has been subjected to sustained theological critique. (See, influentially, Kathryn Tanner, *God and Creation in Christian Theology* [Oxford: Basil Blackwell, 1988].) In other words, while I do not wish to impose on Nagel a theistic stance that he wishes to reject, it is not clear that theists need necessarily consider themselves to be in disagreement with him.

offers one indication of what this might look like.³⁴ God, writes Coakley, "is that-without-which-there-would-be-no-evolution-at-all," "the perpetual invitation and lure of the creation to return to its source in the Father."³⁵ The present reflections are another contribution in this direction. Of course, any stance that plays up cooperation while conveniently overlooking the waste and suffering endemic to nature is Polyannish.³⁶ I take it to be the case that Christians may permissibly continue to confess God's goodness together with God's radical transcendence and humankind's radical finitude, but these remain acts of confession. These acts of confession are enlivened by reflection that is rooted in traditions of theological reflection but open to new observations and theories, including those coming from the natural and human sciences. How do the recent developments in evolutionary and comparative anthropology I have briefly surveyed here shape our perceptions of human nature and its place within the natural world? They make possible new ways of appreciating how humans are not distinct from, but rather part of, the natural world. Beyond this, they allow us to grasp and reflect on the fact that the evolutionary process has been such as to make possible the emergence of uncalculating forms of generosity and cooperation. In human beings, we witness the universe waking up and becoming conscious of itself; here and now, it has become possible hypothetically to reconstruct the emergence of these forms of cooperation and to know and love their goodness.

Life with God

What does this have to do, though, with regarding nature not as complete in itself but, rather, as ecstatically oriented to God? McKenny is content, following Barth, to gesture to "life with God" as the end for which our natures suit us. But the Christian doctrines of creation, redemption, and eschatological consummation imply a dynamic shape to this life with God. I am suggesting that we now have new ways of construing the world in its creaturely *exitus* from and *reditus* to God,

---

34. Sarah Coakley, "Sacrifice Regained: Evolution, Cooperation, and God," *Gifford Lectures*, 2012, https://www.giffordlectures.org/lectures/sacrifice-regained-evolution-cooperation-and-god; see also *Evolution, Games, and God*, ed. Sarah Coakley and Martin Nowak (Cambridge, MA: Harvard University Press, 2013). I am reluctant to idealize self-sacrifice in the ways that Coakley does, however.

35. Sarah Coakley, "Evolution, Providence, and the Trinity: From Natural Cooperation to Natural Theology," *ABC Religion and Ethics*, February 6, 2019, https://www.abc.net.au/religion/evolution,-providence-and-the-trinity/10787616.

36. John Schneider, *Animal Suffering and the Darwinian Problem of Evil* (Cambridge: Cambridge University Press), 46. The realities of evolution and natural selection do pose significant challenges to inherited understandings of God's providential care for creation, but I will not be addressing such problems here, or offering a new theory of theistic evolution.

picking up on an old Neoplatonic theme long ago taken up and elaborated by Christian theologians. And this, in turn, offers further orientation both to our own evolutionary past and to our future biotechnological interventions.

McKenny suggests that the good that God purposes for humans in bringing a creature of their nature into being and destining it for eschatological fulfillment is life with God. But life with God takes different forms, and can be experienced by creatures of many natures. Particularly generative in this context is the theological anthropology developed by David Kelsey. Kelsey argues that "the goodness of actual living human bodies is grounded in exactly the same way, and is of the same sort, as the goodness of all other creatures: it is grounded in God's self-commitment to valuing creatures in delight with them for what they are, valuing them in the free and delighted intimacy and the intimate and attentive freedom of God's creative ongoing active relating to them."[37] God has created what is genuinely other than God and in creating it, enters into relationship with it, a relationship of "attentive delight" that requires nothing of it apart from its God-grounded existence. The goodness of creation, in other words, is grounded wholly in God's affirmative attention; it requires no teleological unfolding on the part of creatures in order to earn that attention, because the relationship is wholly established via *God's* active relating to creaturely being.[38]

The goodness and dignity of each creature is thus fully grounded in God's appreciative delight. But it is also true that creatures by their very existence reflect their creator; "the heavens are telling the glory of God," as the Psalmist has it. That is to say, creation glorifies its creator by its very being. This reflection, this glorification, is the primary mode in which the reditus of creation takes place; that which has come forth from God as God's free self-expression grounding the existence of that which is not God, reflects in finite refracted forms God's uncreated goodness and beauty. But this generic statement is insufficient; each creaturely kind reflects and glorifies God in distinctive ways. Human beings are capable of grasping, of knowingly appreciating, the created giftedness of their being; "we each are called to respond faithfully in the presence of, and in company with, our neighbors, to the faithfulness of God's creativity."[39] Human beings thus have on this account a particular vocation, that of accountability to God for the gift of creation. In its most explicit form, this is grateful worship, a particular instance of the broader way in which creation glorifies God by the mere fact of its existence. But this vocation of accountability is also expressed by way of moral agency as such. For to be a moral agent is to be accountable for one's actions to other reason-

---

37. David Kelsey, *Eccentric Existence: A Theological Anthropology* (Louisville: Westminster John Knox, 2009), 270.

38. For Kelsey, this is reflective of the Wisdom tradition's theology of creation, which forms one of three distinct strands in his theological anthropology, together with a second strand devoted to anthropology through the lens of God's relating to bring creation to eschatological consummation and a third through God's relating to redeem.

39. Kelsey, *Eccentric Existence*, 274.

givers, if not explicitly to God. It is thus to take up a stance, at one and the same time active and reflective, on one's own being in the world as this unfolds in time. If all of creation reflects and thereby glorifies its creator, accountability is one particular form that this reflective response takes. When accountability takes the explicit form of worship, knowledge and love of God and of creation in relation to God, its creator, it in effect gathers up all of creation in grateful appreciation for God's creative self-gift. Worship is one distinctive form of creation's reditus to God, proper to creatures with moral agency.

Jesus Christ, the Inbreaking Reign of God

Might we have a reason for pursuing objective goods that are not good for us as we now are, but which "we acknowledge to be superior, such that we consider it to be a gain to become a being that can enjoy them"?[40] Aristotle, for instance, considered uninterrupted contemplation to be divine and beyond the reach of even the most virtuous, perfected human being, yet not beyond human desire; something that was not "good for" human beings could nevertheless quite intelligibly be affirmed as good absolutely, indeed better than the human good. Aristotle, of course, thought the mixed life the best to which human beings could aspire. But why should transhumanists accept such limitations? Why seek what is good for us, given the kind of creatures we currently are, rather than a better, higher good? Such reflections flounder if guidance is sought purely in what is "good for" an existing nature. Given the dynamic character of natures, our natures as such do not give us adequate reason to affirm them as they are, rather than changing them.

No transformation of a nature is required, McKenny emphasizes, in order to actualize the possibilities of this already-suitable nature.[41] Were such a transformation required, the goodness of creation would be in question. McKenny suggests that the key is to locate the normative significance of human nature "in a good that is found in the role of that nature, still as it is, in our life with God."[42] Our natures as they are, are already suitable to life with God. This is confirmed by the incarnation: "our nature relates us to God's own life, which in Jesus Christ both transcends us from outside, as the divine life in which we participate, and embraces us, as the human life that is lived with and for us."[43] To seek to transform human nature is to reject in some fundamental way the Word's assumption of human nature in the incarnation.

Human nature is already suitable for life with God, indeed, for the special form of life with God characteristic of these creatures who are finite embodied moral agents. Yet it is also the case that humans have a vocation to accountability in their

---

40. McKenny, *Biotechnology, Human Nature, and Christian Ethics*, 94.
41. Ibid., 189.
42. Ibid., 109.
43. Ibid., 148.

existing as finite embodied moral agents.⁴⁴ Human beings are not simply to receive their being from God, but to gather up all of creation in doxological gratitude, knowing and loving themselves, one another, and all of creation in relation to God. The actualization of human nature is this responsive self-relating to God. Christians confess that this vocation is perfectly realized in Christ.

What does Jesus reveal of life with God, according to McKenny? The heart of this is the claim that human life with God is properly lived by imaging God, and that human beings image God by conforming to Jesus Christ.⁴⁵ Further, McKenny follows Barth in affirming that human determination for life with God has been perfectly fulfilled by Jesus Christ in time.⁴⁶ We are called to confirm what Jesus Christ has already accomplished on our behalf and in our place.⁴⁷ Barth regards various aspects of human creaturely nature as properly to be embraced as they are, given the vocation to confirm what Christ has accomplished: human relationality, human existence as body-soul composite, and human temporality. In various ways, McKenny, following Barth, argues that the vocation to image the image of God that is Jesus Christ calls human beings to accept "the goodness of human finitude," rather than seeking to transform human nature.

Yet, McKenny acknowledges one "major theological liability" of this stance: "it is questionable whether its insistence that our life with God is lived entirely in (and not just through) our nature as created by God allows for any eschatological transformation of our nature into the divine likeness."⁴⁸ I want to press on this point. There is a proper place for human agency in anticipation of the eschaton, even if divine agency alone ushers in eschatological consummation. Christians properly look here, as in all things, to Jesus. For Jesus does not simply accept, or call others to accept, the goodness of human finitude, of human relationality as body-soul composite in time. Rather, he preaches the inbreaking kingdom of heaven, and lives a life in anticipation of God's reign. Jesus teaches love not just of neighbor but also of enemy. He teaches forgiveness, not revenge. He reveals God not as ultimate alpha male but as generous servant-leader, empowering rather than dominating God's people. He lands on the cross, yet death does not render the final verdict on his "fitness." Appropriate responsiveness to God is thus revealed as requiring self-involving self-commitment to prostitutes and tax collectors, widows, vulnerable children, and others on the lowest rungs of society. If social selection theory is correct, Jesus engaged in the kind of teaching and preaching that *has already molded* human nature in the direction of greater cooperation, but which at the same time is *continuing to mold* it. He does so in ways that call out not just selfish and dominating behavior, but that also reveal the shadow side of the egalitarian hunter-gatherer ethic itself: its tendency to demonize out-groups and stigmatize

---

44. *Each* form of life with God is special in its own characteristic way.
45. McKenny, *Biotechnology, Human Nature, and Christian Ethics*, 150–1.
46. Ibid., 157.
47. Ibid., 158.
48. Ibid., 181.

nonconformists within the group, its inventiveness in devising rationalizations for placing certain individuals and groups beyond the pale of moral concern.

Conclusion

We do not need to choose between "rendering our nature more suitable to our good" and "actualizing possibilities of our already-suitable nature that instantiate our good."[49] What we can and must do is attempt to discern, amid those things which we have always been doing, those things that constitute appropriate responsiveness and accountability to God *and God's inbreaking reign*, and seek to nurture and strengthen these. If the human vocation is not to some self-enclosed self-realization, but, rather, to the realization of creation's good not as curved in on itself but as opened to God, what is more critical than to discern the character of God whom Christians confess to have been revealed in Jesus Christ?

What is it to live in faithful accountability to God in light of the recognition of how humans have shaped and continue to shape human nature through their social interactions? How do we begin to do knowingly what we have always been doing unknowingly? For starters, with a deep appreciation for our great capacity for self-deception, for framing as generosity what, in fact, favors ourselves and those near and dear, for framing as godly what shores up the privileges of the wealthy and powerful, for grinding the face of the poor in our eagerness to build temples ostensibly glorifying God but, in fact, glorifying our own strength and might. Uses of biotechnology that further exacerbate the gap between rich and poor, the powerful and the weak, those who comply with arbitrary markers of group identity, and those who defy them, are to be rejected. Even more, to invest resources in the development of technologies we can foresee will be used in these ways, rather than in the dismantling of unjust privilege and inequality, is to work against, not to anticipate, God's reign. The doxological attitude, which seeks to know and love creation precisely as creation, as God's creative self-gift grounding finite being in all its fragile and fleeting existence, summons us in all humility to take up the vocation to confirm what Christ has accomplished in taking on flesh, to witness in our being and doing to God's inbreaking reversal of might makes right.[50]

---

49. Ibid., 189.

50. This project/publication was made possible through the support of grant #61661 from the John Templeton Foundation. The opinions expressed in this publication are those of the author(s) and do not necessarily reflect the views of the John Templeton Foundation.

Chapter 12

ENHANCEMENT, QUANTIFICATION, AND THE IMAGE OF GOD
A THEOLOGICAL ANALYSIS OF THE BIOSTATISTICAL VISION OF HUMAN NATURE

Paul Scherz

An increasing number of technologies seek to extend our abilities beyond the normal human range, like performance-enhancing drugs extending athletic accomplishment. Such human enhancement is one of the central concerns of contemporary theoretical bioethics, especially theological bioethics. Transhumanists celebrate the possibility of transcending current human capacities, seeing in it boundless possibilities for human freedom and creativity.[1] Yet, many other theorists, often called bioconservatives, fear the hubris of this quest because of the risk of unintended consequences, possibilities for growing inequality, and the way that it may shift understandings of human flourishing.

Few scholars have done as much to clarify the assumptions and frameworks underlying both sides of this debate as Gerald McKenny. In *To Relieve the Human Condition*, he traced the historical origins of contemporary medicine, and thus enhancement, to a Baconian project of using technology to increase human autonomy and decrease suffering. His *Biotechnology, Human Nature, and Christian Ethics* provides an account of the concepts of human nature and its normativity that underlie various positions in the enhancement debate. In his analysis, there are three major positions in the literature: human nature is valuable in its givenness, as a foundation for rights and flourishing, or as enabling freedom for manipulation. His own position is that human nature is valuable because it is our current nature that enables us to image God, preparing us for the life with God that God gives through grace. There is no need to technologically enhance ourselves to reach our

---

1. In this chapter, I am using the term transhumanist broadly to include anyone who would support enhancement. Examples of prominent transhumanists would include Ray Kurzweil, Nick Bostrom, Julian Savulescu, and Max More. Transhumanism is a diverse movement with many internal disputes, and many who would support enhancement technologies disclaim the broader aims of the transhumanist movement.

final end, and any alteration that one may pursue must be judged according to whether it aligns, or at least does not interfere, with that end.[2]

In this chapter, I expand on McKenny's critique of one particular understanding of human nature, the biostatistical view, that spans many of the normative positions he describes. This framework requires human traits to be described quantitatively. The project of enhancement itself may be impossible without such a biostatistical redescription. Yet, I argue that such a quantitative understanding subtly shifts how we think of these traits, especially insofar as it requires us to eliminate many of the qualitative aspects of mental life. As they are redescribed in quantitative terms, it ceases to become apparent how these characteristics could contribute to life with God. Theologians must therefore be careful when engaging the discourse of enhancement that their own understandings of human character and experience are not shifted as well.

The Biostatistical Concept of Human Nature

McKenny describes Francis Fukuyama as one of the scholars who sees human nature as foundational to our shared understanding of human rights. Fukuyama equates human nature with a range of species-specific values for different biological and behavioral variables.[3] There is a normal distribution of height, human vision perceives a range of wavelengths and a constrained distance, there is a maximal and average life span, emotional responses tend to fall within a certain range, and so forth. Enhancement, in this biostatistical view, is the attempt to shift the distributions of these values or to radically diverge from this normal range. With the rise of biotechnology, Fukuyama fears that "large genetic variations between individuals will narrow and become clustered within certain distinct social groups," because only the wealthy will be able to afford these enhancements.[4] These distinct human groupings might undermine human equality. Alternatively, by shifting emotional responses, technology might undermine our shared morality.[5] Though some variation in a population is inevitable, major shifts might undermine the shared concept of what it means to be human.

McKenny argues that such a biostatistical view is inadequate and raises problems from the perspective of disability rights. It seems to allow only people who lie within a certain range to flourish and count as normal. Drawing on the work of Georges Canguilhem, McKenny suggests that even people with profound disabilities or diseases, who greatly diverge from general norms of health and

---

2. Gerald McKenny, *Biotechnology, Human Nature, and Christian Ethics* (New York: Cambridge University Press, 2018), 176.

3. Francis Fukuyama, *Our Posthuman Future* (New York: Farrar, Straus and Giroux, 2002), 129–47.

4. Ibid., 156.

5. Ibid., 172–4.

fitness, are able to flourish.[6] Living things shape and adapt to their environment. In Canguilhem's terms, they are norm-generating rather than merely subject to biostatistical norms. Despite disease, humans and other living things are able to impose new norms on their surroundings, find a new state for a flourishing life. People can reach distinctive states of well-being even if they might be abnormal from a population perspective. The biostatistical framework is thus a dangerous ally for bioconservatives, as it itself can demean the worth of those with disabilities.

This danger becomes more apparent when one realizes that it is not only, or even primarily, bioconservatives who embrace a biostatistical view. Rather, it is central to transhumanism and its reductionist vision of the person. This should be no surprise. The positivist understanding of science underlying the transhumanist project is at heart mathematical. As Edmund Husserl had earlier argued, the modern technological worldview that McKenny describes in terms of the Baconian project arose from Galileo's restrictive mathematical analysis of the world in terms of primary qualities like extension.[7] Qualitative features of human existence, feeling and affect, formal or final causes, consciousness, and other aspects of the lifeworld must be transformed into quantities open to mathematical modeling if they are to succumb to the gaze of science modeled on physics. Only thus imagined can technology be predictably applied to manipulate the world.[8]

The eugenics movement attempted to apply these mathematical techniques to complex human traits, such as intelligence. Doing so required eugenicists to move beyond deterministic Newtonian laws to a more statistical understanding of human populations. Francis Galton, Karl Pearson, and other eugenic researchers investigated the distribution of valuable and negative traits in a population, developing much of modern mathematical statistics along the way.[9] The goal of this research was to determine how to shift the distribution of traits in a way that would foster more exceptional figures, to select reproductive pairs who would have more intelligent children on average. Transhumanism is the heir of this biostatistical model, embracing this same framework of attempting to accentuate certain parts of a quantitative distribution, even if not explicitly. The most important commonality is that human health, functioning, and experience must be mathematically describable because, as the business adage suggests, "If

---

6. For discussion of Fukuyama, see McKenny, *Biotechnology, Human Nature, and Christian Ethics*, 81–6. For Canguilhem, see McKenny, *Biotechnology, Human Nature, and Christian Ethics*, 114–15; and Georges Canguilhem, *The Normal and the Pathological* (New York: Zone Books, 1989).

7. Edmund Husserl, *The Crisis of European Sciences and Transcendental Phenomenology* (Evanston: Northwestern University Press, 1970).

8. For an analysis of this tendency, see Joseph E. Davis, "Toward the Elimination of Subjectivity: From Francis Bacon to AI," *Social Research* 86, no. 4 (2019): 845–69.

9. Theodore Porter, *The Rise of Statistical Thinking, 1820–1900* (Princeton: Princeton University Press, 1986), 270–314; Daniel Kevles, *In the Name of Eugenics: Genetics and the Uses of Human Heredity* (Cambridge, MA: Harvard University Press, 1995), 1–40.

you can't measure it, you can't improve it." Thus, bioconservatives like Fukuyama are only following the transhumanist or at least the Baconian lead in translating human nature into biostatistical norms.

This biostatistical framework is not innocent. Beyond the concerns McKenny discusses, it tends to shift ethical conversations and our self-understanding. Translating qualitative features of human existence into quantitative terms leads to a fundamental misunderstanding of these characteristics, especially when viewed from the perspective of the Christian philosophical and theological tradition. In some cases, seeking mere quantitative extension misses what is most important about a trait, as when one considers life or memory. In other instances, especially in regard to mental capacities, it results in a pseudo-quantifiability, as these metrics either do not exist or perform poorly. The next sections explore a number of these misdescriptions, showing how they prevent us from understanding the role these unquantifiable characteristics serve in life with God.[10] The danger is that once medical and scientific descriptions work their way into popular accounts, more and more people will accept them as true. We risk alienating ourselves from experience, setting forth policy on a misfounded basis, and distracting ourselves from our ultimate end.

The Limits of the Paradigm of Physical Enhancement

The quantitative model of enhancement is plausible for many of our physical characteristics. There are medically important numerical indicators of bodily function, such as blood glucose level, blood pressure, or pulse. Height is a clearly quantifiable trait distributed across a population in a normal curve. One's place in this distribution can be modified by interventions such as Human Growth Hormone. Sports tend to have clear quantitative goals, such as world record times, distance and number of home runs, or amount of weight lifted. Particular interventions allow athletes to extend their abilities beyond established quantitative limits: steroids allow for more training and EPO injections increase the oxygen-carrying capacity of the blood and, thus, endurance. The physical body can be manipulated like other physical things.

As one moves away from bodily mechanics, though, this quantitative model becomes less plausible, in part because it fails to appreciate our social and spiritual nature, the internal goods of practices, and how capacities relate to other human

---

10. I will compare transhumanist, quantitative models of traits to a number of strands of Christian thought, although primarily to ideas found in the broadly Thomistic tradition. Here I follow McKenny, who has compared transhumanist to both Barthian and Thomistic thought. See Gerald McKenny, "Transcendence, Technological Enhancement, and Christian Theology," in *Transhumanism and Transcendence: Christian Hope in an Age of Technological Enhancement*, ed. Ronald Cole-Turner (Washington: Georgetown University Press, 2011), 177–92; McKenny, *Biotechnology, Human Nature, and Christian Ethics*, 157–76.

ends.¹¹ For example, perhaps the foremost goal of transhumanists is life extension. McKenny and others have shown how such a quest can interfere with our relationship with God and others by denying human finitude, human dependence, and the rhythms of the life cycle.¹² In so doing, it undermines virtues dependent on an acceptance of mortality and vulnerability.¹³ These problems arise because this technological project focuses on the number of days or years survived rather than the quality, intensity, or virtue of the life lived. The goal becomes bare life rather than the good life sought by classical philosophy.¹⁴ A common principle in the philosophical and theological tradition was that the quality of a life did not depend on how long one lived. Indeed, concern over length of life itself was understood as tending toward vice and unhappiness. As Seneca said, "No man can have a peaceful life who thinks too much about lengthening it."¹⁵ Such concerns lead to a focus on the future, an anxious quest to pile up experiences, and distraction from living in the present moment.¹⁶ Thus, a focus on the quantity of life lived undermines the ability to live well. Other visions of the good life are not so easily quantified.

Memory Expansion

Mental faculties are especially problematic for this model of quantitative extension. Consider memory. For many transhumanists, memory is a mere recording of information—the more, the better. It consists of facts, data, like the bits on a hard drive. As merely information, memory can be transmuted into digital form. A National Science Foundation-sponsored report imagines that researchers could

---

11. President's Council on Bioethics, *Beyond Therapy: Biotechnology and the Pursuit of Happiness* (Washington: President's Council on Bioethics, 2003).

12. McKenny, *Biotechnology, Human Nature, and Christian Ethics*, 166–70; Gilbert Meilaender, *Should We Live Forever?: The Ethical Ambiguities of Aging* (Grand Rapids: Eerdmans, 2013).

13. McKenny, *Biotechnology, Human Nature, and Christian Ethics*, 102–3; Leon Kass, *Life, Liberty, and the Defense of Dignity* (San Francisco: Encounter, 2002); Martha Nussbaum, *The Therapy of Desire: Theory and Practice in Hellenistic Ethics* (Princeton: Princeton University Press, 1996).

14. For the bare versus good life distinction, see Hannah Arendt, *The Human Condition* (Chicago: University of Chicago Press, 1998); Giorgio Agamben, *Homo Sacer: Sovereign Power and Bare Life*, trans. Daniel Heller-Roazen (Stanford: Stanford University Press, 1998).

15. Seneca, *Epistles 1–65*, trans. Richard M. Gummere, Loeb Classical Library 75 (Cambridge: Loeb Classical Library, 1917), 4.4.

16. Paul Scherz, "Living Indefinitely and Living Fully: Laudato Si' and the Value of the Present in Christian, Stoic, and Transhumanist Temporalities," *Theological Studies* 79, no. 2 (June 1, 2018): 356–75.

design additional memory units that are compatible with the architecture of human memory. A detailed understanding of how human memory works ... will enable capacity to be increased, just as you now plug additional memory cards into your PC. For installation, a means of doing microsurgery is required. ... If your brain comes with 20 petabytes factory-installed, wouldn't 200 petabytes be better?[17]

Ray Kurzweil envisions nanobots that could extend memory by connecting the brain to internet cloud storage.[18] Such technologies could allow for nearly perfect recall of both objective data and the subjective details of one's own past. Indeed, these are viewed as the same. Lifeloggers already seek this goal of a total objective record of a life by recording and saving all the details of their daily lives: emails, video, Fitbit recordings, etc.[19] Computers are important for this model both as a technology and as metaphor.[20] Factual and experiential memories are imagined as the kind of data that can be stored on a hard drive, allowing for the augmentation of memory by digital devices because all that matters is the amount of recall one has.

But what is memory? Contemporary psychological research recognizes that the transhumanist account is too simplistic.[21] People with exceptional memory of all of the details of their lives find this amazing power unhelpful.[22] They become lost in the minutiae of previous days, perhaps less able to distinguish the important from unimportant aspects of life or to remember other kinds of information. Other transhumanists recognize this more complex role for memory. Memory of experience plays a critical role in our interpretation of who we are. Many seek to augment our power over this interpretation by using neuroscientific tools to erase traumatic or unhelpful memories. Even here, though, a memory is conceptualized

---

17. Mihail Roco and William Sims Bainbridge, *Converging Technologies for Improving Human Performance: Nanotechnology, Biotechnology, Information Technology and Cognitive Science* (Arlington: NSF, 2002), 168.

18. Ray Kurzweil, *The Future of Intelligence, Artificial and Natural* (Innovation Global, 2019), Available online: https://www.youtube.com/watch?v=Kd17c5m4kdM.

19. Roco and Bainbridge, *Converging Technologies for Improving Human Performance*, 168; Ray Kurzweil, *The Singularity is Near* (New York: Viking, 2005), 326–30; Ray Kurzweil, "How You Can Be a Danielle: Chapter 5: And Record Your Life," in *Danielle: A Novel by Ray Kurzweil*, Available online: https://www.danielleworld.com/how-you-can-be-a-danielle/chapter-5-and-record-your-life-ray-kurzweil-novel.

20. For a recent discussion of the broader role of such technological metaphors in brain research, see Jeffrey Bishop, "Of Minds and Brains and Cocreation: Psychopharmaceuticals and Modern Technological Imaginaries," *Christian Bioethics* 24, no. 3 (2018): 224–45.

21. For an overview, see President's Council on Bioethics, *Beyond Therapy*, 211–21.

22. Elizabeth Parker, Larry Cahill, and James McGaugh, "A Case of Unusual Autobiographical Remembering," *Neurocase* 12, no. 1 (2006): 35–49.

as data to be erased from the hard drive of the mind. Thus, transhumanists remained tied to an unhelpful, quantitative, computer-derived model of memory.

If one looks more deeply into the classical and Christian tradition, one finds multiple understandings and practical uses of memory.[23] Some aspects of this tradition frame recall in terms similar to data storage: metaphors of memory as a storehouse or a book. In such models, though, qualitative aspects were understood as essential to memory's operation. For example, the arts of memory that stretched from ancient Greece into the Renaissance consisted of mnemonic devices for rhetoricians to memorize speeches. The rhetorician created an image of a spatial location like a street or palace in his mind, placing different facts or parts of the speech, conceived in striking images, in different locations so that later he could imaginatively walk through the space held in memory and find the argument he needed. In this framework, memory was both structured and qualified by sensory and emotional features. As Mary Carruthers notes of this tradition,

> Nor does the language of computation adequately describe what a memory was thought to be.... Successful memory schemes all acknowledge the importance of tagging material emotionally as well as schematically.... Successful recollection requires that one recognize that every kind of mental representation ... is in its composition sensory and emotional.[24]

The scholar used pictures, slow sounds, or the placement on a page to engrave memories. Memory's function was tied to the senses, emotion, and experience.

The inadequacy of the metaphor of memory as a hard drive that should be ever quantitatively expanded becomes clearer in the Stoic framework of memory. Seneca recounts Demetrius the Cynic's argument that the would-be sage must turn away from useless knowledge. Instead, he must meditate on knowledge that serves a morally formative purpose: "[I]t is far better for us to possess only a few maxims of philosophy that are nevertheless always at our command and in use, than to acquire vast knowledge that notwithstanding serves no practical purpose."[25] The student must not seek merely the quantitative increase of any sort of knowledge, but focus on only the knowledge that will shape his moral worldview, aiding him on the way to virtue. Stoic authors recommended memorizing a stock of short aphorisms, not only in order to shape one's moral worldview but primarily so that

---

23. For historical understandings of memory, see Frances Yates, *The Art of Memory* (Chicago: University of Chicago Press, 1966); and Mary Carruthers, *The Book of Memory* (New York: Cambridge University Press, 1990).

24. Carruthers, *The Book of Memory*, 59–60.

25. Seneca, *Seneca: Moral Essays, Volume III. De Beneficiis*, trans. John W. Basore (Cambridge: Loeb Classical Library, 1935), 7.1.3. This opinion does not stop Seneca from writing a long work on natural philosophy, since it revealed moral meanings in nature. See Gareth D. Williams, *The Cosmic Viewpoint: A Study of Seneca's Natural Questions* (New York: Oxford University Press, 2012).

they would also be ready to hand in the case of emergency. "[T]hese are the precepts that he must never let go . . . and make a part of himself, and by daily meditation reach the point where these wholesome maxims occur to him of their own accord, and are promptly at hand whenever they are desired."[26] These memory tools could resteady him in a time of need, allowing him to properly evaluate the situation, calm his passions, and act appropriately. Having lots of proverbs, a quantitative increase, would be ineffective here. What one needs are a few good ones and a memory that is finely honed so that these will leap to mind in the crisis. This tie to action indicates one of the failures of the transhumanist model. It is predicated on a concept of reason and memory as theoretical rather than practical. Memory on the transhumanist account can be just an inert storehouse because it is not ordered toward action. Yet, as the ancient and medieval tradition saw, memory is essential to practical reason, one of prudence's associated virtues.[27] It is not mere information, but something that seeps into the soul, shaping dispositions and orientations to action.

It is this tie to action rather than merely knowledge that causes Henri Bergson to argue that we cannot think of memory merely in terms of the brain storing discrete memories.[28] Memory allows us to gain an influence on the flow of the present in order to shape the future.[29] It is thus much more deeply tied to the self than a collection of computer data. It belongs to the realm of spirit. Such a conception of memory as a place where "I meet myself" is also found in Augustine.[30] Though drawing on the metaphor of memory as a storehouse of images, Augustine recognized it as a vast, limitless region, asking "Who can reach its uttermost depth?"[31] It was a mystery to him rather than a cleanly legible hard drive. It is in these depths that he must delve to find God,[32] though ultimately God is so intimately linked to the ground of being that Augustine could not find Him there, and so had to ascend beyond it.[33] It is this depth of memory, its tie to the essential self that made it the obvious parallel of God the Father in

---

26. Seneca, *Seneca*, 7.2.1. For such practices in Stoic philosophy, see Michel Foucault, *The Hermeneutics of the Subject: Lectures at the Collège de France, 1981–82*, trans. Burchell (New York: Palgrave Macmillan, 2005); and Pierre Hadot, *Philosophy as a Way of Life: Spiritual Exercises from Socrates to Foucault*, trans. Arnold Davidson (Cambridge: Blackwell, 1995).

27. See discussions in Yates, *The Art of Memory*; and Carruthers, *The Book of Memory*.

28. Henri Bergson, *Matter and Memory*, trans. Nancy Margaret Paul and W. Scott Palmer (New York: MacMillan, 1913), 80–1.

29. Ibid., 296.

30. Augustine, *Confessions*, trans. F. J. Sheed, 2nd ed. (Indianapolis: Hackett, 2006), 10.8.14.

31. Ibid., 10.8.15.

32. "For behold Thou wert within me." Augustine, *Confessions*, 10.27.

33. Ibid., 10.17.

Augustine's model of the Trinity as memory, understanding, and will.[34] For the Christian tradition, memory is a complex place where we interpret our past in light of God's work and seek God through reflection on these works and our spiritual capacities.

As this last point suggests, the transformation of memory into a hard drive full of data in the transhumanist project is not a mere conceptual mistake. It has consequences for how one envisions action. It impacts theological anthropology. Ultimately, it can shape our understanding of God. One cannot understand spirit if one thinks of knowledge only in terms of information. Thus the turn to a quantitative rather than qualitative vision of memory has profound consequences. It is in many ways a necessary shift in emphasis for transhumanists, though, because it is unclear how technology would improve memory in its relation to either practical reason or spirituality.

Mental Forces of Thought and Desire

Transhumanists interpret other aspects of the mind in terms of a quantity of energy or power. For example, Charles Spearman, a student of Galton, quantified intelligence, reducing it to the correlation of scores on intelligence tests. There is a long-running debate over this definition of intelligence, involving the quality of the tests, their statistical analysis, and its use in invidious racial comparisons.[35] Most importantly for this chapter, it quantifies intelligence and conceptualizes it as a form of mental energy.[36] Intelligence becomes set by biology as a sort of power for computation. The extensive debate over whether researchers can accurately test intelligence has not stopped this paradigm from reshaping institutions, with performance testing dominating recent educational reforms. Indeed, many actors now argue that behavioral genetics is necessary in educational reforms, and a company now offers preimplantation genetic testing to determine where one's child might sit in the distribution of intelligence.[37] More importantly for my argument, this view excludes models of intelligence central to the Christian tradition, such

---

34. Augustine, *The Trinity*, ed. John Rotelle, trans. Edmund Hill (New York: New City Press, 2012), 10.

35. For a history of this concept and critiques, see John Horn and John McArdle, "Understanding Human Intelligence Since Spearman," in *Factor Analysis at 100: Historical Developments and Future Directions*, ed. Robert Cudeck and Robert MacCallum (Mahwah: Lawrence Erlbaum Associates, 2007), 205–47.

36. H. Wildon Carr, A. Wolf, and C. Spearman, "Symposium: The Nature of Intelligence," *Proceedings of the Aristotelian Society, Supplementary Volumes* 5 (1925): 27.

37. Robert Plomin, *Blueprint: How DNA Makes Us Who We Are* (Cambridge, MA: MIT Press, 2018); Antonio Regalado, "The World's First Gattaca Baby Tests Are Finally Here," *MIT Technology Review*, November 8, 2019.

as the intellect as the capacity to grasp abstract forms, the interpretive ability of practical reason, or the tie between the intellect and contemplation.[38]

This reductive idea of mental energy is applied to other traits, even when they cannot be immediately quantified. Prominent transhumanists Ingmar Persson and Julian Savalescu, for example, draw on discussions of self-control using questionable ideas of will power as a quantitative resource, meaning that "exerting self-control consumes a limited resource, reducing the amount available for subsequent self-control efforts."[39] This ego-depletion theory has recently been challenged,[40] but the important point is that desires and the will are understood as brute quantitative forces that oppose one another. This is characteristic of many modern theories of desire, in which, as Thomas Pfau describes, desires and passions cease to result from a hermeneutic, cognitive process shaped by engagement with tradition and, instead, become blind forces battling each other based on the strength of their individual drive.[41] This conception is in sharp contrast with classical philosophical and theological understandings of the relation of will and intellect, which envisions an interaction between character, interpretation of a situation, and judgment.

Another realm where the problems of a quantitative rather than qualitative framework can be seen is in arguments over so-called ethical enhancement. Savulescu and Persson are concerned that the increased powers of technology will make us more dangerous. Selfishly or villainously used, such enhanced capabilities could be disastrous. Thus, they argue that humans need moral enhancement. There are different versions of this project, but one of the most prominent ones aims at increasing altruism, the disposition "to sympathize with other beings, to want their lives to go well . . . for their own sakes."[42] The idea is that human motivation is split between selfish egoism and moral altruism. Following behavioral genetics and sociobiology, Persson and Savulescu understand these dispositions to be

---

38. For a fuller discussion of these problems, see Paul Scherz, "Life as an Intelligence Test: Intelligence, Education, and Behavioral Genetics," *Culture, Medicine, and Psychiatry* 46, no. 1 (2022): 59–75.

39. Ingmar Persson and Julian Savulescu, "The Perils of Cognitive Enhancement and the Urgent Imperative to Enhance the Moral Character of Humanity," *Journal of Applied Philosophy* 25, no. 3 (2008): 164. For the origins of the ego-depletion theory, see Roy Baumeister, Ellen Bratslavsky, Mark Muraven, and Dianne Tice, "Ego Depletion: Is the Active Self a Limited Resource?" *Journal of Personality and Social Psychology* 74, no. 5 (1998): 1252–65.

40. For example, Martin Hagger et al., "A Multilab Preregistered Replication of the Ego-Depletion Effect," *Perspectives on Psychological Science* 11, no. 4 (2016): 546–73.

41. Thomas Pfau, *Minding the Modern* (Notre Dame: University of Notre Dame Press, 2013), 139.

42. Persson and Savulescu, "The Perils of Cognitive Enhancement," 168. Unfortunately, they abstain from a detailed explanation of the moral psychology that they use, so it must be inferred.

hardwired into the brain.[43] Through biotechnological interventions, such as pharmaceuticals like oxytocin and SSRIs, or genetic manipulation of genes tied to traits such as aggression, they propose to increase altruism and thus shape people to use their powers to benefit others.[44]

There are many problems with this framework.[45] Most obviously, it raises important concerns about the freedom of those modified. For example, increased altruism could be manipulated by authoritarian societies to encourage people to sacrifice themselves for the state. More importantly from a conceptual perspective, though, moral action is not only about basic motivations, passions pushing a person in one direction or another. Instead, action also involves complex cognitive and contextual elements for interpreting situations and judging the best path forward. Without these cognitive components, altruistically driven action can badly misfire as people misjudge duty and the good in specific situations. Many moral errors occur despite the intention to help others.

This model has even greater problems from a Christian perspective like that of the Thomistic tradition.[46] From this perspective, the basic egoism-altruism dichotomy is an artifact of modern individualism, which imagines separated individuals who are motivated well or poorly in relation to one another and thus seeks to encourage other-directed motivation. This dichotomy neglects our relational nature, the fact that love for others fulfills one's own good. The highest form of relation is charity, in which one loves others through one's love for God. Charity requires willing the good of another, but this is not simply an inarticulate private motivational drive, as is altruism. Charity aims at communion with the other, a relation of mutual self-giving that images the Trinitarian relation. The person "cannot fully find himself except through a sincere gift of himself."[47] In such a communion, one benefits insofar as one gives to the other. As with the friendship upon which Aquinas conceptually modeled it, through charity the beloved becomes another self, so the egoism-altruism, self-other distinction becomes ethically irrelevant. The paradigm of this communion is the Church, understood as the Body of Christ,

---

43. Ingmar Persson and Julian Savulescu, "Moral Hard-Wiring and Moral Enhancement," *Bioethics* 31, no. 4 (2017): 286–95.

44. Persson and Savulescu, "The Perils of Cognitive Enhancement," 172.

45. The objections in this paragraph have been best developed by philosopher John Harris, *How to Be Good: The Possibility of Moral Enhancement* (New York: Oxford University Press, 2016). Harris, though generally supportive of human enhancement, is not a transhumanist.

46. For a range of opinions on this understanding of altruism and cooperation, see Martin Nowak and Sarah Coakley, eds. *Evolution, Games, and God: The Principle of Cooperation* (Cambridge, MA: Harvard University Press, 2013).

47. David J. O'Brien and Thomas A. Shannon, eds., "Gaudium et Spes," in *Catholic Social Thought: The Documentary Heritage* (Maryknoll: Orbis, 2010), 24.

united by charity. Each member is joined together, participating in the whole, including the sufferings and merits of each other member.[48]

More to the point of this chapter, charity cannot be understood as a quantitatively variable force. The virtue of charity can be increased, but it is not a quantitative increase by addition.[49] Instead, Aquinas describes this increase in terms of partaking more in the form of charity, participating to a greater degree in the virtue of charity, through both charitable actions and the gift of grace. One's soul, especially one's will, takes on a particular shape or form, developing potentialities that ultimately transcend human capabilities, so that God causes "the likeness of the Holy Ghost to be more perfectly participated by the soul."[50] This is a qualitative shift, a shift in the mode and end of action. Even beyond the problem of its foundation in grace, it is hard to imagine how technology would enable a greater participation in a form or mode of action.

It is a mistake to envision interpersonal communion as something that could be quantitatively increased. It is not mere interactions or good feelings, but a qualitative conception in which one can only more deeply participate. In the classical and Christian tradition, developing a virtue was never thought of in quantitative terms. Instead, the metaphors always involved taking on a certain form of what it is good to be. One polishes the mirror of the soul to remove blemishes, takes on a likeness, or imitates an exemplar. This change cannot come from the outside so to speak, from a manipulation of a bodily process. It involves a change of heart.

Conclusion

Transhumanists make some promises of qualitative enhancements, but these seem to be the least worked out, the most promissory, and the most difficult to imagine as technologically achievable. Transhumanist artists promise new forms of art that will arise through the transformation of the body. Yet, the artistic work one sees tied to transhumanist projects does not excite optimism. Nick Bostrum promises new realms of subjective experience and new creative works that will emerge from increased intelligence, such as "music that is to Mozart what Mozart is to bad

---

48. For discussion of the practical implications of this model, see John Paul II, "Salvifici Doloris," 1984, 19–27, https://w2.vatican.va/content/john-paul-ii/en/apost_letters/1984/documents/hf_jp-ii_apl_11021984_salvifici-doloris.html.

49. Thomas Aquinas, *Summa Theologica*, trans. Dominicans of the English Province (New York: Benziger Bros., 1947), II-II.24.5.

50. Aquinas, II-II.24.5 ad 3. For a good discussion that contrasts Aquinas' idea of virtue as participation with theories of maximization, see Mary Hirschfeld, *Aquinas and the Market* (Cambridge: Harvard University Press, 2018), 95–117.

Muzak."⁵¹ Yet, based in the relationship to history and technology, Muzak would seem closer to transhumanist visions of progress: it is historically later and more technologically mediated.⁵² These projections of qualitative enhancement are merely speculation based on little evidence. The predictions of expanded sensory experience are most understandable, because more quantifiable: infrared vision, greater sensitivity to light, etc. They are also far less exciting. As one gets further afield from standard experience, like using echolocation, it becomes less clear why the development would be desirable. There are certain utilitarian applications, such as the military use of night vision, but it is hard to see this as contributing much to a broader project of human flourishing.

Most of the claims for enhancement thus depend on describing human characteristics in a quantitative manner, which, beyond a few bodily characteristics, generally leads to a misdescription or at least a very parochial description alien to the understanding of these features present in much of the Christian philosophical and theological tradition as well as in other cultures. Once these characteristics are thought of in a qualitative way, it becomes less clear how technology would improve them. What technology would make the necessary aphorism always ready to hand, develop a striking image, provide the proper interpretation of the past, or help one reach God through an internal path? How would technology help one to extract an intellectual essence? What technology would form one in charity, or help one better participate in the Body of Christ? It is thus unclear, as McKenny argues, how any biotechnological enhancement would further one's life with God.

All people already possess the seeds of these capacities. They just need to grow in them by participating more deeply in the form of the virtues, by allowing their dispositions to take on the right shape, by interpreting the world in a more correct manner. It is unclear how technologies would be of any use in these endeavors. The only way to truly go beyond these aspects of human existence technologically, to exceed human nature, would be for technologies to allow a completely altered form of phenomenological existence. And this is what some transhumanists promise. But at this point, these writers are necessarily silent about what this kind of existence would be like. Lacking such a description, though, it is unclear why we should value, desire, or work for such an altered form of existence. It can only arise from a blind faith in progress or a deep self-hatred, a hatred of our way of being in the world.⁵³

Christian ethicists thus have much to lose by taking the transhumanist framings of these issues at face value. As McKenny noted in an early paper on this

---

51. Nick Bostrom, "Why I Want to Be a Posthuman When I Grow Up," in *The Transhumanist Reader*, ed. Max More and Natasha Vita-More (Malden: Wiley-Blackwell, 2013), 32.

52. In general, this points to the failure in transhumanism to understand the role of classic works in artistic traditions as scholars such as Alasdair MacIntyre or David Tracy discuss.

53. McKenny, "Transcendence, Technological Enhancement, and Christian Theology."

topic, technological projects "turn inchoate desires and purposes into determinate projects that come to assume a certain priority and urgency (including a moral priority and urgency) in our lives. . . . Biomedical technology . . . increasingly sets the agenda for how we understand and act on ourselves."[54] It is necessary, as he has done, to turn to a proper phenomenology of our capacities.[55] Otherwise, Christians will misunderstand human experience and become distracted from their ultimate goal: eternal life received as a fruit of our relationship with Christ. It would be wise to follow McKenny by refocusing our efforts to judge technologies by their ability to contribute to that end. Insofar as ethicists critique transhumanism, it should not be done on the grounds that it would surpass human nature. Rather, the problem is that because of its biostatistical framing it misrepresents what it means to be human.[56]

---

54. Gerald McKenny, "Technologies of Desire: Theology, Ethics, and the Enhancement of Human Traits," *Theology Today* 59, no. 1 (2002): 102.

55. Gerald McKenny, *To Relieve the Human Condition: Bioethics, Technology, and the Body* (Albany: State University of New York Press, 1997), 211–26.

56. I would like to thank Michael Mawson and Paul Martens for organizing this volume and inviting me to be a part of it. Joseph Davis and Cristina Batt provided helpful comments on earlier versions of this chapter. Most of all, I would like to thank Jerry McKenny with whom I first explored many of the topics I address here.

Chapter 13

THE NORMATIVE STATUS OF HUMAN BIOLOGICAL NATURE AND ECOLOGY

Paul Martens

I first learned about Van Rensselaer Potter from Gerald McKenny. We were sitting in an overly crowded restaurant at a forgettable American Academy of Religion Annual Meeting eating the sort of unremarkable food one eats late on a Saturday night. That particular conversation, however, has stuck with me like a Texas grass burr sticks to new shoelaces. McKenny remarked that we were nearing the fiftieth anniversary of the invention of the term "bioethics," which was coined in 1970 by Potter.[1] I smiled and nodded approvingly as if I knew exactly what he was talking about. He continued, immediately qualifying his remark by noting that bioethics, for Potter, was expansive and inclusive of the depth and breadth of ecology. Again, I nodded approvingly in my ignorance, and the conversation continued in another direction.

Immediately after that conversation, I sought out Potter's *Bioethics: Bridge to the Future* and *Global Bioethics: Building on the Leopold Legacy*.[2] In them, I discovered an articulation of bioethics as "biology combined with diverse humanistic knowledge forging a science that sets a system of medical and environmental priorities for acceptable survival."[3] While Potter is no theological ethicist and his

---

1. This claim is not uncontested, and some suggest a polygenesis of the term. See, for example, W. T. Reich, "The Word 'Bioethics': Its Birth and the Legacies of Those Who Shaped It," *Kennedy Institute of Ethics Journal* 4, no. 4 (1994): 319–35; and Reich, "The Word 'Bioethics': The Struggle Over Its Earliest Meanings," *Kennedy Institute of Ethics Journal* 5, no. 1 (1995): 19–34.

2. Van Rensselaer Potter, *Bioethics: A Bridge to the Future* (Englewood Cliffs: Prentice Hall, 1971); and Potter, *Global Bioethics: Building on the Leopold Legacy* (East Lansing: Michigan State University Press, 1988).

3. This is the definition offered boldly on the front cover of Potter's *Global Bioethics*. The closest the text itself comes to reiterating this definition is the slightly different claim that bioethics is "a system of morality based on biological knowledge and human values, with the human species accepting responsibility for its own survival and for the preservation of the natural environment" (153–4).

texts certainly show their age, it seemed to me that he pointed toward a trajectory that theologically trained bioethicists have generally ignored. And, what really began to haunt me was a simple question: even though McKenny has written extensively on bioethics for years and he has known about Potter's work for many of those same years, why did he never follow Potter's provocation by self-consciously narrating bioethics within the larger context of the natural world? Or, to rephrase in a slightly more critical tone, is there something in McKenny's understanding of bioethics that forecloses the possibility of integrating it organically within broader ecological considerations?

Shortly thereafter, I realized that McKenny had started writing about human biological nature and the normative significance of created order.[4] I immediately wondered: were these the first steps toward an expanded notion of bioethics in McKenny's thought, whether intended or not? In the pages that follow, I attempt to continue the conversation with McKenny around Potter's basic insight that began on that nondescript November weekend by reconsidering the ecological entailments of McKenny's appeal to the normative status of human biological nature. To do so, the following analysis requires three steps: (1) clarifying McKenny's definition of human biological nature; (2) testing entailments of McKenny's category in relation to developments in evolutionary biology; and (3) offering a preliminary assessment of the possibility of expanding McKenny's notion of the normative status of human biological nature to engage the full biological context of human nature.

The Normative Status of Human Biological Nature

McKenny's full-throated embrace of human biological nature is articulated with predictable precision in *Biotechnology, Human Nature, and Christian Ethics*.[5] In the context and for the purposes of evaluating biotechnological advances, McKenny appeals to a particular understanding of the normative status of human biological nature.[6] To be clear, the normative significance "has to do (though not exclusively

---

4. One of the earliest articles in this vein is "Evolution, Biotechnology, and the Normative Significance of Created Order," *Toronto Journal of Theology* 31, no. 1 (2015): 15–26. And, over the years, it appears that McKenny's work at Notre Dame's Reilly Center for Science, Technology, and Values frequently placed him in conversations that would be fruitful for this exploration. See, for example, Phillip R. Sloan, Gerald McKenny, and Kathleen Eggleson, eds., *Darwin in the Twenty-First Century: Nature, Humanity, God* (Notre Dame: University of Notre Dame Press, 2015).

5. Gerald McKenny, *Biotechnology, Human Nature, and Christian Ethics* (Cambridge: Cambridge University Press, 2018).

6. One of McKenny's concerns with the consistent use of "human biological nature" seems to be that the insertion of "biological" might narrow or constrain all that is meant by human nature to the biological (*Biotechnology, Human Nature, and Christian Ethics*, 3).

or reductively) with the biological aspect of human nature as a constituent of the created order or the human person; as a ground of human rights or good, of personal identity, or of agency; or as a bearer of the meaning or purpose for which God created human beings."[7] In a more crass framing, he is simply asking something like: what is the point of our "biological functions and traits and the characteristics and capacities they underwrite" in light of biotechnology?[8]

To be clear, McKenny consistently holds the baseline theological convictions that (a) human nature is created by God and (b) ethical reflection therefore arises "as a requirement of respect for God as Creator and for what God has created."[9] The critical interventions and constructive suggestions offered by McKenny cannot be understood or sustained apart from these convictions. Of course, there are possible disagreements with either the basic convictions or McKenny's conclusions drawn from these convictions. The following thought project, however, will assume both the basic convictions internal to McKenny's position and the constructive posture he derives from them in an attempt to extrapolate potential trajectories for integrating bioethics within the broader concerns of ecology. Therefore, illuminating the detailed contours of McKenny's construction of human biological nature is the first and fundamental step of my argument.

By the time McKenny arrives at his preferred understanding of human biological nature in *Biotechnology, Human Nature, and Christian Ethics*, he has already examined three competing options. In essence, he has flagged the two polar extremes as off limits—human nature as given and completed (NS_1) and human nature as indetermined, open-ended, and malleable (NS_3)—while arguing that human nature itself is insufficient to ground genuine human goods or rights (NS_2).[10] Against this background, McKenny argues that

> our creaturely nature suits or equips us for a particular form of life with God that was God's purpose in creating us. However they may have come about in time (and whatever is eventually to become of them in time . . .), we have the natural

Undoubtedly, this is a well-founded concern. On the other hand, one might also raise the concern that eliding the language of "biological" here might have the opposite effect, namely, it might narrow or constrain the notion of human nature in a way that ignores or undermines its inescapable rootedness in biological existence. We will return to this concern in the pages that follow.

7. McKenny, *Biotechnology, Human Nature, and Christian Ethics*, 13.
8. Ibid., 24.
9. Ibid.
10. McKenny codes the normative status of these positions with (NS_x). In this context, I will prescind from evaluating the accuracy of McKenny's selection of illustrative representatives for each of these competing positions. My argument is primarily interested in McKenny's own construction, though I would also note that McKenny himself recognizes the heuristic and typological nature of his description as distinct from the theological dexterity of individual representatives.

traits and powers we happen to have because it is these traits and powers, created by God, that constitute our *capacity* to enjoy the life with God for which God has determined us (that is, the traits and power in, by, or through which we live our life with God) even as the actual *capability* to enjoy that life (that is, the ability or power to bring about and maintain our life with God) depends entirely on God's grace and is not given with our creaturely capacity.[11]

In short, McKenny's preferred normative status (NS_4) is linked to human biological nature "as the condition for the particular form of life with God for which God created us"; it is good to the extent that it suits human beings for life with God; it is a finished work to the extent that it is the nature through which, by God's grace, we enjoy God.[12]

Throughout his account of NS_4, McKenny reiterates a common refrain: "life with God." Whether exemplified in the union of human life with God's own life in Jesus Christ,[13] or described in the form of imitation, witness,[14] fellowship,[15] or imaging God,[16] the determining purpose of human biological nature is life with God. This life, however long it lasts, is lived out in the metanarrative of creation and redemption,[17] while the unconditional capability for such a life is found beyond itself in God's grace.[18] Substantively, the refrain contextualizes and bounds natural life; rhetorically, the repeated nature of the refrain emphasizes precisely how "woefully brief" biological life is in relation to God's eternal life.[19] Yet, even though finite, NS_4 assumes that our biological nature is created for life with God.

To illuminate precisely how this is the case, McKenny draws upon Karl Barth's anthropology and its correspondence to the threefold nature of Christ: relationality, body-soul composition, and temporality. Each of these anthropological aspects entails some normative force within human biological nature. By taking on temporality, God in Christ shares eternity with humanity. By raising Jesus from the dead, God frees humans from the boundedness of temporality. Temporality, therefore, is incorporated within and subordinated to the intra-Trinitarian relationship of love that God in Godself shares with humanity. In temporality, humans image and participate in life with God by sharing the gift of God's love. Or, in McKenny's terms, "human temporality exhibits the same thing as relationality, albeit in a derivative form."[20]

---

11. McKenny, *Biotechnology, Human Nature, and Christian Ethics*, 147–8.
12. Ibid., 148.
13. Ibid.
14. Ibid., 151.
15. Ibid., 159.
16. Ibid., 151–2.
17. Ibid., 152.
18. Ibid., 147.
19. Ibid., 161.
20. Ibid., 166.

Stepping back, it ought to be noted that McKenny is aware that his attention to temporality is asymmetrical to the attention he pays to the other aspects of Barth's anthropology. Yet, attention to temporality seems to be the most important anthropological aspect for articulating a normative response to biotechnology. Attending to the limits of temporality serves the purposes of (a) highlighting that humans, as created by God, already have the natural capacities necessary for life with God (and therefore nothing more provided by biotechnology is necessary) and (b) the recognition of impending death ought to determine the actions that characterize the shape of how one images Christ during one's life (and therefore the fixation of prolonging or radically altering life is a refusal of life with God as intended). In sum, McKenny concludes that "whatever case may be made for the contribution of biotechnological enhancement to the meaning and purpose of our biological nature will not be made on the grounds that the relevant intervention renders our characteristics or capacities better suited to life with God than they now are."[21]

Placing Human Biological Nature

As *Biotechnology, Human Nature, and Christian Ethics* draws to a close, McKenny readily admits that Barth's account of human nature is somewhat abstract.[22] And, McKenny's use of temporality as the primary means of situating human life, of giving a name to human situatedness, has a tendency to also render the normative entailments necessary for "life with God" rather abstract. Certainly, within debates about the desired quality and prolongation of individual lives, a strong affirmation of the limits of one's biological life might be necessary. In the context of human biological existence within creation ecologically considered,[23] however, this claim may be more ambiguous. To claim that "life with God" is the purpose of human existence, it may be necessary to reiterate the limits of biological life against idolizations of conservation, resilience, and sustainability, on one hand, and against acquisitive and extractive consumption on the other. Yet, temporalities in the global context are radically uneven and increasingly correlated qualitatively and quantitatively with how much power one has in the process of ecological engineering. For example, the wealthiest and highest polluting countries enjoy the prospect of more and healthier temporality than the poorest and frequently lowest polluting countries.[24]

---

21. Ibid., 179–80.
22. Ibid., 182.
23. What I mean to imply here is that the biological nature of an individual human being is necessarily intertwined within a larger biological web without which human biological nature could not exist. I take this claim to be noncontroversial but underappreciated.
24. This is not to claim that a uniform allotment of temporality is assumed in discussions about biotechnology. Rather, it is to claim that placing humans in a particular environment

To my mind, this reality points to the limits of Barth's anthropological framework as it is employed to articulate the normative status of human biological nature. Specifically, what I mean here is that the biological place of humans in creation is underdeveloped in NS_4. After all, space and matter are correlated to time and would necessarily be intimately involved and morally implicated in any qualitative or quantitative analysis of temporal existence. In theological terms, one might also say that the strong emphasis on an eschatological telos present in Barth's version of NS_4 rhetorically, and perhaps substantively, tilts the entire discussion away from attending carefully to the earthly placement of human life within the biological context of creation. Along these lines, McKenny's persistent use of "created" and "natural" in place of biological seems inadvertently to introduce a conceptual slippage of sorts, since both terms can also be used to reference human nature as it exists beyond the limits of temporal biological existence.

All that said, one might step back at this point and ask a fairly straightforward question like the following: While I recognize environmental destruction is a really bad thing, have we not made an artificial and probably unfair transition in the argument by exporting McKenny's notion of NS_4 into a categorically different context beyond his engagement with biotechnology? Perhaps. But, I do not think this is the case, and here is why: if McKenny, against the positive interventions of biotechnology, argues for an account of human biological nature sufficient for life with God, it stands to reason that he would also be interested in arguing, against the deleterious effects of ecological destruction, that an account of human biological nature sufficient for life with God ought to be preserved. In short, the ecological context of human biological existence is not simply an optional expansion of McKenny's engagement with biotechnology. It is integral to McKenny's concern with both the goodness of creation (which seems obvious) and the volatility of the category of human biological nature (which seems less obvious). I will address the latter concern, first, by introducing the concept of niche construction and its potential to revise human biological nature as we know it.

Very briefly, niche construction has much in common with ecosystem engineering. In both cases, organisms actively modify environmental conditions, and beaver dams are a classic example of such a modification. The dam is built for the purposes of engineering a revised ecosystem for the beavers. It alters the former river ecosystem in ways that are favorable for the beavers' existence: the deeper water behind the dam protects beavers from select predators, lodges for habitation are built with underwater access in the artificial pond, and food is deposited at the

---

necessarily refuses temporality as an abstraction and acknowledges that temporal limits of human life are frequently conditioned directly and indirectly by the actions of other human beings. On this, the language of slow violence, summarized by Rob Nixon as a violence of delayed destruction—through toxic waste, climate change, deforestation, acidifying oceans, for example—that is dispersed across time and space, is exceptionally helpful. See Nixon, *Slow Violence and the Environmentalism of the Poor* (Cambridge, MA: Harvard University Press, 2011), 2.

bottom of the pond for consumption below the ice during winter months. This kind of ecosystem engineering, however, has consequences well beyond its intended effects for the beavers. Knock-on effects are felt by different species—fish migrations can be interrupted, other species may be affected by local flooding, and changes in water temperature caused by the dams may alter what organisms can survive downstream. Of course, humans perform this type of ecosystem engineering on a much grander scale, and we are just beginning a massive reckoning with this reality.

But this is not the end of the story. The category of niche construction extends beyond ecosystem engineering in a way that reflects its origins in evolutionary biology.[25] Specifically, niche construction theory recognizes that these changes in ecosystems are drivers of selection that may produce novel evolutionary outcomes. In the case of humans, as with other organisms, niche construction directs human evolution, including developments in cognitive capabilities.[26] It allows for feedback loops that are shaped by but also play a significant role in shaping the trajectory of human evolution,[27] and thereby the trajectory of human biological nature. In short, niche construction poses the same challenges to Christian ethics on a local, regional, and global scale that biotechnology poses on an individual level. The timescale of niche construction may have a much wider horizon than popular conceptions of biotechnology, and the indirect character of niche construction may seem benign relative to the direct interventions assumed with biotechnology, yet the very same principles of biotechnology used in medicine are also energetically employed in agricultural, industrial, and environmental contexts, and they have been for millennia, whether intended or not.[28] One might justifiably argue that niche construction itself played a significant role in the emergence of human biological nature as we understand it today.

25. While the term itself was coined by Oxford biologist John Odling-Smee in 1988, prototypical understandings had been circulating decades earlier. See F. J. Odling-Smee, "Niche Constructing Phenotypes," in *The Role of Behavior in Evolution*, ed. Plotkin (Cambridge, MA: MIT Press; 1988), 73–132. In this context, I make no attempt to provide a complex or nuanced understanding of niche construction beyond the basic principles outlined here.

26. Kevin Laland, Blake Mathews, and Marcus W. Feldman, "An Introduction to Niche Construction Theory," *Evolutionary Ecology* 30 (2016): 191–202.

27. See Agustin Fuentes, "Human Niche, Human Behavior, Human Nature," *Interface Focus* 7: 72016013620160136 http://doi.org/10.1098/rsfs.2016.0136

28. In this context, a generic definition of "biotechnology" is assumed: "biotechnology uses either living material or biological products to create new products for their use in various pharmaceutical, medical, agricultural, and environmental applications, with the ultimate goal to benefit humanity." See Ashish Swarup Verma, Shishir Agrahari, Shruti Rastogi, and Anchal Singh, "Biotechnology in the Realm of History," *Journal of Pharmacy and BioAllied Sciences* 3, no. 3 (2011): 321–3. Certainly, the exponential growth of technological capabilities means that biotechnological interventions in medicine have almost immediate and profound impacts in the contemporary world. That said, the same could be said of interventions in the agricultural, industrial, and environmental contexts as well.

With this recognition in view, we return to the connection highlighted by Potter. In his own words: "Bioethics, as I envision it, would attempt to generate wisdom, the knowledge of how to use knowledge for social good from a realistic knowledge of *[human] biological nature* and the biological world."²⁹ Writing in the 1960s, Potter's framing of teenage pregnancy, abortion, population growth, pesticides, and perpetual progress under the umbrella of a science of survival appears radically insufficient—that is, anthropological and utilitarian—on McKenny's terms. Yet, what Potter got right (and what Lisa Sideris points to in a very different way)³⁰ is the deep interdependence between human biological nature and the evolving biological world. This recognition need not be understood as a reversion to NS_3 (human nature as indetermined, open-ended, and malleable), but it might require McKenny to further develop NS_4 in a manner that retains creation as a "good and finished work"³¹ in the context of the ongoing irreversible anthropocentric alterations of our air, land, water, and global biome that will, inevitably, yield either species extinction or evolutionary adaptation that inflects human biological nature. Framed this way, the circumscribed delimitations of potential biotechnological alterations of human biological nature are exploded; framed this way, appeals to a creation-eschatology metanarrative in which God realizes the good rings either morbidly apocalyptic, tragically impassive, or naively optimistic. Yet, I am convinced McKenny embraces none of the above—his account of God's good grace perfecting our nature is too pervasive for these simplistic dispositions.

Continuing the Conversation

As indicated in the opening paragraphs of this brief chapter, the provocation for this line of questioning can be traced indirectly back to McKenny himself. Further, in *Biotechnology, Human Nature, and Christian Ethics*, he slips a very important clarification into the footnotes:

> What happens with and to our creaturely nature is therefore of the greatest significance, and it is our creaturely nature that is directly implicated by biotechnology. The effects of biotechnology on our relationality, body-soul composition, and temporality have to do with the conditions in which we live with God and one another as reconciled sinners and heirs of redemption.³²

---

29. Potter, *Bioethics*, 26 (emphasis mine).
30. See Lisa Sideris, *Environmental Ethics, Ecological Theology, and Natural Selection* (New York: Columbia University Press, 2003).
31. McKenny, *Biotechnology, Human Nature, and Christian Ethics*, 186.
32. Ibid., 171n.

If this is the case, the question is not whether McKenny is already embroiled in ecological ethics but when he will further develop and share his theological reflections about ecology and human nature in print.

On his own terms, the Barthian threefold creaturely nature indicated previously could be a vehicle for such an analysis. But, instead of leaning heavily on temporality (as in the case of biotechnology), perhaps he might develop relationality or the body-soul composition of human nature further in normative directions. His cursory treatment of the normative implications of Barth's affirmation of humans as a body-soul composition in the final pages of his text intimate one possible trajectory. For McKenny, Barth's notion of body-soul composition "requires respect for bodily integrity," and the standard bioethical language of "safety" at least partially captures what this claim implies.[33] In the ecological context, however, anthropogenic threats to bodily integrity are omnipresent—from airborne carcinogens to inorganic compounds floating in water supplies to severe weather caused by climate change—and their causes are diverse and dispersed. Recognizing this, McKenny might then follow the Barthian position sketched by Willis Jenkins, allowing that "God acts redemptively toward humanity, 'pitying and receiving this threatened and needy creature within a threatened cosmos of God's creatures,' by inviting humans into God's nurturing and guarding act for the whole of creation." In this manner, humans become "guardians" of creation, partners in the covenant that testifies that God's Yes as the Creator has been spoken.[34]

Or, in attending to the normative role of relationality in human biological nature, McKenny may find inspiration in the neo-Barthian direction pointed to by Colin Gunton—and appropriated masterfully by Michael Northcott—in which a Trinitarian doctrine of creation reestablishes the ontological ground for materiality, substantiality, and relationality, the latter expanded to all that is created, including the embodiedness of all life. Within this framework, human existence in the interim, as the narrative of redemption unfolds, is continually shaped by the restoration of relationality "between persons and God, and between persons and created order in terms of their own bodies, of human society, and of the embodied life of the biosphere."[35] This conclusion, too, would likely conform to the NS_4 position developed by McKenny in *Biotechnology, Human Nature, and Christian Ethics*.

Whatever the case may be, and whatever trajectory McKenny chooses, I dare to dream that he will carry his conviction that "what happens with and to our creaturely nature is therefore of the greatest significance" into the realm of ecology. My hope is that this brief and long-delayed response to his aside concerning Van Resselaer Potter might provoke attention to that task.

---

33. Ibid., 192.

34. Willis Jenkins, *Ecologies of Grace: Environmental Ethics and Christian Theology* (Oxford: Oxford University Press, 2008), 173–4.

35. Michael Northcott, *The Environment and Christian Ethics* (Cambridge: Cambridge University Press, 1996), 222–3. See also Colin Gunton, *The One, The Three, and the Many: God, Creation, and the Culture of Modernity* (Cambridge: Cambridge University Press, 1993).

LIST OF GERALD MCKENNY'S PUBLICATIONS

Authored Books

Karl Barth's Moral Thought. Oxford: Oxford University Press, 2021.
Biotechnology, Human Nature, and Christian Ethics. Cambridge: Cambridge University Press, 2018.
The Analogy of Grace: Karl Barth's Moral Theology. Oxford: Oxford University Press, 2010.
To Relieve the Human Condition: Bioethics, Technology, and the Body. Albany: State University of New York Press, 1997.

Edited Books and Journal Issues

Darwin in the Twenty-First Century: Nature, Humanity, and God, edited by Phillip R. Sloan, Gerald McKenny, and Kathleen K. Eggleson. Notre Dame: University of Notre Dame Press, 2015.
Altering Nature, Vol. 1: Concepts of "Nature" and the "Natural" in Biotechnology Debates, and Vol. 2: Religion, Biotechnology, and Public Policy, edited by Baruch A. Brody, B. Andrew Lustig, and Gerald P. McKenny. New York: Springer Science Press, 2008.
"Genre and Persuasion in Religious Ethics." [Special issue] *Journal of Religious Ethics* 33 (2005): 398–407.
The Ethical, edited by Edith Wyschogrod and Gerald P. McKenny. New York: Blackwell Publishers, 2003.
"Enhancements and the Quest for Perfection." [Special topic issue] *Christian Bioethics* 4, no. 2 (1999): 99–103.
Theological Analyses of the Clinical Encounter, edited by Gerald P. McKenny and Jonathan R. Sande. Dordrecht: Kluwer Academic Press, 1994.

Journal Articles and Book Chapters

"Barth on Love." In *The Wiley Blackwell Companion to Karl Barth: Barth and Dogmatics*, edited by George Hunsinger and Keith L. Johnson, 381–91. Hoboken: Wiley Blackwell, 2020.
"The Rich Young Ruler and Christian Ethics: A Proposal." *Journal of the Society of Christian Ethics* 40, no. 1 (2020): 59–76.
"Ethics." In *The Oxford Handbook of Karl Barth*, edited by Paul Dafydd Jones and Paul T. Nimmo, 482–98. Oxford: Oxford University Press, 2019.

"Freedom, Responsibility, and Moral Agency." In *The Oxford Handbook of Dietrich Bonhoeffer*, edited by Philip Ziegler and Michael Mawson, 306–20. Oxford: Oxford University Press, 2019.

"Human Nature and Biotechnological Enhancement: Some Theological Considerations." *Studies in Christian Ethics* 32, no. 2 (2019): 229–40.

"Finitude, Freedom, and Biomedicine: An Engagement with Gilbert Meilaender's Bioethics." *Studies in Christian Ethics* 30, no. 2 (2017): 148–57.

"Karl Barth and the Plight of Protestant Ethics." In *Freedom of a Christian Ethicist*, edited by Brian Brock and Michael Mawson, 17–38. London: T&T Clark Bloomsbury, 2016.

"The Strength to Be Patient." [Coauthored with Stanley Hauerwas] *Christian Bioethics* 22 (2016): 5–20.

"Creation, Evolution, and Biotechnology: Can Christian Conceptions of Created Order Rule Out Biotechnological Alteration of Human Nature?" *Toronto Journal of Theology* 31 (2015): 15–26.

"Freed by God for God: Human Agency in Karl Barth's Evangelical Theology and Other Late Writings." In *Karl Barth in America: The 50th Anniversary of Barth's Evangelical Theology*, edited by Bruce McCormack and Clifford Anderson, 119–38. Grand Rapids: Eerdmans, 2015.

"Response to Paul Nimmo" (response to Paul Nimmo's review article of The Analogy of Grace), *Scottish Journal of Theology* 68 (2015): 98–105.

"Karl Barth's Concept of Responsibility." In *"Kein Mensch, der der Verantwortung entgehen könnte." Verantwortungsethik in theologischer, philosophischer und religionswissenschaftlicher Perspektive*, edited by Jürgen Boomgaarden and Martin Leiner, 67–93. Freiburg: Herder-Verlag, 2014.

"Biotechnology and the Normative Significance of Human Nature: A Contribution from Theological Anthropology." *Studies in Christian Ethics* 26 (2013): 18–36.

"Disability and the Christian Ethics of Solidarity." *Fu Jen International Religious Studies* 6 (2012): 1–20.

"Transcendence, Technological Enhancement, and Christian Theology." In *Transhumanism and Transcendence: Christian Hope in an Age of Technological Enhancement*, edited by Ronald Cole-Turner, 177–92. Washington: Georgetown University Press, 2011.

"Desire for the Transcendent: Engelhardt and Christian Ethics." In *At the Roots of Christian Bioethics: Critical Essays on the Thought of H. Tristram Engelhardt, Jr.*, edited by Mark J. Cherry and Ana I. Smith, 105–31. Beverly: Scrivener Publishing, 2009.

"Moral Disagreement and the Limits of Reason: Reflections on MacIntyre and Ratzinger." In *Intractable Disputes about the Natural Law: Alasdair MacIntyre and Critics*, edited by Lawrence Cunningham, 195–226. Notre Dame: University of Notre Dame Press, 2009.

"Nature as Given, Nature as Guide, Nature as Natural Kinds: Return to Nature in the Ethics of Human Biotechnology." In *Without Nature? A New Condition for Theology*, edited by David Albertson and Cabell King, 152–77. New York: Fordham University Press, 2009.

"Biodiversity and Biotechnology." Authored by Nicholas Agar, David Lodge, Gerald McKenny, and LaReesa Wolfenbarger. In *Altering Nature: How Religions Assess Biotechnology*, vol. 2, coedited by Baruch A. Brody, B. Andrew Lustig, and Gerald McKenny, 285–319. New York: Springer Science Press, 2008.

"(Re)placing Ethics: Jean-Luc Marion and the Horizon of Modern Ethics." In *Counter-Experiences: Reading Jean-Luc Marion*, edited by Kevin Hart, 339–55. Notre Dame: University of Notre Dame Press, 2007.

"Biomedical Enhancement Technologies: Beyond Humanism and Posthumanism." In *Science and Religion in the Age of Crisis: Proceedings of the Fourth Yoko Civilization International Conference*, vol. 2, 129–41. Yoko Civilization Institute, 2007 (revised version published as "Ethics of Regenerative Medicine: Beyond Humanism and Posthumanism." In *The Bioethics of Regenerative Medicine*, edited by King-Tak Ip, 155–69. Springer Science Press, 2009).

"Genre and Persuasion in Religious Ethics: An Introduction." *Journal of Religious Ethics* 33 (2005): 397–407 (reprinted in *Comparative Religious Ethics, Vol. III: Meaning and Understanding in Comparative Religious Ethics*, edited by Charles Mathewes, Matthew Puffer, and Mark Storslee. New York: Routledge, 2015).

"Responsibility." In *The Oxford Handbook of Theological Ethics*, edited by Gilbert Meilaender and William Werpehowski, 237–53. Oxford: Oxford University Press, 2005.

"Technology." In *A Companion to Religious Ethics*, edited by William Schweiker, 459–68. Hoboken: Blackwell Publishers, 2004.

"Ethical Considerations in the Integration of Religion and Psychotherapy: Three Perspectives." Authored by James W. Lomax, Samuel E. Karff, and Gerald P. McKenny, *Psychiatric Clinics of North America* 25 (2002): 547–59.

"Technologies of Desire: Theology, Ethics, and the Enhancement of Human Traits." *Theology Today* 59 (2002): 90–103.

"Religion and Gene Therapy: The End of One Debate, the Beginning of Another." In *A Companion to Genetics*, edited by Justine Burley and John Harris, 287–301. Blackwell Publishers, 2002.

"Critical Care Medicine and the Catholic Tradition: Reflections on the Consensus Statement." *Christian Bioethics* 7 (2001): 203–9.

"Divine Grace, Human Care, and the Limits of Morality: A Protestant Perspective on Physician-Assisted Suicide." In *Considering Religious Traditions in Bioethics: Christian and Jewish Voices*, edited by Mary Jo Iozzio, 107–17. Scranton: University of Scranton Press, 2001.

"Religion, Biotechnology, and the Integrity of Nature: A Critical Examination." In *Claiming Power over Life: Religion and Biotechnology Policy*, edited by Mark J. Hanson, 169–91. Washington: Georgetown University Press, 2001.

"Heterogeneity and Ethical Deliberation: Casuistry, Narrative, and Event in the Ethics of Karl Barth." *Annual of the Society of Christian Ethics* 20 (2000): 205–24.

"Human Enhancement Uses of Biotechnology, Ethics, Therapy vs. Enhancement." In *Encyclopedia of Ethical, Legal and Policy Issues in Biotechnology*, edited by Thomas Murray and Maxwell J. Mehlman, 507–15. Hoboken: Wiley & Sons, 2000.

"Gene Therapy, Ethics, Religious Perspectives." In *The Encyclopedia of Ethical, Legal, and Policy Issues in Biotechnology*, edited by Thomas Murray and Maxwell Mehlman, 300–11. Hoboken: Wiley and Sons, 2000.

"The Integrity of the Body: Critical Remarks on a Persistent Theme in Bioethics." In *Persons and Their Bodies: Rights, Responsibilities, Relationships*, edited by Thomas Bole and Mark J. Cherry, 353–61. New York: Kluwer Academic Press, 1999.

"A Bad Disease, a Fatal Cure: Sterilization may be Permissible but the Autonomy of Medicine is Not." *Christian Bioethics* 4 (1998): 100–9.

"Enhancements and the Ethical Significance of Vulnerability." In *Enhancing Human Capacities: Conceptual Complexities and Ethical Implications*, edited by Eric Parens, 222–37. Washington: Georgetown University Press, 1998.

"Bioethics, the Body, and the Legacy of Bacon." In *On Moral Medicine*, 2nd edition, edited by Stephen E. Lammers and Allen Verhey, 308–23. Grand Rapids: Eerdmans, 1998.

Reprinted in *On Moral Medicine*, 3rd edition, edited by M. Therese Lysaught, Joseph J. Kotva, Jr., with Stephen E. Lammers and Allen Verhey, 398–409. Grand Rapids: Eerdmans, 2012.

"An Anthropological Bioethics: Hermeneutical or Critical? A Response to Carl Elliott." In *The Philosophy of Medicine and Bioethics*, edited by Chester Burns and Ronald Carson, 213–20. Kluwer Academic Press, 1997.

"Technology, Authority and the Loss of Tradition: Religious and Cultural Roots of American Bioethics." In *Japanese and Western Bioethics: Studies in Moral Diversity*, edited by Kazumasa Hoshino, 73–87. Amsterdam: Kluwer Academic Press, 1997.

"Physician-Assisted Death: A Pyrrhic Victory for Secular Bioethics." In *Theology and Secular Bioethics*, edited by Earl E. Shelp, 145–58. Amsterdam: Kluwer Academic Press, 1996.

"Religious and Cultural Roots of American Bioethics." In *Report from the US-Japan Bioethics Congress—1994 Tokyo Conference*, 89–99. US-Japan Bioethics Congress, 1995, Tokyo (in Japanese).

"Whose Tradition? Which Enlightenment? What Content? Hauerwas, Engelhardt, Capaldi, and the Future of Christian Bioethics." *Christian Bioethics* 1 (1995): 84–96.

"Theology, Ethics, and the Clinical Encounter." In *Theological Analyses of the Clinical Encounter*, edited by Gerald P. McKenny and Jonathan R. Sande, vii–xx. Amsterdam: Kluwer Academic Press, 1994.

"Personal Religious Positions: Protestantism." In *On the New Frontiers of Genetics and Religion*, J. Robert Nelson, 163–6. Grand Rapids: Eerdmans, 1994.

"A Qualified Bioethic? Particularity in James Gustafson and Stanley Hauerwas." *Journal of Medicine and Philosophy* 18 (1993): 511–29.

"Applied Ethics and Its Discontents," *Second Opinion* 17, no. 2 (October, 1991): 131–5.

"From Consensus to Consent: A Plea for a More Communicative Ethic." *Soundings* 74 (1991): 427–57.

"Theological Objectivism as Empirical Theology: H. Richard Niebuhr and the Liberal Tradition." *American Journal of Theology and Philosophy* 12 (1991): 19–33.

"Values Interpretation: A New Role for Hospital Ministry." Authored by Christopher G. Fichtner and Gerald McKenny, *Journal of Religion and Health* 30 (1991): 109–18.

BIBLIOGRAPHY

Adams, Robert. *Finite and Infinite Goods: A Framework for Ethics*. Oxford: Oxford University Press, 1999.
Adams, Robert. "Saints." *The Journal of Philosophy* 81, no. 7 (1984): 392–401.
Agamben, Giorgio. *Homo Sacer. Sovereign Power and Bare Life*. Translated by Daniel Heller-Roazen. Stanford: Stanford University Press, 1998.
Alter, Robert. *The Hebrew Bible, Vol. 1: The Five Books of Moses: A Translation with Commentary*. New York: W. W. Norton, 2019.
Arendt, Hannah. *The Human Condition*. Chicago: University of Chicago Press, 1998.
Aristotle. *Nicomachean Ethics*. Translated by W. D. Ross. Oxford: Oxford University Press, 1961.
Arner, Neil. "Precedents and Prospects for Incorporating Natural Law in Protestant Ethics." *Scottish Journal of Theology* 69, no. 4 (2016): 375–88.
Aquinas, Thomas. *Commentary on Aristotle's Metaphysics*. South Bend: St. Augustine's Press, 1995.
Aquinas, Thomas. *Summa Theologica*. Translated by Fathers of the English Dominican Province. Westminster: Christian Classics, 1981.
Augustine. *The City of God against the Pagans*. Translated and edited by R. W. Dyson. Cambridge: Cambridge University Press, 1998.
Augustine. *Confessions*, 2nd ed. Translated by F. J. Sheed. Indianapolis: Hackett, 2006.
Augustine. *Teaching Christianity*. Translated by Edmund Hill. New York: New City Press, 1996.
Augustine. *The Trinity*. Edited by John Rotelle. Translated by Edmund Hill. New York: New City Press, 2012.
Ballor, Jordan. "Christ in Creation: Bonhoeffer's Orders of Preservation and Natural Theology." *Journal of Religion* 86, no. 1 (2006): 1–22.
Banman, Joel. *Reading in the Presence of Christ: A Study of Bonhoeffer's Bibliology and Exegesis*. London: T&T Clark Bloomsbury, 2021.
Barclay, John. *Paul and the Gift*. Grand Rapids: Eerdmans, 2015.
Baron, Marcia. "A Kantian Take on the Supererogatory." *Journal of Applied Philosophy* 33, no. 4 (November 2016): 347–62.
Barth, Karl. *Church Dogmatics*, 14 Volumes. Edited by Geoffrey William Bromiley and Thomas F. Torrance. Edinburgh: T&T Clark, 1956–1975.
Barth, Karl. *Community, State, and Church: Three Essays*. Garden City: Anchor Books, 1960.
Barth, Karl. *Ethics*. Translated by Geoffrey Bromiley. New York: Seabury Press, 1981.
Barth, Karl. *The Holy Spirit and the Christian Life*. Translated by R. Birch Hoyle. Louisville: Westminster John Knox, 1993.
Barth, Karl. "The Righteousness of God." In *The Word of God and the Word of Man*, translated by Douglas Horton, 9–27. Gloucester: Peter Smith, 1978.

Baumeister, Roy, Ellen Bratslavsky, Mark Muraven, and Dianne Tice. "Ego Depletion: Is the Active Self a Limited Resource?" *Journal of Personality and Social Psychology* 74, no. 5 (1998): 1252–65.

Blankenhorn, Bernhard O. P. *Mystery of Union with God: Dionysian Mysticism in St. Albert the Great and Thomas Aquinas*. Washington: Catholic University of America Press, 2015.

Bedford-Strohm, Heinrich. "Biotechnology and Public Theology: A Dialogue with Dietrich Bonhoeffer." In *Bonhoeffer and the Biosciences: An Initial Exploration*, edited by Ralph K. Wüstenberg, Stefan Heuser, and Ester Hornung, 133–45. Pieterlen: Peter Lang, 2010.

Bergson, Henri. *Matter and Memory*. Translated by Nancy Margaret Paul and W. Scott Palmer. New York: MacMillan, 1913.

Biggar, Nigel. *The Hastening that Waits: Karl Barth's Ethics*. Oxford: Oxford University Press, 1993.

Bishop, Jeffrey. "Of Minds and Brains and Cocreation: Psychopharmaceuticals and Modern Technological Imaginaries." *Christian Bioethics* 24, no. 3 (2018): 224–45.

Boehm, Christopher. *Moral Origins: The Evolution of Virtue, Altruism, and Shame*. New York: Basic Books, 2012.

Bonhoeffer, Dietrich. *Conspiracy and Imprisonment, 1940–1945, DBWE 16*. Edited by Mark S. Brocker. Translated by Lisa E. Dahill. Minneapolis: Fortress Press, 2006.

Bonhoeffer, Dietrich. *Creation and Fall, DBWE 3*. Edited by John de Gruchy. Translated by Douglas Stephen Bax. Minneapolis: Fortress Press, 1997.

Bonhoeffer, Dietrich. *Ethics, DBWE 6*. Edited by Clifford Green. Translated by Reinhard Krauss, Charles West, and Douglas W. Stott. Minneapolis: Fortress Press, 2006.

Bonhoeffer, Dietrich. *Ethik, DBW 6*. Edited by Isle Tödt, Heinz Eduard Tödt, Ernst Feil, and Clifford Green. München: Chr. Kaiser Verlag, 1992.

Bonhoeffer, Dietrich. *Life Together, DBWE 5*. Edited by Geffrey B. Kelly. Translated by Daniel W. Bloesch and James H. Burtness. Minneapolis: Fortress Press, 1996.

Bonner, Gerald. "Augustine's Conception of Deification." *Journal of Theological Studies* 37, no. 2 (1986): 369–86.

Bostrom, Nick. "Why I Want to Be a Posthuman When I Grow Up." In *The Transhumanist Reader*, edited by Max More and Natasha Vita-More, 28–53. Malden: Wiley-Blackwell, 2013.

Bowles, S. and H. Gintis. *A Cooperative Species: Human Reciprocity and Its Evolution*. Princeton: Princeton University Press, 2011.

Bowlin, John. *Contingency and Fortune in Aquinas' Ethics*. Cambridge: Cambridge University Press 1999.

Boyle, Leonard E. O. P. "The Setting of the *Summa Theologiae* of St. Thomas—Revisited." In *The Ethics of Aquinas*, edited by Stephen J. Pope, 17–29. Washington: Georgetown University Press, 2001.

Brock, Brian. "Discipline, Sport, and the Religion of Winners: Paul on Running to Win the Prize, 1 Corinthians 9:24-27." *Studies in Christian Ethics* 25, no. 1 (2012): 4–19.

Brock, Brian and Stanley Hauerwas. *Beginnings: Interrogating Hauerwas*. Edited by Kevin Hargaden. London: T&T Clark Bloomsbury, 2017.

Brown, Peter. *Through the Eye of the Needle: Wealth, the Fall of Rome, and the Making of Christianity in the West, 350–550 AD*. Oxford: Oxford University Press, 2012.

Bultmann, Rudolf. *Theology of the New Testament*, Vol. I. New York: Charles Scribner's Sons, 1951.

Bynum, Caroline Walker. *The Resurrection of the Body in Western Christianity, 200–1336*. New York: Columbia University Press, 1995.

Calvin, John. *Institutes of the Christian Tradition*. Edited by John T. McNeill. Translated by Ford Lewis Battles. Louisville: Westminster John Knox, 1960.
Canguilhem, Georges. *The Normal and the Pathological*. New York: Zone Books, 1989.
Carr, H. Wildon, A. Wolf, and C. Spearman. "Symposium: The Nature of Intelligence." *Proceedings of the Aristotelian Society, Supplementary Volumes* 5 (1925): 1–27.
Carruthers, Mary. *The Book of Memory*. New York: Cambridge University Press, 1990.
Carpenter, Angela. *Responsive Becoming: Moral Formation in Theological, Evolutionary, and Developmental Perspective*. London: T&T Clark Bloomsbury, 2019.
Chrysostom, John. *On Wealth and Poverty*. Yonkers: St Vladimir Seminary Press, 1999.
Clair, Joseph. "Wolterstorff on Love and Justice: An Augustinian Response." *Journal of Religious Ethics* 41, no. 1 (2013): 138–67.
Clark, Adam C. "The Creator Sovereign in Christ: Dietrich Bonhoeffer and Protestant Natural Law Retrieval." PhD Dissertation, University of Notre Dame, Notre Dame, 2017.
Clough, David. *On Animals: Theological Ethics*, Vol. II. London: T&T Clark Bloomsbury, 2018.
Coakley. "Evolution, Providence, and the Trinity: From Natural Cooperation to Natural Theology." *ABC Religion and Ethics*, February 6, 2019. Available online: https://www.abc.net.au/religion/evolution,-providence-and-the-trinity/10787616 (accessed July 2021).
Coakley, Sarah. "Sacrifice Regained: Evolution, Cooperation, and God." *Gifford Lectures*, 2012. Available online: https://www.giffordlectures.org/lectures/sacrifice-regained-evolution-cooperation-and-god (accessed July 2021).
Condrey, B. J. "The Possibility and Role of Supererogation in Protestant Ethics." PhD Dissertation, University of Edinburgh, 2020.
Connor, William F. "The Natural Life of Man and Its Laws: Conscience and Reason in the Theology of Dietrich Bonhoeffer." PhD Dissertation, Vanderbilt University, Nashville, 1973.
Conti, Greg. "Jean Barbeyrac, Supererogation, and the Search for a Safe Religion." *Modern Intellectual History* 13, no. 1 (2016): 1–31.
Cowley, Christopher, ed. *Supererogation*, Royal Institute of Philosophy Supplement 77. Cambridge: Cambridge University Press, 2015.
Cunningham, Lawrence, ed. *Intractable Disputes About the Natural Law: Alisdair MacIntyre and Critics*. Notre Dame: University of Notre Dame Press, 2009.
Darwall, Stephen. *Morality, Authority, and Law*. Oxford: Oxford University Press, 2013.
Davis, Joseph E. "Toward the Elimination of Subjectivity: From Francis Bacon to AI." *Social Research* 86, no. 4 (2019): 845–69.
Dawkins, Richard. *The Selfish Gene*, 2nd ed. Oxford: Oxford University Press, 1990.
DeJonge, Michael. "Respecting Rights and Fulfilling Duties: Bonhoeffer's *Formed Life* in Bioethical Perspective." In *Bonhoeffer and the Biosciences: An Initial Exploration*, edited by Ralph K. Wüstenberg, Stefan Heuser, and Ester Hornung, 109–22. Pieterlen: Peter Lang, 2010.
De Lubac, Henri. *Corpus Mysticum: The Eucharist and the Church in the Middle Ages*. Translated by G. Simmonds with R. Price and C. Stephens. Edited by L. P. Hemming and S. F. Parsons. Notre Dame: University of Notre Dame Press, 2006.
Dreher, Rod. *The Benedict Option: A Strategy for Christians in a Post-Christian Nation*. New York: Sentinel, 2017.
Drever, Matthew. "Entertaining Violence: Augustine on the Cross of Christ and the Commercialization of Suffering." *The Journal of Religion* 92, no. 3 (2012): 331–61.

Drever, Matthew. *Image, Identity, and the Forming of the Augustinian Soul*. Oxford: Oxford University Press, 2013.
Finnis, John. *Natural Law and Natural Rights*. New York: Oxford University Press, 1980.
Finstuen, Andrew. *Original Sin and Everyday Protestants*. Chapel Hill: University of North Carolina Press, 2009.
Fiorenza, Francis Schussler. "Theology as Responsible Valuation or Reflexive Equilibrium." In *The Legacy of H. Richard Niebuhr*, edited by Ronald Thiemann, 25–32. Minneapolis: Fortress Press, 1991.
Fischer, David Hackett. *Albion's Seed: Four British Folkways in America*. New York: Oxford University Press, 1989.
Flanagan, Owen. *The Really Hard Problem: Meaning in a Material World*. Cambridge, MA: MIT Press, 2007.
Flescher, Andrew. *Heroes, Saints and Ordinary Morality*. Washington: Georgetown University Press, 2003.
Foucault, Michel. *The Hermeneutics of the Subject: Lectures at the Collège de France, 1981–82*. Translated by Burchell. New York: Palgrave Macmillan, 2005.
Frey, Jennifer. "Neo-Aristotelian Ethical Naturalism." In *The Cambridge Companion to Natural Law Ethics*, edited by Tom Angier, 92–110. Cambridge: Cambridge University Press, 2019.
Fuentes, Agustin. "Human Niche, Human Behavior, Human Nature." *Interface Focus* 7: 72016013620160136. Available online: http://doi.org/10.1098/rsfs.2016.0136 (accessed February 2022).
Fukuyama, Francis. *Our Posthuman Future*. New York: Farrar, Straus and Giroux, 2002.
Grabill, Stephen J. *Rediscovering the Natural Law in Reformed Theological Ethics*. Grand Rapids: Eerdmans, 2006.
Grant, Colin. *Altruism and Christian Ethics*. Cambridge: Cambridge University Press, 2001.
Greenberg, Julia R., Katharina Hamann, Felix Warneken, and Michael Tomasello. "Chimpanzee Helping in Collaborative and Noncollaborative Contexts." *Animal Behaviour* 80, no. 5 (2010): 873–80.
Grisez, Germain. *The Way of the Lord Jesus: Vol. 1, Christian Moral Principles*. Chicago: IL: Franciscan Herald Press, 1983.
Gunton, Colin. *The One, The Three, and the Many: God, Creation, and the Culture of Modernity*. Cambridge: Cambridge University Press, 1993.
Gustafson, James M. *Ethics from a Theocentric Perspective, Vol. 1: Theology and Ethics*. Chicago: University of Chicago Press, 1981.
Gustafson, James M. *Ethics from a Theocentric Perspective, Vol. 2: Ethics and Theology*. Chicago: University of Chicago Press, 1984.
Gutierrez, Gustavo. *On Job: God-Talk and the Suffering of the Innocent*. Translated by Matthew J. O'Connell. Maryknoll: Orbis Books, 1987.
Hadot, Pierre. *Philosophy as a Way of Life: Spiritual Exercises from Socrates to Foucault*. Translated by Arnold Davidson. Cambridge: Blackwell, 1995.
Hagger, Martin, Nikos Chatzisarantis, Hugo Alberts et al. "A Multilab Preregistered Replication of the Ego-Depletion Effect." *Perspectives on Psychological Science* 11, no. 4 (2016): 546–73.
Hamann, Katharina, Felix Warneken, Julia R. Greenberg, and Michael Tomasello. "Collaboration Encourages Equal Sharing in Children but not in Chimpanzees." *Nature* 476 (2011): 328–31.
Harman, Elizabeth. "Morally Permissible Moral Mistakes." *Ethics* (January 2016): 366–93.
Harris, John. *How to Be Good: The Possibility of Moral Enhancement*. New York: Oxford University Press, 2016.

Hauerwas, Stanley. *Approaching the End: Eschatological Reflections on Church, Politics, and Life*. Grand Rapids: Eerdmans, 2013.
Hauerwas, Stanley. *Hannah's Child: A Theologian's Memoir*. Grand Rapids: Eerdmans, 2010.
Hauerwas, Stanley. "How 'Christian Ethics' Came to Be." In *The Hauerwas Reader*, edited by John Berkman and Michael Cartwright, 37–50. Durham: Duke University Press, 2001.
Hauerwas, Stanley. *Naming the Silences: God, Medicine, and the Problem of Suffering*. London: Continuum, 2004.
Hauerwas, Stanley. *The Peaceable Kingdom: A Primer in Christian Ethics*. Notre Dame: University of Notre Dame Press, 1981.
Hauerwas, Stanley. *Suffering Presence: Theological Reflections on Medicine, the Mentally Handicapped, and the Church*. Notre Dame: University of Notre Dame Press, 1986.
Hauerwas, Stanley. "Suffering Presence: Twenty-five Years Later." In *Approaching the End: Eschatological Reflections on Church, Politics, and Life*, 176–91. Grand Rapids: Eerdmans, 2013.
Hauerwas, Stanley. *With the Grain of the Universe: The Church's Witness and Natural Theology*. Grand Rapids: Brazos Press, 2001.
Hauerwas, Stanley. *The Work of Theology*. Grand Rapids: Eerdmans, 2015.
Hauerwas, Stanley and David Burrell. "From System to Story." In *Why Narrative? Readings In Narrative Theology*, edited by Stanley Hauerwas and L. Gregory Jones, 158–90. Grand Rapids: Eerdmans Publishing, 1989.
Hauerwas, Stanley and Gerald McKenny. "The Strength to be Patient." *Christian Bioethics* 22, no. 1 (2016): 5–20.
Hawthorne, John and Daniel Nolan. "What Would Teleological Causation Be?" In *Metaphysical Essays*, edited by John Hawthorne, 265–83. Oxford: Oxford University Press, 2006.
Herdt, Jennifer. *Assuming Responsibility: Ecstatic Eudaimonism and the Call to Live Well*. Oxford: Oxford University Press, 2022.
Herdt, Jennifer. "Hauerwas Among the Virtues." *Journal of Religious Ethics* 40, no. 2 (2012): 202–27.
Herdt, Jennifer. *Putting on Virtue: The Legacy of the Splendid Vices*. Chicago: University of Chicago Press, 2008.
Heyd, David. "Supererogation." In *The Stanford Encyclopedia of Philosophy*, edited by Edward N. Zalta, Winter 2019 ed. Available online: https://plato.stanford.edu/archives/win2019/entries/supererogation/.
Heyd, David. *Supererogation: Its Status in Ethical Theory*. Cambridge: Cambridge University Press, 1982.
Hill, Thomas E. Jr., *Dignity and Practical Reason*. Ithaca: Cornell University Press, 1992.
Hinze, Christine Firer. *Radical Sufficiency: Work, Livelihood, and U.S. Catholic Economic Ethic*. Washington: Georgetown University Press 2021.
Hirschfeld, Mary. *Aquinas and the Market*. Cambridge, MA: Harvard University Press, 2018.
Hittinger, Russell. *The First Grace: Rediscovering Natural Law in a Post-Christian World*. Wilmington: ISI Books, 2003.
Hogan, Terry and Mark Timmons. "Untying the Knot from the Inside Out: Reflections on the 'Paradox of Supererogation.'" *Social Philosophy and Policy* 27 (2010): 29–63.
Horn, John, and John McArdle. "Understanding Human Intelligence Since Spearman." In *Factor Analysis at 100: Historical Developments and Future Directions*, edited by Robert Cudeck and Robert MacCallum, 205–47. Mahwah: Lawrence Erlbaum Associates, 2007.

Hruschka, Joachim "Supererogation and Meritorious Duties." *Annual Review of Law and Ethics* 6 (1998): 93–108.
Hunsinger, George. "A Tale of Two Simultaneities: Justification and Sanctification in Calvin and Barth." *Zeitschrift Für Dialektische Theologie* 18, no. 3 (2002): 316–38.
Husserl, Edmund. *The Crisis of European Sciences and Transcendental Phenomenology*. Evanston: Northwestern University Press, 1970.
Illich, Ivan. *The Rivers North of the Future: The Testament of Ivan Illich as told to David Cayley*. Toronto: House of Anansi Press, 2005.
International Theological Commission. "In Search of a Universal Ethic: A New Look at the Natural Law." Available online: https://www.vatican.va/roman_ curia/congregations/cfaith/cti_ documents/rc_con_cfaith_doc_20090520_legge-naturale en.html (accessed July 2021).
Jackson, Timothy P. *Love Disconsoled: Meditations on Christian Charity*. Cambridge: Cambridge University Press, 1999.
Jenkins, Willis. *Ecologies of Grace: Environmental Ethics and Christian Theology*. Oxford: Oxford University Press, 2008.
Jennings, Willie. "A Rich Disciple? Barth on the Rich Young Ruler." In *Reading the Gospels with Karl Barth*, edited by Daniel L. Migliore, 56–66. Grand Rapids: Eerdmans, 2017.
John, Paul II. "Salvifici Doloris." 1984. Available online: https://w2.vatican.va/content/john-paul-ii/en/apost_letters/1984/documents/hf_jp-ii_apl_11021984_salvifici-doloris.html (accessed July 2021).
John, Paul II. "Veritatis Splendor." 1993. Available online: https://www.vatican.va/content/john-paul-ii/en/encyclicals/documents/hf_jp-ii_enc_06081993_veritatis-splendor.html (accessed July 2021).
Kant, Immanuel. *Groundwork of the Metaphysics of Morals*. Translated and edited by Mary Gregor, 7–51. New York: Cambridge University Press, 1997.
Kass, Leon. *Life, Liberty, and the Defense of Dignity*. San Francisco: Encounter, 2002.
Kekes, John. *The Examined Life*. University Park: Pennsylvania State University Press, 1988.
Kelsey, David. *Eccentric Existence: A Theological Anthropology*. Louisville: Westminster John Knox, 2009.
Kevles, Daniel. *In the Name of Eugenics: Genetics and the Uses of Human Heredity*. Cambridge, MA: Harvard University Press, 1995.
King, Martin Luther Jr. *I Have a Dream: Speeches and Writings that Changed the World*. Edited by James Melvin Washington, 83–100. San Francisco: HarperSanFrancisco, 1992.
Korsgaard, Christine. *The Sources of Normativity*. Cambridge: Cambridge University Press, 1996.
Kroeker, P. Travis. *Messianic Political Theology and Diaspora Ethics: Essays in Exile*. Eugene: Cascade Books, 2017.
Kurzweil, Ray. "How You Can Be a Danielle: Chapter 5: And Record Your Life." *Danielle: A Novel by Ray Kurzweil*. Available online: https://www.danielleworld.com/how-you-can-be-a-danielle/chapter-5-and-record-your-life-ray-kurzweil-novel (accessed July 2021).
Kurzweil, Ray. "The Future of Intelligence, Artificial and Natural." *Innovation Global*, 2019. Available online: https://www.youtube.com/watch?v=Kd17c5m4kdM (accessed July 2021).
Kurzweil, Ray. *The Singularity Is Near*. New York: Viking, 2005.
Laland, Kevin, Blake Mathews, and Marcus W. Feldman. "An Introduction to Niche Construction Theory." *Evolutionary Ecology* 30 (2016): 191–202.

Lennox, James. *Aristotle's Philosophy of Biology*. Cambridge: Cambridge University Press, 2001.
Little, David. "The Law of Supererogation." In *The Love Commandments: Essays in Christian Ethics and Moral Philosophy*, edited by Edmund N. Santurri and William Werpehowski, 157–81. Washington: Georgetown University Press, 1992.
Lovin, Robin. *Christian Faith and Public Choices: The Social Ethics of Barth, Brunner, and Bonhoeffer*. Minneapolis: Fortress, 1984.
Luther, Martin. *The Large Catechism*. Translated by Robert H. Fischer. Philadelphia: Fortress Press, 1959.
Luther, Martin. *Luther's Basic Theological Writings*. Edited by Timothy Lull. Minneapolis: Fortress Press, 1989.
Luther, Martin. *Treatise on Good Works*. Translated by Scott H. Hendrix. Minneapolis: Fortress Press, 2012.
Luther, Martin. "Two Kinds of Righteousness." In *Luther's Works*, edited by Harold J. Grimm (General Editor: Helmut T. Lehmann), Vol. 31, 298–301. Philadelphia: Fortress Press, 1957.
Marga, Amy. "Barth and Roman Catholicism." In *The Wiley Blackwell Companion to Karl Barth: Barth in Dialogue*, edited by George Hunsinger and Keith L. Johnson, Vol. 2, 845–55. Hoboken: Wiley Blackwell, 2020.
Mauldin, Joshua. *Barth, Bonhoeffer, and Modern Politics*. Oxford: Oxford University Press, 2021.
McCormack, Bruce. *Orthodox and Modern: Studies in the Theology of Karl Barth*. Grand Rapids: Baker Academic, 2008.
McCormack, Bruce and Thomas Joseph White, eds. *Thomas Aquinas and Karl Barth: An Unofficial Dialogue*. Grand Rapids: Eerdmans, 2013.
McKenny, Gerald. *The Analogy of Grace: Karl Barth's Moral Theology*. New York: Oxford University Press, 2010.
McKenny, Gerald. *Biotechnology, Human Nature, and Christian Ethics*. Cambridge: Cambridge University Press, 2018.
McKenny, Gerald. "Biotechnology and the Normative Significance of Human Nature: A Contribution from Theological Anthropology." *Studies in Christian Ethics* 26, no. 1 (2013): 18–36.
McKenny, Gerald. "Evolution, Biotechnology, and the Normative Significance of Created Order." *Toronto Journal of Theology* 31, no. 1 (2015): 15–26.
McKenny, Gerald. "Human Nature and Biotechnological Enhancement: Some Theological Considerations." *Studies in Christian Ethics* 32, no. 2 (2019): 229–40.
McKenny, Gerald. "Karl Barth and the Plight of Protestant Ethics." In *The Freedom of a Christian Ethicist: The Future of a Reformation Legacy*, edited by Brian Brock and Michael Mawson, 17–38. London: T&T Clark Bloomsbury, 2018.
McKenny, Gerald. *Karl Barth's Moral Thought*. New York: Oxford University Press, 2021.
McKenny, Gerald. "Moral Disagreement and the Limits of Reason: Reflections on MacIntyre and Ratzinger." In *Intractable Disputes About the Natural Law*, edited by Lawrence Cunningham, 195–226. Notre Dame: University of Notre Dame Press, 2009.
McKenny, Gerald. "Technologies of Desire: Theology, Ethics, and the Enhancement of Human Traits." *Theology Today* 59, no. 1 (2002): 90–103.
McKenny, Gerald "Technology." In *The Blackwell Companion to Religious Ethics*, edited by William Schweiker, 459–68. Oxford: Blackwell Publishing, 2005.
McKenny, Gerald. *To Relive the Human Condition: Bioethics, Technology, and the Body*. New York: SUNY, 1997.

McKenny, Gerald. "Transcendence, Technological Enhancement, and Christian Theology." In *Transhumanism and Transcendence: Christian Hope in an Age of Technological Enhancement*, edited by Ronald Cole-Turner, 177–92. Washington: Georgetown University Press, 2011.

Meconi, David Vincent. *The One Christ: St. Augustine's Theology of Deification*. Washington: Catholic University of America Press, 2013.

Meilaender, Gilbert. *The Freedom of a Christian*. Grand Rapids: Brazos Press, 2006.

Meilaender, Gilbert. *Should We Live Forever? The Ethical Ambiguities of Aging*. Grand Rapids: Eerdmans, 2013.

Meilaender, Gilbert. *The Theory and Practice of Virtue*. Notre Dame: University of Notre Dame Press, 1984.

Mellema, Gregory. *Beyond the Call of Duty: Supererogation, Obligation, and Offence*. Albany: SUNY Press, 1991.

Mellema, Gregory. "Supererogation and Theism." *International Journal of Philosophy and Theology* 5, no. 1 (2017): 1–7.

Milbank, John. *The Word Made Strange: Theology, Language, Culture*. Oxford: Blackwell, 1997.

Mortimer, Sarah. "Counsels of Perfection and Reformation Political Thought." *The Historical Journal* 62, no. 2 (2019): 311–30.

Mumford, James. "The Experience of Obligation: The Enduring Promise of Levinas for Theological Ethics." *Studies in Christian Ethics* 33, no. 3 (2019): 352–69.

Nagel, Thomas. *Mind and Cosmos*. Oxford: Oxford University Press, 2012.

Neuhaus, Richard John. *The Naked Public Square: Religion and Democracy in America*. Grand Rapids: William B. Eerdmans, 1984.

Niebuhr, H. Richard. *The Responsible Self: An Essay in Christian Moral Philosophy*. New York: Harper and Row, 1963.

Niebuhr, H. Richard. *The Social Sources of Denominationalism*. New York: Henry Holt and Company, 1929.

Nightingale, Andrea. *Once Out of Nature: Augustine on Time and the Body*. Chicago: University of Chicago Press, 2011.

Nixon, Rob. *Slow Violence and the Environmentalism of the Poor*. Cambridge, MA: Harvard University Press, 2011.

Northcott, Michael. *The Environment and Christian Ethics*. Cambridge: Cambridge University Press, 1996.

Nowak, Martin, and Sarah Coakley, eds. *Evolution, Games, and God: The Principle of Cooperation*. Cambridge, MA: Harvard University Press, 2013.

Nunziato, Joshua. *Augustine and the Economy of Sacrifice: Ancient and Modern Perspectives*. Cambridge: Cambridge University Press, 2019.

Nussbaum, Martha. *The Therapy of Desire: Theory and Practice in Hellenistic Ethics*. Princeton: Princeton University Press, 1996.

O'Brien, David J., and Thomas A. Shannon, eds. "Gaudium et Spes." In *Catholic Social Thought: The Documentary Heritage*, 166–237. Maryknoll: Orbis, 2010.

O'Connell, Mark. *To Be a Machine: Adventures Among Cyborgs, Utopians, Hackers, and the Futurists Solving the Modest Problem of Death*. London: Granta, 2017.

O'Donovan, Oliver. *Resurrection and Moral Order: An Outline for Evangelical Ethics*, 2nd ed. Grand Rapids: Eerdmans, 1994.

O'Meara, Thomas F. O. P. "Virtues in the Theology of Thomas Aquinas." *Theological Studies* 58 (1997): 254–85.

Odling-Smee, F. J. "Niche Constructing Phenotypes." In *The Role of Behavior in Evolution*, edited by H. C. Plotkin, 73–132. Cambridge, MA: MIT Press, 1988.
Olshoorn, Johan. "Grotius on Natural Law and Supererogation." *Journal of the History of Philosophy* 57, no. 3 (2019): 443–69.
Outka, Gene. *Agape: An Ethical Analysis*. New Haven: Yale University Press, 1977.
Outka, Gene and Paul Ramsey, eds. *Norm and Context in Christian Ethics*. New York: Charles Scribner's Sons, 1968.
Parker, Elizabeth, Larry Cahill, and James McGaugh. "A Case of Unusual Autobiographical Remembering." *Neurocase* 12, no. 1 (2006): 35–49.
Pasnau, Robert. *Thomas Aquinas on Human Nature: A Philosophical Study of Summa Theologiae 1a 75–89*. Cambridge: Cambridge University Press, 2002.
Persson, Ingmar, and Julian Savulescu. "Moral Hard-Wiring and Moral Enhancement." *Bioethics* 31, no. 4 (2017): 286–95.
Persson, Ingmar, and Julian Savulescu. "The Perils of Cognitive Enhancement and the Urgent Imperative to Enhance the Moral Character of Humanity." *Journal of Applied Philosophy* 25, no. 3 (2008): 162–77.
Pieper, Josef. *Faith, Hope, Love*. San Francisco: Ignatius Press, 1997.
Pinckaers, Servais, O. P. *The Sources of Christian Ethics*. Translated by Sr. Mary Thomas Noble O. P. Washington: The Catholic University of America, 1995.
Pfau, Thomas. *Minding the Modern*. Notre Dame: University of Notre Dame Press, 2013.
Plomin, Robert. *Blueprint: How DNA Makes Us Who We Are*. Cambridge, MA: MIT Press, 2018.
Pope, Stephen. "Reason and Natural Law." In *The Oxford Handbook of Theological Ethics*, edited by Gilbert Meilaender and William Werpehowski, 148–67. Oxford: Oxford University Press, 2007.
Porter, Jean. *Justice as a Virtue: A Thomistic Perspective*. Grand Rapids: Eerdmans, 2016.
Porter, Jean. *Ministers of the Law: A Natural Law Theory of Legal Authority*. Grand Rapids: Eerdmans, 2010.
Porter, Jean. "Moral Virtues, Charity, and Grace: Why the Infused and Acquired Virtues Cannot Co-Exist." *Journal of Moral Theology* 8, no. 2 (2019): 40–66.
Porter, Jean. *Natural and Divine Law: Reclaiming the Tradition for Christian Ethics*. Grand Rapids: Eerdmans, 1999.
Porter, Jean. *Nature as Reason: A Thomistic Theory of Natural Law*. Grand Rapids: Eerdmans, 2005.
Porter, Jean. "Responsibility, Passion, and Sin: A Reassessment of Abelard's *Ethics*." *The Journal of Religious Ethics* 28, no. 3 (2000): 367–94.
Porter, Jean. "Virtue and Sin: The Connection of the Virtues and the Case of the Flawed Saint." *The Journal of Religion* 75, no. 4 (1995): 521–39.
Porter, Jean. "Virtue Ethics and Its Significance for Spirituality: A Survey and Assessment of Recent Work." *The Way Supplement* 88 (1997): 26–35.
Porter, Theodore. *The Rise of Statistical Thinking, 1820–1900*. Princeton: Princeton University Press, 1986.
Potter, Van Rensselaer. *Bioethics: A Bridge to the Future*. Englewood Cliffs: Prentice Hall, 1971.
Potter, Van Rensselaer. *Global Bioethics: Building on the Leopold Legacy*. East Lansing: Michigan State University Press, 1988.
President's Council on Bioethics. *Beyond Therapy: Biotechnology and the Pursuit of Happiness*. Washington: President's Council on Bioethics, 2003.

Putnam, Robert. *Bowling Alone: The Collapse and Revival of American Community*. New York: Simon and Schuster, 2000.
Putnam, Robert. *Upswing: How America Came Together A Century Ago and How We Can Do It Again*. New York: Simon and Schuster, 2020.
Rawls, John. *A Theory of Justice*. Cambridge, MA: Harvard University Press, 1971.
Reed, Esther. *The Ethics of Human Rights: Contested Doctrinal and Moral Issues*. Waco: Baylor University Press, 2007.
Regalado, Antonio. "The World's First Gattaca Baby Tests Are Finally Here." *MIT Technology Review*, November 8, 2019.
Reich, W. T. "The Word 'Bioethics': Its Birth and the Legacies of Those Who Shaped It." *Kennedy Institute of Ethics Journal* 4, no. 4 (1994): 319–35.
Reich, W. T. "The Word 'Bioethics': The Struggle Over Its Earliest Meanings." *Kennedy Institute of Ethics Journal* 5, no. 1 (1995): 19–34.
Rhonheimer, Martin. *Natural Law and Practical Reason: A Thomist View of Moral Autonomy*. Translated by Gerald Malsbary. New York: Fordham University Press, 2000.
Roberts, J. Deotis. *Bonhoeffer and King: Speaking Truth to Power*. Louisville: Westminster John Knox Press, 2005.
Roco, Mihail and William Sims Bainbridge. *Converging Technologies for Improving Human Performance: Nanotechnology, Biotechnology, Information Technology and Cognitive Science*. Arlington: National Science Foundation, 2002.
Rogers, Eugene F. *Aquinas and the Supreme Court: Race, Gender, and the Failure of Natural Law in Thomas's Biblical Commentaries*. Oxford: Wiley-Blackwell, 2013.
Rogers, Eugene F. *Thomas Aquinas and Karl Barth: Sacred Doctrine and the Natural Knowledge of God*. Notre Dame: University of Notre Dame Press, 1995.
Sandel, Michael. *The Case against Perfection: Ethics in the Age of Genetic Engineering*. Cambridge, MA: Harvard University Press, 2007.
Scherz, Paul. "Living Indefinitely and Living Fully: Laudato Si' and the Value of the Present in Christian, Stoic, and Transhumanist Temporalities." *Theological Studies* 79, no. 2 (June 1, 2018): 356–75.
Schmidt, Marco F. H. and Michael Tomasello. "Young Children Enforce Social Norms." *Current Directions in Psychological Science* 21, no. 4 (2012): 232–36.
Schneewind, Jerome. "Misfortunes of Virtue." *Ethics* 101, no. 1 (October 1990): 42–63.
Schneider, John. *Animal Suffering and the Darwinian Problem of Evil*. Cambridge: Cambridge University Press, 2020.
Schumaker, Millard. *Sharing Without Reckoning: Imperfect Right and the Norms of Reciprocity*. Toronto: Wilfrid Laurier University Press, 1992.
Seneca. *Epistles*, 1–65. Translated by Richard M. Gummere. Loeb Classical Library 75. Cambridge: Loeb Classical Library, 1917.
Seneca. *Moral Essays, Volume III. De Beneficiis*. Translated by John W. Basore. Cambridge: Loeb Classical Library, 1935.
Showers, Carolin J. and Virgil Zeigler-Hill. "Organization of Self-knowledge: Features, Functions, and Flexibility." In *Handbook of Self and Identity*, edited by Mark R. Leary and June Price Tangney, 47–67. New York: The Guilford Press, 2003.
Sideris, Lisa. *Environmental Ethics, Ecological Theology, and Natural Selection*. New York: Columbia University Press, 2003.
Sloan, Phillip R., Gerald McKenny, and Kathleen Eggleson, eds. *Darwin in the Twenty-First Century: Nature, Humanity, God*. Notre Dame: University of Notre Dame Press, 2015.

Song, Robert. "Review of Gerald McKenny's *Biotechnology, Human Nature and Christian Ethics*." *Theology* 123, no. 1 (2020): 46–7.
Stangl, Rebecca. "Neo-Aristotelian Supererogation." *Ethics* 126 (January 2016): 339–65.
Stendahl, Krister. "The Apostle Paul and the Introspective Conscience of the West." *The Harvard Theological Review* 56, no. 3 (1963): 199–215.
Stewart-Kroeker, Sarah. "Love of and for the Martyrs: Resurrected Wounds and the 'Order' of Restoration." *Studia Patristica* 116 (2022): 91–8.
Stewart-Kroeker, Sarah. *Pilgrimage as Moral and Aesthetic Formation in Augustine's Thought*. Oxford: Oxford University Press, 2017.
Stiegler, Bernard. *Technics and Time, 1: The Fault of Epimetheus*. Translated by Richard Beardsworth and George Collins. Stanford: Stanford University Press, 1998.
Sytsma, David S. "John Calvin and Virtue Ethics: Augustinian and Aristotelian Themes." *Journal of Religious Ethics* 48, no. 3 (2020): 519–56.
Tanner, Kathryn. *Christ the Key*. Cambridge: Cambridge University Press, 2009.
Tanner, Kathryn. *God and Creation in Christian Theology*. Oxford: Basil Blackwell, 1988.
Tanner, Kathryn. "In the Image of the Invisible." In *Apophatic Bodies: Negative Theology, Incarnation, and Relationality*, edited by Chris Boesel and Catherine Keller, 117–35. New York: Fordham University Press, 2009.
Tanner, Kathryn. *Jesus, Humanity and The Trinity*. Minneapolis: Fortress, 2001.
Taylor, Charles. *A Secular Age*. Cambridge, MA: Harvard University Press, 2007.
Taylor, Charles. *Sources of the Self: The Making of Modern Identity*. Cambridge: Cambridge University Press, 1989.
Thurman, Howard. *Jesus and the Disinherited*. New York: Abingdon-Cokesbury, 1949.
Timmons, Mark and Robert N. Johnson. *Reason, Value, and Respect: Kantian Themes from the Philosophy of Thomas E. Hill, Jr*. Oxford: Oxford University Press, 2015.
Tranter, Samuel. *Oliver O'Donovan's Moral Theology: Tensions and Triumphs*. London: T&T Clark Bloomsbury, 2020.
Tödt, Heinz Eduard. *Authentic Faith: Bonhoeffer's Theological Ethics in Context*. Translated by David Stassen and Isle Tödt. Grand Rapids: Eerdmans, 2007.
Tomasello, Michael. *A Natural History of Human Thinking*. Cambridge, MA: Harvard University Press, 2014.
Torell, Jean-Pierre, O. P. *Christ and Spiritualty in St. Thomas Aquinas*. Washington: Catholic University of America Press, 2011.
Ulrich, Hans. "The Form of Ethical Life." In *The Oxford Handbook of Dietrich Bonhoeffer*, edited by Michael Mawson and Philip G. Ziegler, 289–305. Oxford: Oxford University Press, 2019.
Urmson, J. O. "Saints and Heroes." In *Moral Concepts*, edited by Joel Feinberg, 60–73. Oxford: Oxford University Press, 1969.
van den Heuvel, Steven. *Bonhoeffer's Christocentric Theology and Fundamental Debates in Environmental Ethics*. Eugene: Pickwick Publications, 2017.
Verma, Ashish Swarup, Shishir Agrahari, Shruti Rastogi, and Anchal Singh. "Biotechnology in the Realm of History." *Journal of Pharmacy and BioAllied Sciences* 3, no. 3 (2011): 321–3.
Volck, Brian. *Attending Others: A Doctor's Education in Bodies and Words*. Eugene: Cascade, 2020.
Vosloo, Robert. "Body and Health in the Light of the Theology of Dietrich Bonhoeffer." *Religion and Theology* 13, 1 (2006): 23–7.
Wadell, Paul J. *Happiness and the Christian Moral Life: An Introduction to Christian Ethics*. Lanham: Rowman & Littlefield, 2012.

Wannenwetsch, Bernd. "My Strength is Made Perfect in Weakness: Bonhoeffer and the War over Disabled Life." In *Disability in the Christian Tradition: A Reader*, edited by Brian Brock and John Swinton, 353–90. Grand Rapids: Eerdmans, 2012.

Webb, Stephen. *The Gifting God: A Trinitarian Ethics of Excess*. Oxford: Oxford University Press, 1996.

Webster, John. *Barth's Ethics of Reconciliation*. Cambridge: Cambridge University Press, 1995.

Webster, John. "God and Conscience." In *Word and Church: Essays in Christian Dogmatics*, 233–62. Edinburgh: T&T Clark, 2001.

Webster, John. *Karl Barth's Moral Theology: Human Action in Barth's Thought*. Grand Rapids: Eerdmans, 1998.

Williams, Gareth D. *The Cosmic Viewpoint: A Study of Seneca's Natural Questions*. New York: Oxford University Press, 2012.

Wilson, Eric Entrican and Lara Denis. "Kant and Hume on Morality." *Stanford Encyclopedia of Philosophy*. Available online: https://plato.stanford.edu/entries/kant-hume-morality/ (accessed July 2021).

Wittman, Tyler R. *God and Creation in the Theology of Thomas Aquinas and Karl Barth*. New York: Cambridge University Press, 2018.

Wolf, Susan. "Moral Saints." *The Journal of Philosophy* 79, no. 8 (August 1982): 419–39.

Wood, Donald. "This Ability: Barth on the Concrete Freedom of Human Life." In *Disability in the Christian Tradition: A Reader*, edited by Brian Brock and John Swinton, 391–426. Grand Rapids: Eerdmans, 2012.

Yates, Frances. *The Art of Memory*. Chicago: University of Chicago Press, 1966.

Zachman, Randall. *The Assurance of Faith*. Louisville: Westminster John Knox Press, 2005.

Zahl, Simeon. "Non-Competitive Agency and Luther's Experiential Argument Against Virtue." *Modern Theology* 35 (2019): 199–222.

Zimmermann, Jens. "The Cultural Context for Re-Envisioning Christian Humanism." In *Re-Envisioning Christian Humanism*, edited by Jens Zimmermann, 137–60. Oxford: Oxford University Press, 2017.

Zimmermann, Jens. *Dietrich Bonhoeffer's Christian Humanism*. Oxford: Oxford University Press, 2019.

Zimmermann, Jens. "Recovering the Natural for Politics: Bonhoeffer and the Natural Law Tradition." In *Dietrich Bonhoeffer, Theology, and Political Resistance*, edited by Lori Brandt Hale and W. David Hall, 27–48. Lanham: Lexington, 2020.

CONTRIBUTORS

Angela Carpenter is Assistant Professor of Religion at Hope College. She is the author of *Responsive Becoming: Moral Formation in Theological, Evolutionary, and Developmental Perspective* (2019).

Eric Gregory is Professor of Religion and former chair of the Council of the Humanities at Princeton University. He is the author of *Politics and the Order of Love: An Augustinian Ethic of Democratic Citizenship* (2008).

Stanley Hauerwas is Gilbert T. Rowe Professor Emeritus of Divinity and Law at Duke University. Some of his recent books include *Approaching the End: Eschatological Reflection on Church, Politics, and Life* (2013), *The Work of Theology* (2015), and *Beginnings: Interrogating Hauerwas* (with Brian Brock, 2017).

Jennifer A. Herdt is Gilbert L. Stark Professor of Christian Ethics at Yale Divinity School. Her books include *Putting on Virtue: The Legacy of the Splendid Vices* (2008), *Forming Humanity: Redeeming the German Bildung Tradition* (2019), and *Assuming Responsibility: Ecstatic Eudaimonism and the Call to Live Well* (2022).

Travis Kroeker is Professor of Religious Studies and Member of the Institute on Globalization and the Human Condition at McMaster University. He is the author of *Messianic Political Theology and Diaspora Ethics* (2017) and, with Bruce Ward, *Remembering the End: Dostoevsky as Prophet to Modernity* (2001).

Robin W. Lovin is Cary Maguire University Professor Emeritus of Ethics at Southern Methodist University and a Visiting Scholar in Theology at Loyola University Chicago. He is the author of *Christian Realism and the New Realities* (2008), *An Introduction to Christian Ethics: Goals, Duties, and Virtues* (2011), and *What Do We Do When Nobody Is Listening?* (2022).

Paul Martens is Associate Professor of Religion and Director of Interdisciplinary Programs at Baylor University. His publications include *The Heterodox Yoder* (2012) and *Reading Kierkegaard I: Fear and Trembling* (2017).

Michael Mawson is Senior Lecturer in Theology and Research Fellow in the Public and Contextual Theology Research Centre, Charles Sturt University, Australia, and Research Fellow for the Theology for Southern Africa Initiative at the University of the Free State, South Africa. He is the author of *Christ Existing as Community:*

Bonhoeffer's Ecclesiology (2018) and coeditor of *The Oxford Handbook of Dietrich Bonhoeffer* (2019).

Gilbert Meilaender is Senior Research Professor of Theology at Valparaiso University. His publications include *Friendship: A Study in Theological Ethics* (1981) and *Thy Will Be Done: The Ten Commandments and the Christian Life* (2020).

Jeffrey Morgan is Assistant Professor of Theology at Saint Joseph's College of Maine. He is the author of *The Single Individual and the Searcher of Hearts: A Retrieval of Conscience in the Work of Immanuel Kant and Soren Kierkegaard* (2020).

Stephen J. Pope is Professor of Theological Ethics at Boston College. He is the author of *A Step Along the Way: Models of Christian Service* (2015) and *Human Evolution and Christian Ethics* (2007), and editor of *Solidarity and Hope: Jon Sobrino's Challenge to Christian Theology* (2008).

Jean Porter is John A. O'Brien Professor of Theology at the University of Notre Dame. Her publications include *Ministers of the Law: A Natural Law Theory of Legal Authority* (2011), *The Perfection of Desire: Habit, Reason, and Virtue in Aquinas's Summa Theologiae* (2018), and *Justice as Virtue: A Thomistic Perspective* (2016).

Paul Scherz is Associate Professor of Moral Theology and Ethics at the Catholic University of America. He is the author of *Science and Christian Ethics* (2019) and coeditor with Joseph E. Davis of *The Evening of Life: The Challenges of Aging and Dying Well* (2020).

INDEX

accountability   35, 37, 40, 43, 51, 55, 170, 171, 173
Adams, Robert   58, 62
agency, human   2, 3, 5, 13, 15, 19–21, 23, 25–7, 29–32, 35–7, 88, 89, 96, 116, 161, 166–7, 170–2, 191
altruism   55, 164, 184–5
Anthropocene   88, 102–3
anthropology   82, 164, 196
    comparative   5, 169
    theological   19, 26–7, 88, 116, 118, 145, 147, 161, 170, 183, 192–4
antinomianism   24, 53
apocalyptic   5, 88, 91–3, 95, 99–103, 196
Aquinas, Thomas   5, 63–4, 85, 104–6, 112, 116–17, 126–9, 132–41, 185–6
Aristotle   107, 127–9, 132, 171; *see also* ethics, aristotelian
Augustine   5, 9–11, 62, 65–6, 87–103, 108, 114, 143, 182–3
    City of God   97–101
    De trinitate   92
authority   35, 41–51, 84, 101, 108, 114, 118, 120, 122
autonomy   8–9, 11, 36, 57, 88–9, 102, 106–7, 110, 118, 175; *see also* freedom

Baconian Project, the   4, 7, 83, 175, 177–8
Barth, Karl
    Chruch Dogmatics   13, 17
bioconservative   175, 177–8
bioethics; *see under* ethics, bioethics
biostatistics   5, 175–8
biotechnology   4–5, 7–11, 18, 87–91, 94–6, 100, 102–3, 106–11, 125–7, 130–1, 139, 143–8, 159, 161, 165, 173, 176, 185, 187, 190–7; *see also* enhancement

body (embodiment)   2, 4, 7, 81–5, 96–101, 128–9, 147, 156–7, 167, 172, 178, 192, 196–7
    resurrected   97–9, 186
Bonhoeffer, Dietrich   5, 45, 73–6, 78–9, 83–4, 144, 149–59
    Life Together   73–4
    "Natural Life"   144, 149–59

calling   44–6, 48–50, 76–7, 79; *see also* vocation
Calvin, John, (Calvininsm)   1–2, 8, 13, 17, 20, 23, 29, 30, 41, 59–67
Canguilhem, Georges   176–7
Carruthers, Mary   181–2
charity   59, 78, 133–5, 138, 140, 185–7
Christology   64, 91, 115, 144–5, 148, 151
church   31, 36, 43, 48–51, 62, 69–79, 83, 97, 116, 119, 185; *see also* ecclesiology
civil law; *see under* law
Coakley, Sarah   169, 185
command, divine   3, 12, 29, 32, 37–8, 45, 49, 51–3, 62, 65, 120–2; *see also* ethics, divine command
conscience   3, 24, 35–52, 120, 122, 157, 163
cooperation   78, 136, 162–5, 168–9, 172, 185; *see also* hyper-cooperativity
covenant   2, 11, 20, 26–8, 32, 46, 59, 152, 159, 197
    of grace   46, 121, 146
creation   11, 16, 26, 29, 31, 38, 41, 45–6, 60, 76, 88–9, 91, 94–103, 108–10, 114–18, 125, 130, 132, 139, 145, 150, 152, 158–9, 161, 165–73, 192–7
cross   13, 72, 89, 101–2, 172

Darwin, Charles   167–9
death   4, 10, 16, 25, 85, 96–101, 128–9, 172, 193

Decalogue; *see* Ten Commandments
deification   88–94, 96–102, 110, 117, 145, 158
deontology   57–8
dignity   73, 88–9, 93, 107–8, 115, 145, 157, 170
disability   2, 176–7
discernment   9, 22, 32, 36, 45, 122, 150, 155–9, 173
discipleship   63–6
divine law; *see under* law
duty   54–62, 65–7, 71, 76, 85, 116, 156, 185

ecclesiology   48, 51, 53, 70, 90; *see also* church
ecology   5, 189–97
economics   60, 71, 76, 118
Eden   94–7
election, divine   7, 11–12, 15, 28, 31, 119–20
embodiment; *see* body
enhancement   11, 89–90, 98, 106–11, 130, 143–8, 159, 175–88, 193
equality   76, 107, 162, 173, 175–6
eschatology   5, 17–18, 38–43, 51, 57, 60, 88–9, 101, 108, 110, 117–19, 141, 148, 159, 161, 165–72, 194–6
ethics
    aristotelian-thomistic   112, 128
    bioethics   2, 4, 8, 9, 12, 54, 60, 81–3, 88–9, 102, 125–6, 156, 175, 179–80, 185, 189–90, 196–7
    communitarian   36
    divine command   62, 121
    medical   2, 81
    natural law   62, 82, 123, 168
    philosophical   111, 143
    Protestant   16, 54, 59–62, 65, 67, 151
    theological   30, 36, 54, 58, 135, 149, 161
    virtue   55, 60, 62, 66, 111, 116
eudaimonia (eudaimonism)   65, 107
evolution   5, 108, 110, 112–13, 125, 129, 161–70, 190, 195–6

fairness   8–11, 88–9, 102
faith (faithfulness)   11, 14–18, 23–5, 29, 32, 45, 57, 59, 69–79, 95, 99, 105, 110, 134, 157, 170, 173, 187

flourishing, human   4, 108, 112–13, 116–19, 127, 130–1, 134, 143, 150, 156, 166, 168, 175–7, 187
forgiveness   10, 15–17, 21–4, 29, 59, 119, 172
form
    accidental   133
    substantial   127, 134
formation   4, 19–23, 30–3, 43, 70–9, 85, 96, 134–7, 167
Foucault, Michel   2, 4, 83, 182
freedom
    human   11, 23–7, 42–3, 53, 57, 61, 71, 76, 78–9, 83, 88, 97, 99, 119–21, 135, 137–40, 152, 154, 156–8, 175, 185
friendship (friends)   26, 46, 75–6, 85, 133, 139–40, 185
Fukuyama, Francis   108, 143, 176–8

Galton, Francis   177
generosity   31, 58, 163–5, 169, 173
Gospel   14, 16, 53, 58, 63, 72, 78, 116, 151
Grant, Colin   58
gratitude   26–31, 42, 44, 46, 48–50, 119, 172
Gustafson, James   2, 4, 7, 59, 69, 73, 77, 82, 87, 105
Gunton, Colin   197

Habermas, Jurgen   107, 143
habit   133–6
habituation   25, 32, 84
happiness   106, 110, 112, 115–19, 130–3, 140, 179
Hauerwas, Stanley   2, 4, 36, 60, 70–1, 114
    Naming the Silences: God, Medicine, and the Problem of Suffering   83
    Suffering Presence: Theological Reflections on Medicine, the Mentally Handicapped, and the Chruch   4, 81
Holy Spirit (Spirit)   10, 13–17, 31–2, 38–44, 69, 116, 119–20, 135, 138, 145–6, 148, 150
hope   25, 70, 72, 97
Hruschka, Joachim   67
hubris   108, 175; *see also* pride
human agency; *see* agency
humanism (humanistic)   22, 118, 189; *see also* transhumanism

human nature, normativity of 4, 58, 107–23, 152, 159, 175
  NS1 4, 102, 106–9, 143–4, 147–8, 151, 166, 191
  NS2 4–5, 106–10, 118, 143–4, 148, 156, 167, 191
  NS3 5, 106, 108–10, 143–6, 148, 166, 191, 196
  NS4 5, 106–7, 110–11, 114, 118–19, 144–59, 192, 194, 196–7
humility 21, 31, 47–9, 91, 100–2, 114, 173
Husserl, Edmund 177
hyper-cooperativity 162

Illich, Ivan 95
imago dei 5, 64, 87–93, 95–6, 98, 100, 102–3, 108–9, 114, 119, 138, 145–6, 152, 162, 172, 175–87
immortality 90–2, 94, 98–9, 102; *see also* mortality
incarnation 87, 89, 91–2, 94–5, 97–103, 116, 151, 162, 171
individualism 36–7, 51, 185
inequality 173, 175; *see also* equality
injustice 60, 66, 91; *see also* justice

Jackson, Timothy P. 61–2
Jenkins, Willis 197
John Paul II 122
justice 12–16, 49, 55, 59–60, 66, 76, 78–9, 91, 94, 118; *see also* injustice
justification 2, 8–16, 29–30, 53, 62, 76, 98, 114–15, 153

Kant, Immanuel 41, 55, 60–2, 66, 107, 119, 156
Kass, Leon 4, 7, 82, 108, 143, 179
Kelsey, David 170
kenosis 89–93, 97, 100, 102
Kolbert, Elizabeth 102
Korsgaard, Christine 167
Kurzweil, Ray 175, 180

law
  civil 118
  God's, divine 27, 107, 115, 117–18, 121
  moral 10, 54, 63–7, 107, 119
  natural 54, 62–4, 67, 82–5, 106–7, 109–21, 123, 150–1, 155
Leder, Drew 4, 82
Lennox, James 129
limitation, human 94, 136, 161, 165, 171
Little, David 61
Logos 89, 91, 97, 100
love 16–17, 23–4, 26, 28, 53, 59, 61–6, 72, 89–96, 99–102, 119, 121, 132–8, 146–7, 169, 171–3, 185, 192
Lovin, Robin 4, 150
Luther, Martin 1–3, 8–10, 13, 15–17, 20, 23–9, 32, 57, 59–62, 136, 149

MacIntyre, Alasdair 2, 83, 187
McKenny, Gerald
  The Analogy of Grace: Karl Barth's Moral Theology 1, 7, 109
  Biotechnology, Human Nature and Christain Ethics 4, 9, 87, 106–7, 125, 140, 143, 161, 175, 190–1, 193, 196–7
  To Relieve the Human Condition: Biotechnology and the Body 4, 7, 82, 108, 175
marriage 46, 65, 113, 149, 157, 164
medical ethics; *see under* ethics
medicine 2, 4–5, 81–5, 175, 195
Meilaender, Gilbert 3
Mellema, Gregory 56, 59, 61
memory 178–83
metaphysics 93, 112, 126, 132–4, 139
morality 11, 18, 55–8, 60, 113–15, 157, 167, 176, 189

Nagel, Thomas 168
natural law; *see under* law
neighbor 24, 44, 46–50, 53, 57, 65, 77–9, 99–100, 119, 163, 170, 172
Neuhaus, Richard John 71
Niebuhr, H. Richard 1, 36, 42, 69
Nightingale, Andrea 91, 95–8
  Once Out of Nature: Augustine on Time and the Body 90
normativity; *see* human nature
Northcott, Michael 197
Nunziato, Joshua 101–2
Nussbaum, Martha 108, 143

obedience   20, 28, 43, 45–6, 50, 119–22
obligation   10, 18, 20–1, 54–62, 107, 110, 114, 116, 120–1, 156–7
O'Connell, Mark   94–5
O'Donovan, Oliver   2, 88, 91, 107, 143, 155
ontology   27, 57–8, 91–5, 111, 118, 197
Outka, Gene   59, 61–2

Pearson, Karl   177
penultimate   43, 74–9, 150, 153, 158–9
perfection   16–17, 21–2, 30, 53–6, 63–4, 89–91, 99–100, 110, 119, 131, 134, 136–7, 140
permission   10–11, 18, 20–1, 27, 55
Persson, Ingmar   184–5
Peterson, Ted   109
Pfau, Thomas   184
phenomenology   2, 187–8
Plato   62, 91–3, 107, 128, 170
Porter, Jean   2, 5, 106–8, 111–19, 123
  Nature as Reason: A Thomistic Theory of Natural Law   106
Potter, Van Rensselaer   189–90, 196–7
prayer   9, 11–12, 18, 22, 32, 74, 116
preservation   117, 128, 135, 138, 150, 152–9, 162, 189
prohibition   64, 66, 94, 119
protestant   2, 4, 9, 13, 16, 22, 24, 53–67, 69–73, 79, 111, 123, 143, 150–1
psychology   5, 19–20, 23–33, 120, 161

Rahner, Karl   59, 109
rationality, human   25, 36, 96, 107, 111, 120, 122, 127–8, 132, 134, 137–8, 147
reconciliation   15–16, 29, 31, 38, 39, 46–8, 91, 100–1, 151, 153
redemption   29, 31, 38, 42, 94, 97, 116, 153, 165, 169, 192, 196–7
Reformation   3, 9–10, 13–15, 19–20, 23–7, 32, 53–4, 60, 62, 67, 70, 73
resurrection
  eschatological   97–100, 148, 159
  Jesus   10, 16, 102
revelation   36, 89, 95, 101, 112, 115, 118, 121, 151
rights, human   4, 54, 57, 71, 76, 106, 118, 130, 143, 149–50, 155–9, 166–7, 175–6, 191

sacrament   23, 30–1, 89–90, 100–1, 119–20
salvation   12, 15, 21–2, 24, 58, 64, 88–9, 95, 97–8, 102, 132, 135, 153
sanctification   8–13, 16, 29–30, 62, 110
Sandel, Michael   107–8, 144
scripture   23, 54, 64, 93
sin   3, 13–14, 17–18, 22–3, 25, 29, 39, 46–8, 53, 70, 91–6, 111, 116–17, 138, 140, 158–9, 165
  simul justus et peccator   39, 47
Spearman, Charles   183
suffering   4, 83, 85, 90–2, 99, 101, 109, 169, 175, 186
supererogation   3, 4, 53–67

Tanner, Kathryn   5, 58, 87, 89–97, 110, 114, 125, 141, 144–51, 158–9, 168
  Christ the Key   92, 114
Taylor, Charles   53–4
technology; *see* biotechnology
Ten Commandments, the   63, 66
theological anthropology; *see under* anthropology
Tomasello, Michael   163
transcendence   74, 88, 102, 161, 166–9, 178
transhuman (transhumanist)   88, 90–1, 93–8, 102–3, 171, 175, 177–88
trinity   71, 89–92, 101, 115, 145, 169, 183, 185, 192, 197

Urmson, J. O.   55, 57, 61
utilitarianism   55, 60, 187, 196

values   57, 70–2, 114, 131, 135, 140, 176, 190
virtue   22, 25–6, 29–30, 32, 55–6, 59–62, 66, 111, 116, 128, 134–5, 146, 162, 179, 181, 186
vocation   4, 22, 53, 61–2, 69–71, 73, 75–9, 89, 95, 111, 170–3

Wolf, Susan   57

Zaner, Richard   4, 82
Zimmerman, Jens   150

www.ingramcontent.com/pod-product-compliance
Lightning Source LLC
Chambersburg PA
CBHW062222300426
44115CB00012BA/2177